Mastering Linux Network Administration

Master the skills and techniques that are required to design, deploy, and administer real Linux-based networks

Jay LaCroix

BIRMINGHAM - MUMBAI

Mastering Linux Network Administration

First published: October 2015

Production reference: 1231015

Published by Packt Publishing Ltd.
Livery Place
35 Livery Street
Birmingham B3 2PB, UK.

ISBN 978-1-78439-959-7

www.packtpub.com

Cover image by Jay LaCroix

Credits

Author

Jay LaCroix

Reviewers

Adriano Dos Santos Gregório

Jitesh Marathe

Sabir Mustafa

Davor Lozić

Mosudi Isiaka

Commissioning Editor

Kartikey Pandey

Acquisition Editor

Harsha Bharwani

Content Development Editor

Sumeet Sawant

Technical Editor

Madhunikita Sunil Chindarkar

Copy Editor

Roshni Banerjee

Project Coordinator

Shweta H Birwatkar

Proofreader

Safis Editing

Indexer

Priya Sane

Production Coordinator

Shantanu N. Zagade

Cover Work

Shantanu N. Zagade

About the Author

Jay LaCroix is a Michigan-born technologist with a focus on Linux and open source software. He has over 13 years of experience working with Linux, including servers, networking, scripting, programming, virtualization, and any open source technology he can get his hands on. He is currently working as a Linux systems engineer and enjoys writing, training, and empowering others to use Linux. He is also the author of *Linux Mint Essentials*.

About the Reviewers

Adriano Dos Santos Gregório is an expert in the field of operating systems, he is curious about new technologies and is passionate about mobile technologies. He has been a Unix administrator since 1999 and he focuses primarily on networking projects with an emphasis on the physical and logical security of various network environments and databases. He has also reviewed some other Packt Publishing books such as *Kali Linux Cookbook* and *Kali Linux CTF Blueprints*.

He is a Microsoft Certified MCSA and MCT Alumni.

> I would like to thank my mother and father, my friends, the many people who are a part of my life, and Packt for this opportunity.

Jitesh Marathe is an IT professional with a bachelor's degree in computer application. He has spent most of his career being a system administrator at various IT companies and he specializes in System and Applications Operations and Support. Jitesh enjoys traveling to new places with his family.

He has also reviewed *Linux Utilities Cookbook, Packt Publishing*.

> I would especially like to thank my loving wife Darshna and son Nihar.

Sabir Mustafa has more than 13 years of work experience in the field of ICT and information technology, which includes:

- Delivery and awareness of information and automation policies to the employees of an organization

- Prepare, deploy, test, and manage solutions

- Conduct continuous tests and upgrades to ensure the protection of configurations and data

- Prepared and updated the technical documentation for teams and the data center

He is currently working as the project lead in a US-based multinational firm, Royal Cyber Inc. His expertise profile includes cloud services, Linux, JBoss Middleware, Windows Servers, and IBM Middleware.

Besides that, he holds a postgraduate degree in MCS (Master in Computer Science) and he is also multi-certified in industry recognized technologies including RHCE, MCSA, and Oracle Enterprise Linux. His hardware expertise includes DELL, HP Server Hardware, and EMC Storage. As a trainer, he has also launched a video training series on RHCSA at `http://urduitacademy.com/`.

He has a strong background in IT implementation in the government sector as well, which includes security policies, centralized SSH authentication using LDAP, data center deployment plans, and SAN storage.

I would like to thank my sweet wife and little kids for their support during the review.

Davor Lozić is a senior software engineer interested in various subjects, especially computer security, algorithms, and data structures. He creates web applications in CakePHP and Ext JS. In his spare time, he loves to read books about modern physics, graph databases such as OrientDB, and other related subjects. You can visit his website at `http://warriorkitty.com` and contact him from there. He likes cats! If you want to talk about any aspect of technology or if you have funny pictures of cats, feel free to contact him.

Mosudi Isiaka is a graduate in electrical and computer engineering from Federal University of Technology, Minna, Niger State, Nigeria. He has demonstrated excellent skills in numerous aspects of Information and Communication Technology. He has very good experience in Local Area Network implementation and management, from a simple network to a mid-level complex network scenario of more than a thousand workstations (Microsoft Windows 7, Microsoft Windows Vista, and Microsoft Windows XP), with Microsoft Windows 2008 Server R2 Active Directory Domain Controllers deployed in more than a single location. He has set up data center infrastructure, VPN, WAN link optimization, a firewall and intrusion detection system, a web/e-mail hosting control panel, an OpenNMS network management application and so on.

He can use open source software and applications to achieve enterprise level network management solutions in scenarios that cover Virtual Private Network (VPN), IP PBX, cloud computing, clustering, virtualization, routing, high availability, customized firewall with advanced web filtering, network load balancing, failover and link aggregation for multiple Internet access solutions, traffic engineering, collaboration suits, Network Attached Storage (NAS), Linux systems administration, virtual networking, and computing.

He is currently employed as a data center manager at One Network Ltd., Nigeria. Mosudi also works with ServerAfrica (`http://www.serverafrica.com`) as a managing consultant (technical). More information about him is available on his website `http://www.mioemi.com`. Contact him at `http://ng.linkedin.com/pub/isiaka-mosudi/1b/7a2/936/`.

He has also reviewed *Mastering Python High Performance* by Fernando Doglio for *Packt Publishing*.

I would like to thank my lovely mother, Mrs. Mosudi R. Ekundayo, for her moral support.

I would also like to thank my colleague, Oyebode Micheal Tosin, for his timely reminders and technical suggestions during reviews.

www.PacktPub.com

Support files, eBooks, discount offers, and more

For support files and downloads related to your book, please visit www.PacktPub.com.

Did you know that Packt offers eBook versions of every book published, with PDF and ePub files available? You can upgrade to the eBook version at www.PacktPub.com and as a print book customer, you are entitled to a discount on the eBook copy. Get in touch with us at service@packtpub.com for more details.

At www.PacktPub.com, you can also read a collection of free technical articles, sign up for a range of free newsletters and receive exclusive discounts and offers on Packt books and eBooks.

https://www2.packtpub.com/books/subscription/packtlib

Do you need instant solutions to your IT questions? PacktLib is Packt's online digital book library. Here, you can search, access, and read Packt's entire library of books.

Why subscribe?

- Fully searchable across every book published by Packt
- Copy and paste, print, and bookmark content
- On demand and accessible via a web browser

Free access for Packt account holders

If you have an account with Packt at www.PacktPub.com, you can use this to access PacktLib today and view 9 entirely free books. Simply use your login credentials for immediate access.

Table of Contents

Preface   **v**

Chapter 1: Setting up Your Environment   **1**

Getting started   **1**
Distributions to consider   **2**
Physical machines versus virtual machines   **3**
Setting up and configuring VirtualBox   **4**
   Acquiring VirtualBox   4
   Downloading and installing the Extension Pack   6
Acquiring and installing Debian 8   **10**
Acquiring and installing CentOS 7   **36**
Summary   **44**

Chapter 2: Revisiting Linux Network Basics   **45**

Understanding the TCP/IP protocol suite   **46**
Naming the network device   **48**
Understanding Linux hostname resolution   **51**
Understanding the net-tools and iproute2 suites   **53**
Manually managing network interfaces   **57**
Managing connections with Network Manager   **64**
Summary   **68**

Chapter 3: Communicating Between Nodes via SSH   **69**

Using OpenSSH   **70**
Installing and configuring OpenSSH   **71**
   Connecting to network hosts via openssh-client   72
The OpenSSH config file   **74**
Understanding and utilizing scp   **75**
   Transferring files to another node via scp   76
   Tunneling traffic via SSH   78

Generating public keys 80
Keeping SSH connections alive 82
Exploring an alternative to SSH – utilizing Mosh (mobile shell) 84
Summary 85

Chapter 4: Setting up a File Server 87
File server considerations 87
NFS v3 versus NFS v4 89
Setting up an NFS server 89
Learning the basics of Samba 97
Setting up a Samba server 98
Mounting network shares 104
Automatically mounting network shares via fstab and systemd 106
Creating networked filesystems with SSHFS 108
Summary 109

Chapter 5: Monitoring System Resources 111
Inspecting and managing processes 112
Understanding load average 114
Checking available memory 117
Using shell-based resource monitors 119
Scanning used storage 126
Introduction to logging 128
Maintaining log size with logrotate 129
Understanding the systemd init system 132
Understanding the systemd journal 135
Summary 135

Chapter 6: Configuring Network Services 137
Planning your IP address layout 137
Installing and configuring a DHCP server 140
Installing and configuring a DNS server 144
Setting up an internal NTP server 152
Summary 157

Chapter 7: Hosting HTTP Content via Apache 159
Installing Apache 159
Configuring Apache 162
Adding modules 166
Setting up virtual hosts 169
Summary 171

Chapter 8: Understanding Advanced Networking Concepts   **173**

Dividing your network into subnets   173
Understanding the CIDR notation   177
Implementing Quality of Service   181
Routing TCP/IP traffic   186
Creating redundant DHCP and DNS servers   190
Summary   194

Chapter 9: Securing Your Network   **195**

Limiting the attack surface   195
Securing OpenSSH   199
Configuring the iptables firewall   203
Protecting system services with fail2ban   206
Understanding SELinux   208
Configuring Apache to utilize SSL   212
Deploying security updates   214
Summary   217

Chapter 10: Troubleshooting Network Issues   **219**

Tracing routing issues   219
Troubleshooting DHCP issues   222
Troubleshooting DNS issues   224
Displaying connection statistics with netstat   225
Scanning your network with Nmap and Zenmap   226
Installing missing firmware on Debian systems   229
Troubleshooting issues with Network Manager   230
Summary   232

Index   **233**

Preface

In this book, we will learn about the concepts that are required to manage real Linux-based networks. The goal is to help the reader grow from a beginner or an intermediate-level Linux user, to someone who can manage and support real Linux-based networks. The book starts with a couple of introductory chapters, in which the reader will set up their environment and then refresh some basics that will serve as the foundation for the rest of the book. From there, more advanced topics will be covered with useful examples, which the reader will be able to follow along with gaining valuable hands on practice.

During this journey, we will cover the tasks that a network administrator will typically perform on the job such as installing Linux, setting up DHCP, sharing files, IP addressing, monitoring resources, and so on. These examples are covered for not one but two popular distributions, Debian and CentOS. Since these two are very popular distributions in the enterprise, the reader will be well prepared to manage networks based on one distribution or the other (and also the countless other distributions based on them).

Finally, the last few chapters will cover the best practices to prevent intrusions and attacks and also troubleshooting to assist you when things go wrong.

What this book covers

Chapter 1, *Setting up Your Environment*, covers the process of setting up your lab environment for use in this book. Installing Debian and CentOS is covered, along with the pros and cons of using virtual machines.

Chapter 2, *Revisiting Linux Network Basics*, refreshes the reader on core Linux concepts that provide a foundation for the rest of the book such as TCP/IP, hostname resolution, and the IP and net tools suites.

Chapter 3, Communicating Between Nodes via SSH, covers all things SSH. In this chapter, we take a look at how to use SSH and how to set up an OpenSSH server to allow other nodes to connect. The scp command is also covered, allowing us to transfer files from one machine to another.

Chapter 4, Setting up a File Server, covers both Samba and NFS. Here, we'll discuss when it's appropriate to use one over the other, as well as the configuring and mounting these shares.

Chapter 5, Monitoring System Resources, deals with the monitoring of resources on our Linux systems such as inspecting free disk space, checking available memory, rotating logs, and viewing journal logs.

Chapter 6, Configuring Network Services, is all about the services that make our network come together. Topics such as DHCP and DNS servers are covered here. NTP is also thrown in for good measure.

Chapter 7, Hosting HTTP Content via Apache, covers Apache, which is currently the most used web server software in the world. Here, we'll not only install Apache, but we'll configure it and manage the modules as well. The virtual hosts are also covered.

Chapter 8, Understanding Advanced Networking Concepts, takes the reader to the next level by discussing more advanced topics such as subnetting, Quality of Service, redundancy in DHCP and DNS, and many more.

Chapter 9, Securing Your Network, deals with hardening our systems in order to prevent unauthorized access. Here, we'll cover iptables, fail2ban, SELinux, and much more.

Chapter 10, Troubleshooting Network Issues, rounds up our journey with some troubleshooting tips you can use if you run into problems.

What you need for this book

This book requires you to have one or more computers at your disposal that are capable of running either Debian or CentOS, preferably both. It really doesn't matter if you run them on a virtual machine or physical hardware, as the only requirement is that you should be able to install one or both of these distributions and access them via a terminal. Root level access is required for these installations.

While you can certainly use any Linux installations you may already have, it's highly recommended to have separate, fresh installations to work with, as some of our topics can be disruptive if they are run on production networks. If you are in doubt, VirtualBox or older machines that you may have lying around will do just fine. Network access is required, but that goes without saying, given the subject matter of this book.

Some general Linux know-how is expected. By no means is the user required to be advanced, as the purpose of this book is to upgrade your existing knowledge. That being said, there are a few things that you should already be familiar with in order to have the smoothest possible experience. First, you should already know how to modify configuration files using a text editor. No assumptions are made in this book as to which text editor you use, it's really up to you. As long as you understand any text editor, whether it be nano, vim, or even gedit—you're in good shape. If you can open a root-owned configuration file, then make changes and save it—you're all set. If in doubt, nano is a great text editor for beginners and only takes a few minutes to learn. For the more advanced users, vim is a good choice. Speaking of root, you should also understand the difference between running commands as a root or a normal user. Also, you should be able to navigate the file system and browse around.

However, even if you need to brush up on the editing of text files or switching to the root user, don't let that stop you. There is quite a bit of knowledge online that you can use to brush up, most text editors available for Linux offer really good documentation.

Who this book is for

This book is targeted at the users who already know the basics of Linux, who want to learn how to manage Linux-based networks or take their skills to the next level. This can either be for the purpose of supporting an all-Linux network or even a mixed environment. This book takes the reader through easier topics such as installing Debian, to the more advanced concepts such as subnetting. By the end of this book, you should have enough knowledge to set up a completely networked environment, including all the components that such a network should feature. If this excites you, then this book is definitely for you!

However, in this book we focus on real-world examples pertaining only to Linux. If your goal is to become certified with Cisco or obtain some other high-level certification, this may not be the best place for you. Here, it's all about practical examples, without focusing too much on the theory. While certification cram books are neat, in this book we get things done – the real things that you will be required to do if asked by your boss or client to implement a Linux network. If that's your goal, you're definitely in the right place.

Conventions

In this book, you will find a number of text styles that distinguish between different kinds of information. Here are some examples of these styles and an explanation of their meaning.

Code words in text, database table names, folder names, filenames, file extensions, pathnames, dummy URLs, user input, and Twitter handles are shown as follows: "In most cases, this will be /dev/sda."

A block of code is set as follows:

```
default-lease-time 86400;
max-lease-time 86400;
option subnet-mask 255.255.252.0;
option broadcast-address 10.10.99.255;
option domain-name "local.lan";
authoritative;
subnet 10.10.96.0 netmask 255.255.252.0 {
    range 10.10.99.100 10.10.99.254;
    option routers 10.10.96.1;
    option domain-name-servers 10.10.96.1;
}
```

Any command-line input or output is written as follows:

```
systemctl status httpd
```

Any command that is required to be run with root previleges will be prefixed with a # character, like this:

```
# yum install httpd
```

New terms and **important words** are shown in bold. Words that you see on the screen, for example, in menus or dialog boxes, appear in the text like this: "Once it's finished, you can save the results by clicking **Scan** and then **Save Scan**."

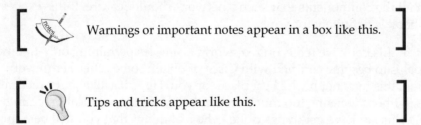

Warnings or important notes appear in a box like this.

Tips and tricks appear like this.

Reader feedback

Feedback from our readers is always welcome. Let us know what you think about this book—what you liked or disliked. Reader feedback is important for us as it helps us develop titles that you will really get the most out of.

To send us general feedback, simply e-mail feedback@packtpub.com, and mention the book's title in the subject of your message.

If there is a topic that you have expertise in and you are interested in either writing or contributing to a book, see our author guide at www.packtpub.com/authors.

Customer support

Now that you are the proud owner of a Packt book, we have a number of things to help you to get the most from your purchase.

Downloading the example code

You can download the example code files from your account at http://www.packtpub.com for all the Packt Publishing books you have purchased. If you purchased this book elsewhere, you can visit http://www.packtpub.com/support and register to have the files e-mailed directly to you.

Downloading the color images of this book

We also provide you with a PDF file that has color images of the screenshots/diagrams used in this book. The color images will help you better understand the changes in the output. You can download this file from http://www.packtpub.com/sites/default/files/downloads/9597OS_ColorImages.pdf.

Errata

Although we have taken every care to ensure the accuracy of our content, mistakes do happen. If you find a mistake in one of our books—maybe a mistake in the text or the code—we would be grateful if you could report this to us. By doing so, you can save other readers from frustration and help us improve subsequent versions of this book. If you find any errata, please report them by visiting http://www.packtpub.com/submit-errata, selecting your book, clicking on the **Errata Submission Form** link, and entering the details of your errata. Once your errata are verified, your submission will be accepted and the errata will be uploaded to our website or added to any list of existing errata under the Errata section of that title.

To view the previously submitted errata, go to https://www.packtpub.com/books/content/support and enter the name of the book in the search field. The required information will appear under the **Errata** section.

Piracy

Piracy of copyrighted material on the Internet is an ongoing problem across all media. At Packt, we take the protection of our copyright and licenses very seriously. If you come across any illegal copies of our works in any form on the Internet, please provide us with the location address or website name immediately so that we can pursue a remedy.

Please contact us at copyright@packtpub.com with a link to the suspected pirated material.

We appreciate your help in protecting our authors and our ability to bring you valuable content.

Questions

If you have a problem with any aspect of this book, you can contact us at questions@packtpub.com, and we will do our best to address the problem.

1
Setting up Your Environment

Welcome to the world of Linux networking! This book will be your guide to perfecting your Linux network management skills. In this chapter, we will go over what's needed to get your environment up and running. We'll talk about several Linux distributions that are of interest to enterprise networking, the things to keep in mind while setting up an environment in your home or office so you can follow along with this book, and some best practices for setting up a few Linux installations that we'll use throughout this book. Basically, we'll lay the groundwork that you'll use to develop your skills.

In this chapter, we will cover:

- Getting started
- Distributions to consider
- Physical machines versus virtual machines
- Setting up and configuring VirtualBox
- Acquiring and installing Debian 8
- Acquiring and installing CentOS 7

Getting started

Network management in Linux is a fun, diverse field that is always changing. While the core components typically remain the same throughout the years (such as the **TCP/IP** protocol), how these services are managed have evolved in each generation, such as the rise of **systemd**. Linux is definitely exciting.

In this chapter, we'll see how to set up your environment. Depending on your experience level, you can skip directly to *Chapter 2, Revisiting Linux Networking Basics*. If you're already comfortable setting up a distribution or two on a physical or **virtual machine**, you already have the knowledge needed to get started. Here, we'll discuss how to install a few distributions of interest for the exercises in this book and some general pointers.

In a nutshell, the more Linux installations you have to work with, the better. While practicing networking concepts, it's a good idea to have as many nodes as possible, so you can test how your configuration changes, will affect your environment. If you are already comfortable installing Linux, feel free to set up some nodes and then I'll meet you in the next chapter.

Distributions to consider

There are over a hundred distributions of Linux in existence today. These include distributions geared specifically toward workstations or servers (or even both) and specialist distributions, which solve a specific task, such as Kali, Mythbuntu, and Clonezilla. Naturally, the first question one might have when studying a concept such as network administration is which distributions to start with.

Let's not focus on any one distribution. In the enterprise, no two data centers are same. Some organizations that utilize Linux might standardize on a specific distribution set (for example, Ubuntu and Ubuntu Server) though it's far more common to see a mix of one or more distributions in use. Distributions such as **SUSE Enterprise Linux**, **Red Hat Enterprise Linux**, **Ubuntu Server**, **CentOS**, and **Debian** are extremely common among servers within Linux-based networks. In my experience, I've seen Debian (as well as its derivatives) and Red Hat-based distributions in use most often.

You are encouraged to experiment and mix up whichever distributions you might favor. There are many candidates, and websites such as `www.distrowatch.com` would give you a list of possibilities. Specifically for the sake of the examples in this book, CentOS and Debian are recommended for your use. In fact, these two distributions are wonderful places to start. You'll get a taste for two different forms of package management (**rpm** and **deb** packages) and familiarize yourself with two of the most popular distributions. Regarding Debian, quite a few distributions are based on it (**Ubuntu**, **Linux Mint**, and others). By learning how to manage a Debian installation, much of that knowledge would be transferable to other distributions should you consider switching. The same can be said about CentOS, which is based on Red Hat. Red Hat is a very popular distribution and since CentOS is created from its source, you're essentially learning it as well. While **Fedora** is more bleeding-edge than Red Hat or CentOS, much of the knowledge will be useful there as well; Fedora is popular as a workstation distribution.

The examples within this book were tested in both CentOS and Debian. Whenever an instruction is specific to a particular distribution, I will let you know. Having a CentOS and Debian installation will suit you for the purposes of this book, but feel free to experiment. As far as individual versions of these distributions are concerned, both CentOS 7 and Debian 8 were used. Install these in your environment or home lab.

Physical machines versus virtual machines

Seeing a section on virtual machines in a networking book may come as somewhat of a surprise. To be fair, it certainly is out of place. In addition to being an important enterprise platform, **virtualization** can also be an invaluable learning tool. In real networks, a technician may test a service in a virtual machine before rolling it out to the environment. For example, a new **DNS** server may begin life as a **VM**, and then once it is tested and proven, moved into an environment for use by the organization. One benefit of this approach is that you can take several snapshots as you develop the solution, and should you mess up and ruin it, you can just restore the snapshot and begin from a known-working state.

As far as mastering our Linux networking skills are concerned, virtual machines allow you to test how a procedure differs from one distribution to another. It's easy to bring up a virtual machine, and it's even easier to trash it. If you're limited by physical hardware, then virtual machines may offer you a chance to build a small virtual network to practice on. Of course, the trade-off with virtual machines is how much RAM they use. However, without a GUI, most Linux distributions will run quite comfortably with just 512 MB RAM. Nowadays, quite a few computers ship with 8 GB or even 16 GB RAM, so you should be able to run several VMs on even the budget computers available today.

To be fair, using virtual machines for purposes of practice and study isn't always ideal. In fact, when studying networking, physical equipment is usually preferred. While you can certainly practice setting up and serving a web page via Apache running in a VM, you wouldn't be able to practice racking switches and routers in such an environment. Whenever possible, try to use physical equipment. However, virtual machines offer a unique chance for you to create a small army of nodes to maintain on your network.

Of course, not everyone has a stack of Dell towers sitting in the closet, ready and waiting for a shiny new Linux install. Depending on what you have at your disposal, you may use all physical machines or a mix of physical and virtual. In this book, no assumptions are made about your inventory. The name of the game is to manage nodes, so set up as many as possible.

In this book, **VirtualBox** is discussed. However, it's by no means the only solution for creating virtual machines. There are other solutions as well, such as **KVM**, **Xen**, **VMware** and others. VirtualBox has the benefit of being free, open source, and cross-platform (it's available for Linux, Mac OS X, and Windows), so there's a good chance it will work in your environment. In most cases, it's even easier to set up than KVM or Xen (but perhaps not nearly as cool). You don't have to use VirtualBox (or even VMs at all, for that matter) in order to follow along with this book. Use whatever solution you prefer. In this book, I try not to limit the instructions to any one specific solution, so the content works for as many people as possible.

Setting up and configuring VirtualBox

If you've decided to use VirtualBox in your environment (either for studying, testing distributions, or evaluating network services before implementation), we will set up our VirtualBox host in this activity.

Acquiring VirtualBox

Downloading and installing VirtualBox is actually fairly straightforward, but each platform has its unique quirks. In Windows, the initial installation is simply a matter of navigating to the following site and downloading the setup file and running through the installation wizard:

```
https://www.virtualbox.org/wiki/Downloads
```

After installation, all you would need to do is skip to the *Downloading and installing the Extension Pack* section of this chapter. Installing on Mac OS X is also straightforward.

For Linux, there are several methods to install VirtualBox. One way is to use your **package manager**, if your distribution already has it available in its repositories. Unfortunately, depending on the version of your distribution, the version of VirtualBox that may be included is very likely to be out of date. For example, Debian typically contains older packages in its repositories, but bleeding-edge distributions such as Arch are more likely to contain the latest and best.

Perhaps a better way of acquiring VirtualBox is to import the repositories that VirtualBox itself provides into your system. The following URL has a list of Debian repositories and even a method of adding a repository for RPM-based distributions (Fedora, Red Hat, and so on):

```
https://www.virtualbox.org/wiki/Linux_Downloads
```

For example, using the instructions on the page as a guide, we can run through the following procedure on a Debian-based system. However, Oracle may change their instructions and repository listing at any time; always consult the previous URL before installation to see if the procedure has changed.

To verify that we will add the correct version, we need to determine which repository to use. This differs based on which distribution you're running, so definitely consult the documentation on the VirtualBox site to ensure you're importing the correct repository.

For Debian 8 "Jessie", we would use the following:

```
deb http://download.virtualbox.org/virtualbox/debian jessie contrib
```

To add this repository to our Debian system, we would use the following command:

```
# echo "deb http://download.virtualbox.org/virtualbox/debian jessie
contrib" > /etc/apt/sources.list.d/virtualbox.list
```

Then, we can add the public key for the repository with the following command:

```
# wget -q https://www.virtualbox.org/download/oracle_vbox.asc -O- | apt-
key add -
```

From now on, we can find Oracle's VirtualBox package in our repositories and install it. To do so, let's first update our package listing with the following command (as root):

```
# apt-get update
```

Then install VirtualBox with the following command:

```
# apt-get install dkms virtualbox-4.3
```

 This same procedure for installation will work for Ubuntu as well, as long as you choose the appropriate matching repository.

For distributions such as Fedora, **Red Hat Enterprise Linux (RHEL)** and openSUSE, Oracle provides similar instructions.

The public key can be downloaded via the following command:

```
# wget -q https://www.virtualbox.org/download/oracle_vbox.asc -O- | rpm
--import -
```

In order to add the repository to a Fedora system, execute the following command:

```
# wget -P /etc/yum/repos.d/ http://download.virtualbox.org/virtualbox/
rpm/fedora/virtualbox.repo
```

After adding the repository, VirtualBox can be installed with the following command:

```
# yum install VirtualBox-4.3
```

In addition, instructions for OpenSUSE and RHEL are also available on the VirtualBox website. See the VirtualBox website for more details at `https://www.virtualbox.org/`.

Downloading and installing the Extension Pack

Oracle offers an **Extension Pack**, which enables USB support as well as support for **Preboot Execution Environment (PXE)** booting. You may or may not need these features. If you think you would benefit from being able to insert a flash drive on your host PC and accessing it from within your VM, it's probably a good idea to install the pack.

 The extension pack isn't built-in to VirtualBox due to licensing issues. Feel free to consult the VirtualBox license should you wish to learn more.

The installation procedure for the extension pack is mostly the same, regardless of whether your host computer is running Linux, Windows, or Mac OS X. However, there is one added step if your host is running Linux, which is to add your user account to the vboxusers group.

1. When you first install VirtualBox, it should have created this group. To verify, execute the following command:

   ```
   cat /etc/group |grep vboxusers
   ```

2. You should see an output similar to the following:

   ```
   vboxusers:x:1000:username
   ```

3. If you don't see the output, create the group with the following command:

   ```
   # groupadd vboxusers
   ```

4. Then, add yourself to that group:

```
# usermod -aG vboxusers yourusername
```

 You'll need to log out and then log in before adding yourself to the vboxusers group takes effect.

Now, you're ready to install the extension pack. Again, this procedure should be the same regardless of your underlying operating system. First, download the Extension Pack from the following URL and save it locally:

```
https://www.virtualbox.org/wiki/Downloads
```

After downloading, follow the next steps:

1. Open VirtualBox and go to **File | Preferences...**.

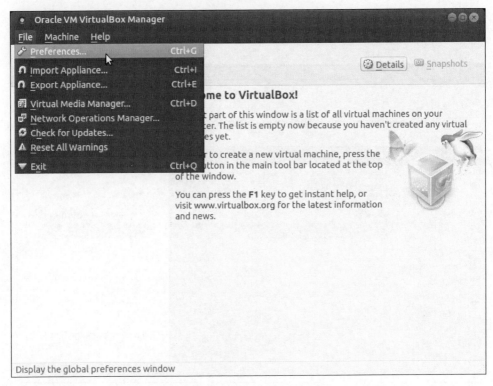

Accessing the file menu in VirtualBox

2. Next, click on **Extensions** and then click on the green triangle icon on the right-hand side.

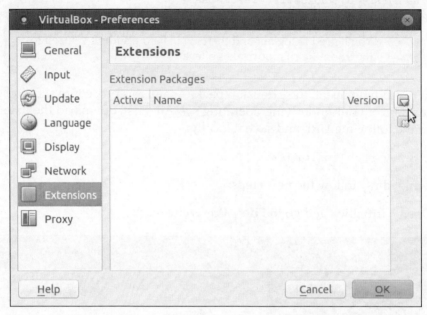

VirtualBox settings

3. Select the extension pack that you downloaded earlier and click on **Open**.

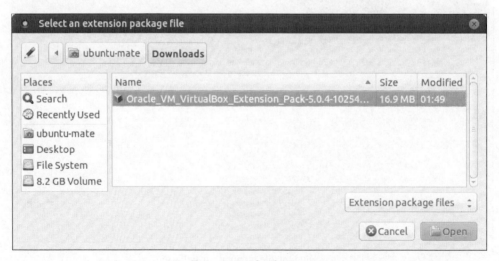

Extension pack selection

4. You'll then be asked to confirm the installation. Click on **Install**.

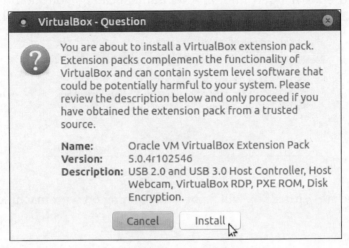

Confirmation of extension pack installation

5. The VirtualBox license agreement will be displayed. Feel free to check it. Then, scroll to the bottom and click on **I Agree** to confirm it.

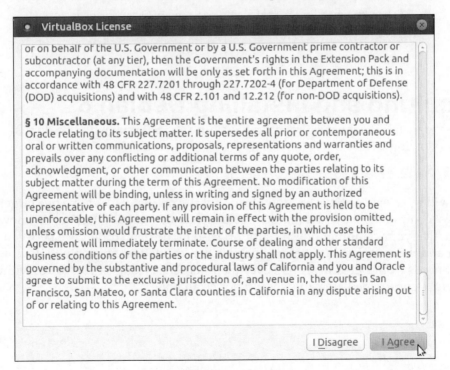

VirtualBox license agreement

6. If you're running Linux, you may be asked for the root or sudo password. If you do, enter it and continue. After authenticating, you should see confirmation that you've successfully installed the extension pack.

Confirmation of successfully installing the VirtualBox extension pack

After this procedure, VirtualBox will be up and running on your machine.

> In some distributions, the password prompt may not appear, causing the installation of the extension pack to fail. If that happens, run VirtualBox with root privileges using the following command:
>
> `sudo VirtualBox`
>
> Then, try installing the extension pack again. Once finished, close VirtualBox and then reopen it as a normal user before continuing.

Acquiring and installing Debian 8

In order to install Debian, we first need to acquire an **ISO image** file. To do that, go the following URL:

`http://www.debian.org/distrib/netinst`

There will be several options for download, but the **netinst** ISO will be our target. For most computers, the 64-bit (amd64) version should suffice—unless you know for sure that your computer doesn't support 64-bit. The main difference between the netinst and the complete installation image is that the netinst version will download what it needs from Debian's servers over the Internet. As long as you're not within a bandwidth-constrained area, this should not be an issue.

Of course, the ISO file by itself is not useful unless you're attaching it to a virtual machine. If you are, then you're ready to go. If you're setting up a physical machine, you'll need to either create a bootable CD with a disc mastering utility of your choice, or create a bootable flash drive.

> Because there is a multitude of different disc mastering utilities available, a complete walkthrough of how to create a bootable CD in your environment is not possible. In most cases, your utility should have an option to burn an ISO image in its menu. The disc will not function as Debian installation media if you simply create a data disc.

The steps for installing Debian 8 are as follows:

1. In a Linux system, you can create a bootable Debian flash drive with the following command:

   ```
   # cp name-of-debian.iso /dev/sd? && sync
   ```

2. Essentially, we're copying the downloaded ISO image directly to a flash drive. Of course, change the file name and target to what is relevant on your system. To determine the device node to use, execute the following command:

   ```
   # fdisk -l
   ```

3. Within the output, you should see the node designation of your flash drive. The output of that command will look like this:

   ```
   Device     Boot Start      End   Sectors  Size Id Type
   /dev/sdb1        2048 60563455 60561408 28.9G 83 Linux
   ```

4. Then, /dev/sdb would be the device to use to create the flash drive. Putting it all together, we would create the flash drive with the following command:

   ```
   # cp name-of-debian.iso /dev/sdb && sync
   ```

Downloading the example code

You can download the example code files from your account at http://www.packtpub.com for all the Packt Publishing books you have purchased. If you purchased this book elsewhere, you can visit http://www.packtpub.com/support and register to have the files e-mailed directly to you.

5. Once you have created bootable media, insert it into your computer and follow your computer's specific directives to access the boot menu and select your Debian media. After it finishes loading, the first screen will ask you to select your language. Choose your language, then click on **Continue**.

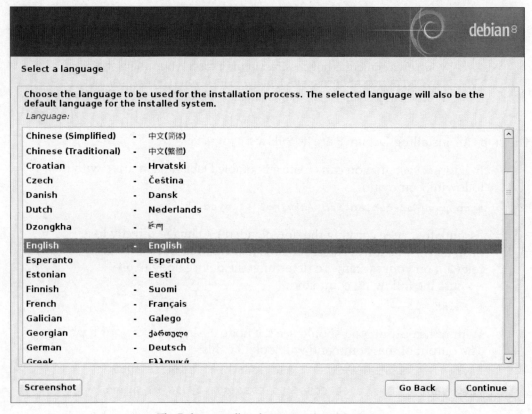

The Debian installer's language selection screen

6. After selecting your language, the next screen will have you choose your location. Select it and then click on **Continue**.

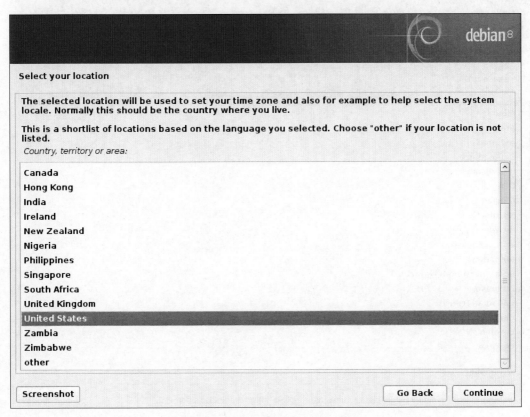

Language selection in the Debian installer

7. Similarly, choose a keymap that fits your keyboard and click on **Continue**.

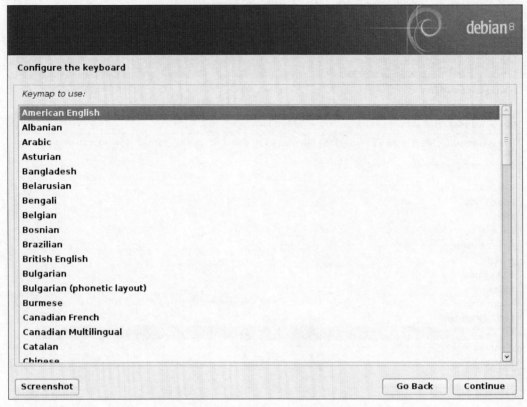

The Debian installer's keyboard selection screen

8. At this point, the Debian installer will detect your hardware, and then allow you to configure your host name. For this option, choose a unique host name that will identify your device on the network. When finished, click on **Continue**.

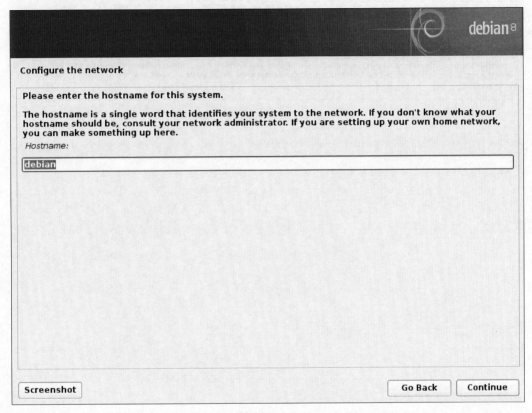

Choosing a hostname during installation of Debian

9. The installer will then ask for your domain name. Enter your domain name here if you have one; otherwise, just leave it blank. Click on **Continue**.

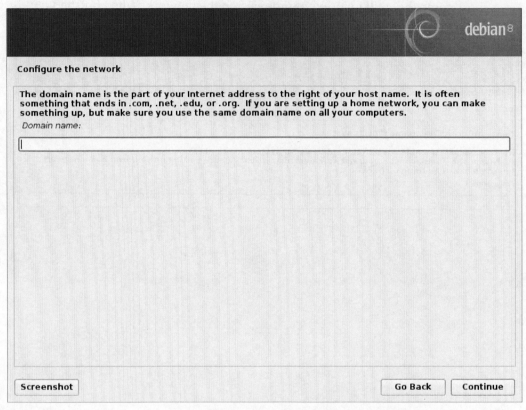

Domain name configuration while installing Debian

10. Next, you'll be asked to set a password for the **root** account. For this, you should create a unique (and preferably randomly generated) password. As you probably know, the root account has full access to the system. After setting the password, click on **Continue**.

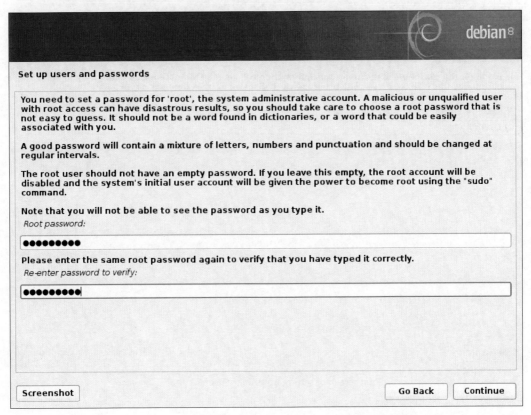

Root password entry during Debian installation

11. In the next three screens, you'll set up your user account. First, you'll enter your first and last name, and then click on **Continue**.

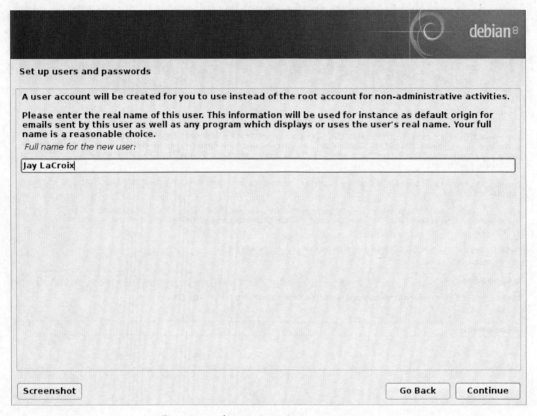

First screen of setting up primary user account

12. Then, type in username and click on **Continue**.

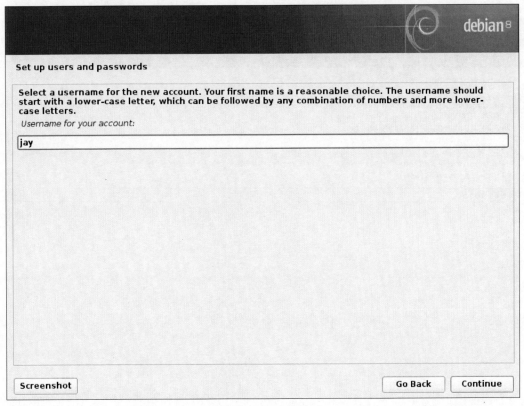

Creating a username

13. The final portion of the user setup section will ask you to create a password. When done, click on **Continue** again.

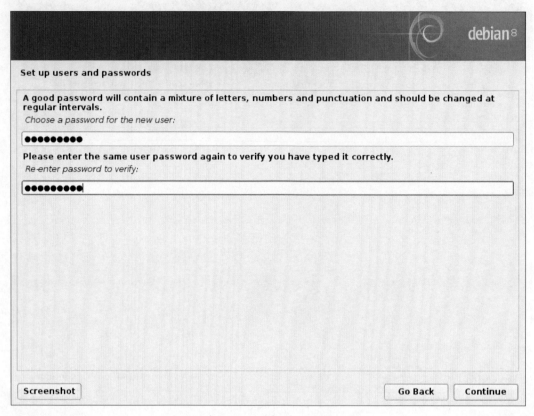

Setting the password for the primary user

14. Next, Debian will try to use **Network Time Protocol (NTP)**, if available, to configure your clock. Then, you'll be presented with a screen to select your time zone. Make sure your time zone is highlighted, and click on **Continue**.

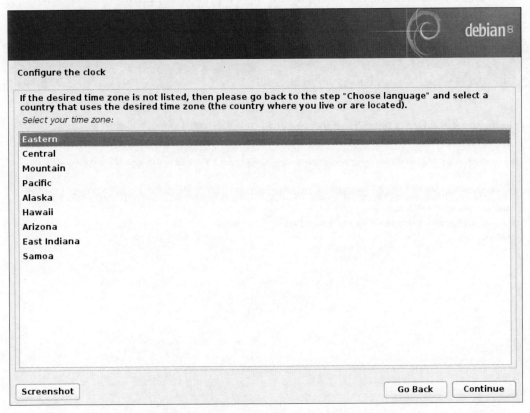

Configuring your location, for the time zone

15. Now, we'll partition our disk. Feel free to partition your disk any way you want, as there are no partitioning requirements as far as this book is concerned. For the sake of this instruction, **Guided - use entire disk**, the default for Debian, is chosen. If you have a preferred partitioning scheme, feel free to use it. When finished, click on **Continue**.

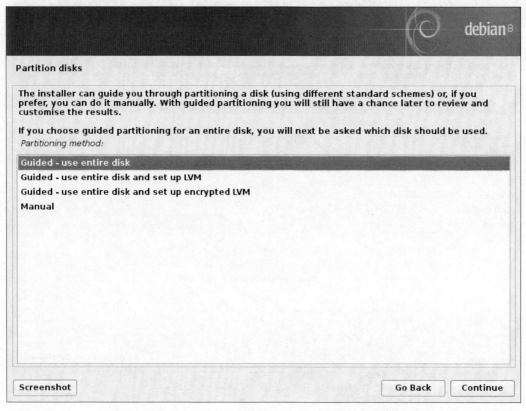

First screen of the partitioning portion of the Debian installation

16. Next, you'll have to select the hard disk on which to install Debian. In this example, there is only one hard disk available in the VM that was used to capture the procedure. If you have more than one disk, select the appropriate disk for installation and click on **Continue**.

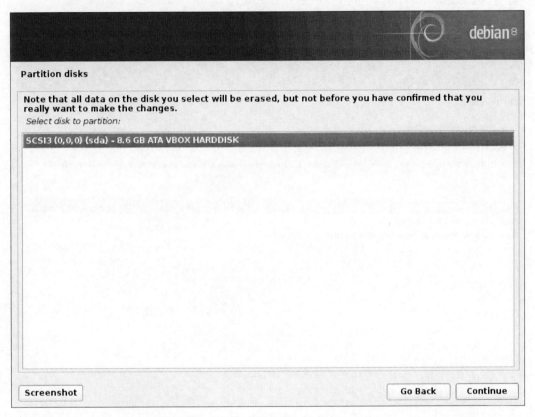

Selecting the target disk for Debian

17. In the next section, the Debian installer will ask if you would like to have a separate /home partition (recommended if you wish to retain files between installations), separate /home, /var, and /tmp partitions, or all files in one partition. This book has no partitioning requirements, so choose the one that best fits your preference. When you've made your selection, click on **Continue**.

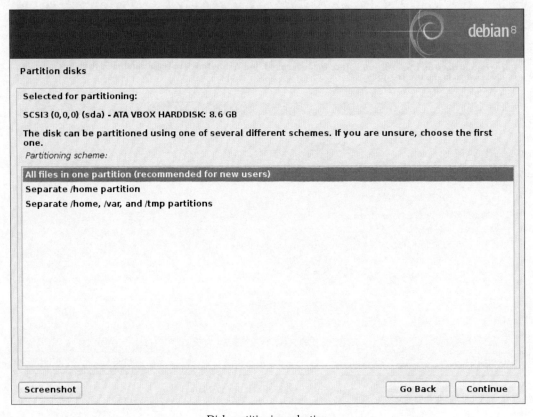

Disk partitioning selection

18. Next, Debian will display a summary of the changes it's about to make. If these changes look good to you, ensure **Finish partitioning and write changes to disk** is highlighted and click on **Continue**.

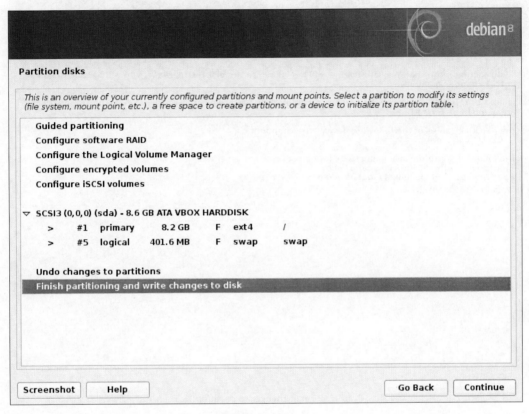

Partitioning overview

19. Then, you'll have to confirm the details again. Select **Yes** and then click on **Continue**.

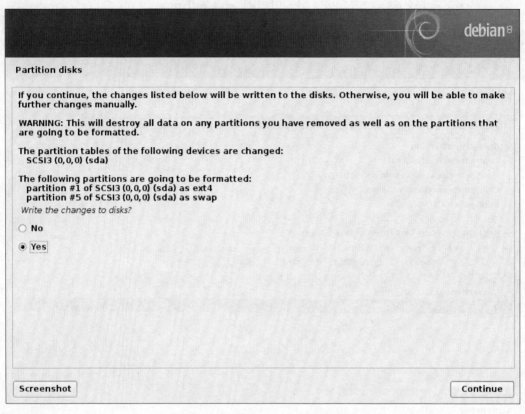

Confirmation of changes to partitioning

20. The base system will be installed next; this might take a little while depending on the speed of your computer and hard disk. Afterwards, you'll be presented with a screen where you'll select the country nearest you in order to set up Debian's package manager.

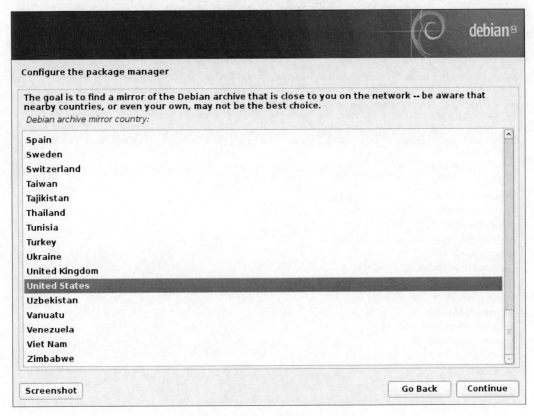

Choosing a location for the package manager

21. Next, you'll select a mirror for Debian's package archives. In most cases, the default selection is usually accurate. So unless it guessed incorrectly, leave the default selection as-is and click on **Continue**.

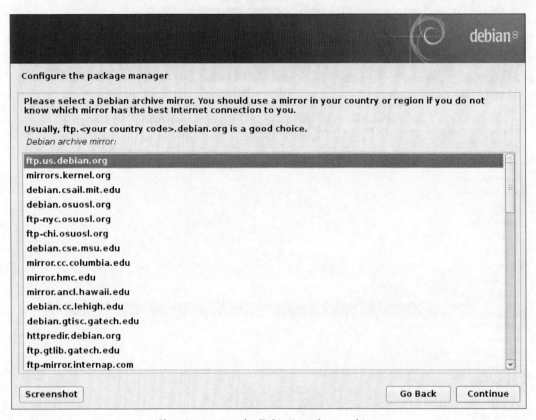

Choosing a mirror for Debian's package archives

22. In the next screen, Debian will give you a chance to configure an HTTP proxy, if you have one. If not, leave it blank.

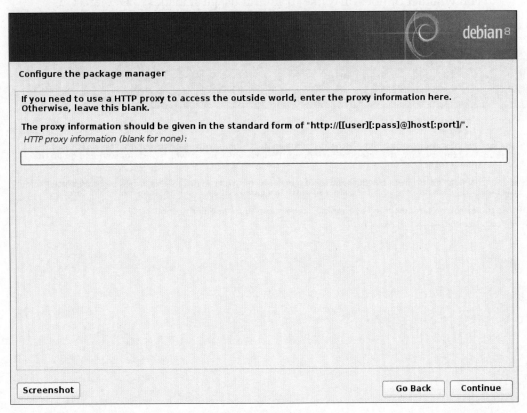

HTTP proxy configuration

23. Next, Debian will configure your package manager and update your sources. After a few progress bars scroll by, you'll see a new screen asking you whether or not you'd like to submit usage statistics to Debian. This information is helpful to Debian's developers, but it's not required. Make your choice and click on **Continue**.

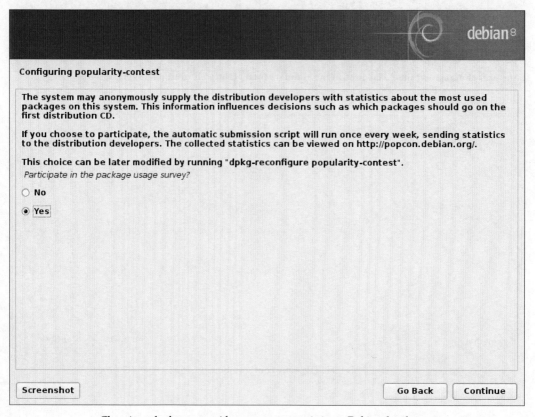

Choosing whether to provide anonymous statistics to Debian developers

The next screen will offer us additional packages that we can add to our system, but these aren't required (it's a good idea to leave standard system utilities enabled, though). Most of the options presented allow us to choose a **desktop environment**, but you are not required to install one. Typically, servers are not installed with a desktop environment. However, if you are setting up a workstation PC, it may be of benefit.

- ° **GNOME**: It is the default desktop environment for Debian. GNOME is state of the art, and offers a unique paradigm for interacting with your computer. GNOME uses virtual workspaces heavily, which allows you to split your workflow between several desktops. Unfortunately, GNOME has relatively modest hardware acceleration requirements; this means if you don't have a modern video card, it won't function properly.

- ° **Xfce**: It is a very lightweight alternative to GNOME, and it has been around for a long time. Xfce is great for computers with lower end processing capabilities. Nowadays, Xfce doesn't see much active development, so it doesn't change much. This means that it is more stable in quite a few cases, though it may not interest those who prefer something with modern features.

- ° **KDE**: It is a modern desktop environment like GNOME, but it resembles the user interface of Windows. Like GNOME, KDE also has relatively modest hardware requirements, though not quite as bad as GNOME. KDE features the **Dolphin** file manager, which is respected by Linux users.

- ° **Cinnamon**: It was originally created as a fork of GNOME, but it has evolved into its own desktop environment with little GNOME dependencies. Cinnamon offers a more traditional style of desktop, with the modern feel of GNOME.

- ° **MATE**: It is a continuation of the older 2.x versions of GNOME. As such, MATE runs well on older machines and sees more development than Xfce. It may not be as stable as Xfce, but it is close.

- ° **LXDEL**: It is also a good choice for older computers, and it is similar to Xfce but not as popular.

Other than the desktop environment choice, it's recommended to select **SSH server** from this list. **Web server** can also be chosen, but you may as well wait until we come to the part of the book in which Apache is discussed, as we'll walk through the installation.

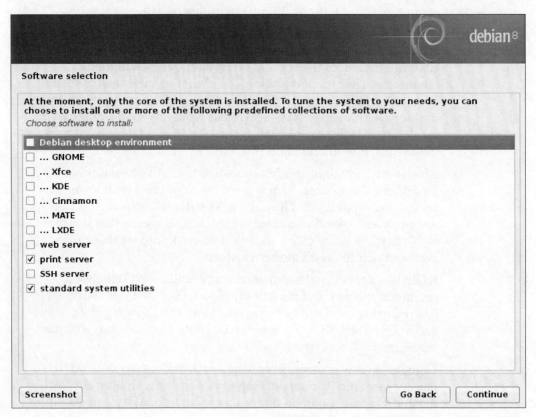

Debian software selection

24. Make your selections and then wait for the rest of the installation procedure to finish, as Debian installs the software you selected in the previous step. Then, it's time to configure GRUB. **GRUB** is an acronym for **Grand Unified Bootloader** and is necessary in order for us to boot our system. You'll be asked whether you'd like to install GRUB into the master boot record (which you more than likely will want to do), so ensure the **Yes** radio box is checked and click on **Continue**.

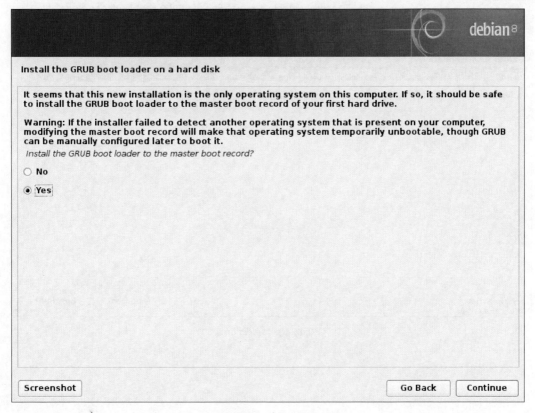

GRUB configuration

25. Next, select a target on which GRUB should be installed. In most cases, this will be /dev/sda.

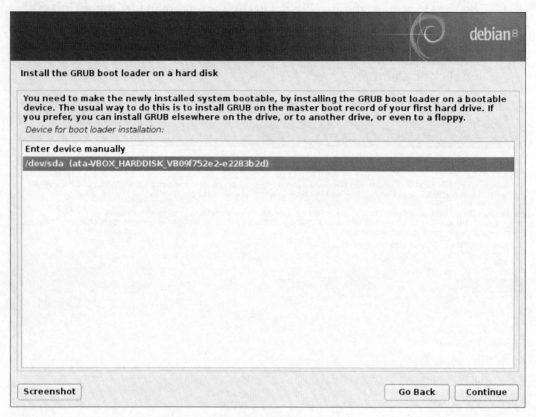

GRUB target selection

26. Whew! We are finally ready to reboot into our new Debian environment. Click on **Continue** one last time and we're off to the races!

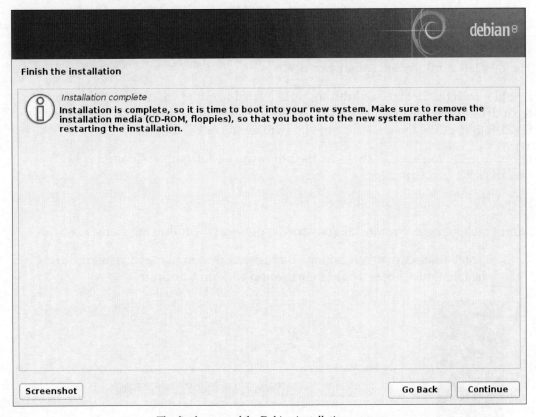

The final screen of the Debian installation process

Acquiring and installing CentOS 7

In this activity, we install CentOS 7 (which has far fewer steps than Debian). To download an ISO, navigate to the following URL:

```
https://www.centos.org/download/
```

The DVD ISO link should satisfy our needs.

Just like with the Debian walkthrough, we'll need to either create a bootable disc or flash drive to get the installation started. Unlike the Debian installer, now we need a DVD-R disc, as the image will be too large to fit onto a CD-R.

If you're installing via a flash drive, the following URL from the CentOS wiki describes the procedure:

```
http://wiki.centos.org/HowTos/InstallFromUSBkey
```

After you boot from your installation media perform the following steps:

1. You'll first see a screen asking you to select the language to be used during installation. Choose your language and click on **Continue**.

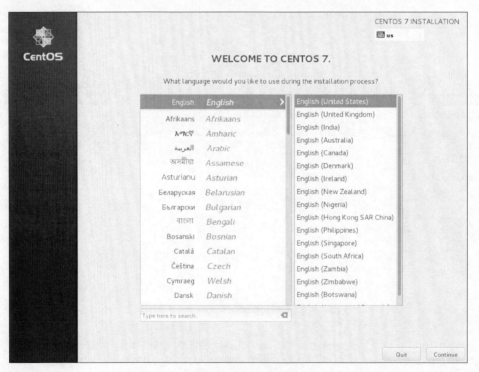

Language selection during CentOS installation

2. The next screen that appears is one of two main sections of the installation. The items shown here (**DATE & TIME, KEYBOARD, LANGUAGE SUPPORT, INSTALLATION SOURCE, SOFTWARE SELECTION, INSTALLATION DESTINATION**, and **NETWORK & HOSTNAME**) can be completed in any order. As you can see in the screenshot, only one section (**INSTALLATION DESTINATION**) is actually required. Basically, you can go through each section listed and complete its task and then click on **Begin Installation** when you're finished. If you choose not to complete a section, its defaults will be used.

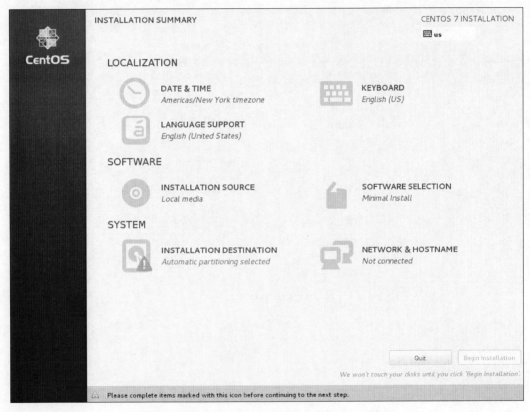

First main section of the CentOS installation procedure

3. For **LANGUAGE SUPPORT**, you'll choose your language. When finished, click on the icon labeled **Done** on the top-left corner.

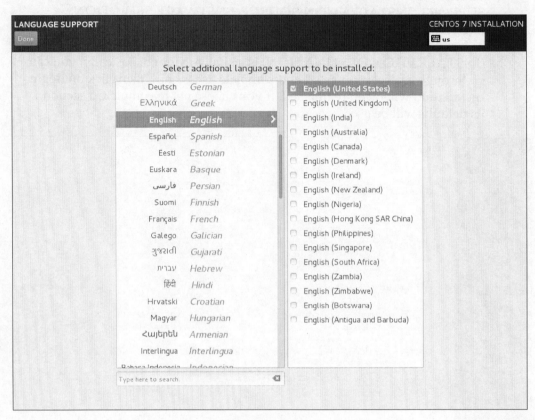

Language selection

4. Don't skip the **NETWORK & HOSTNAME** section. By default, networking isn't even enabled at all, so you can enable it by clicking on the toggle switch next to your interface. Near the bottom, you can type in the desired host name of your computer. When finished, click on **Done**.

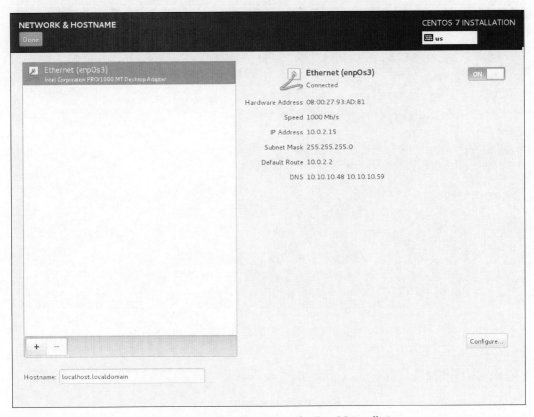

Networking configuration during the CentOS installation

5. In the **DATE & TIME** section, you can set up your clock and location. Keep in mind that if you didn't enable your network interface in the **NETWORK & HOSTNAME** section, you'll be unable to utilize NTP.

Date and time configuration

6. Completing the **INSTALLATION DESTINATION** section is compulsory. Here, you will select which disk to install CentOS onto, as well as your partitioning scheme. In this walkthrough, we'll select a disk and keep the default partitions, but feel free to customize the partition scheme if you prefer.

Disk configuration section of the CentOS installer

7. By default, CentOS will be a **Minimal Install**. This means that there will be no graphical user interface, just the default packages. If you prefer, you can opt for a desktop environment such as GNOME or KDE by selecting the corresponding option.

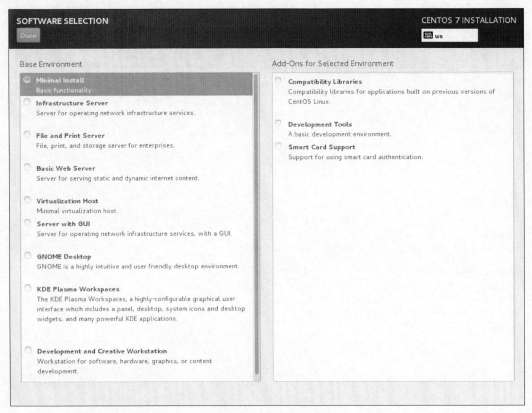

CentOS software selection

8. After you click on **Begin Installation**, you'll be brought to the second main section of the installation procedure while CentOS installs itself onto your system in the background. This section is much smaller and has just two steps. We'll set our root password and create a standard user account.

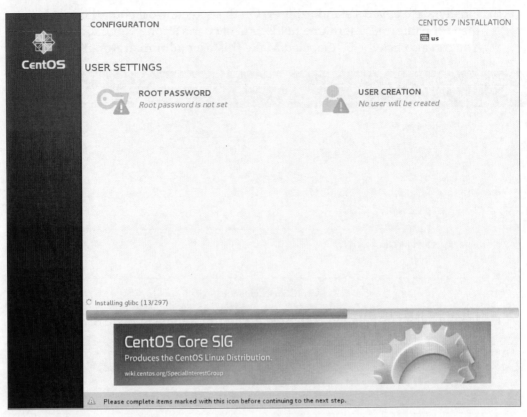

CentOS user configuration

9. For the root password, choose something secure. A password meter will show the presumed strength of the password. Click on **Done** when finished.

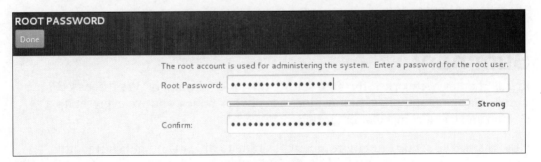

Root password entry

10. Finally, we'll create a standard user. On this screen, we'll enter the values in the **Full name** and **Username** fields, and choose a strong value for **Password**. You can also tick the box labeled **Make this user administrator**, if necessary.

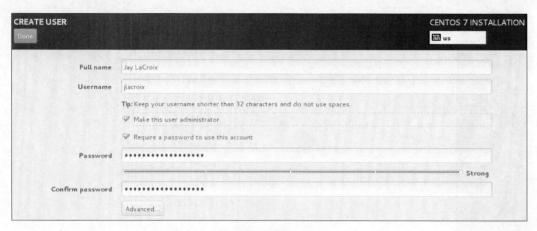

CentOS user creation

11. Finally, when installation is complete, click on **Reboot** and we're all set.

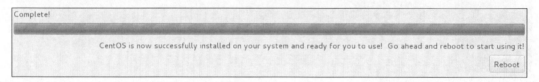

Confirmation of a completed CentOS installation

With that out of the way, feel free to set up as many Linux installations as you may need. In future chapters, we'll use these installations to configure networking and advance our knowledge.

Summary

In this chapter, we worked through setting up our environment. We discussed virtual machines and physical machines as network nodes, and we even set up a Debian and CentOS installation or two.

Now that we've set up our environment, it's time to dive in and get started. In *Chapter 2*, *Revisiting Linux Networking Basics*, we'll cover all the commands we'll need for our journey, for example, configuring network interfaces, manually connecting to networks, and setting up Network Manager. Stay tuned!

2
Revisiting Linux Network Basics

Whether you have a lot of knowledge of Linux networking or you are just getting started, we will round off the basics of Linux networking in this chapter. While the TCP/IP stack in Linux is implemented with the same features as in other platforms, specific tools are used to manage such networks. Here, we'll discuss how Linux handles IP addressing, network device naming, as well as bringing interfaces up and down. In addition, we'll discuss the graphical and nongraphical tools used to manage our interfaces.

In this chapter, we will cover:

- Understanding the TCP/IP protocol suite
- Naming the network device
- Understanding Linux hostname resolution
- Understanding the iproute2 and net-tools suites
- Managing network interfaces manually
- Managing connections with Network Manager

Understanding the TCP/IP protocol suite

TCP/IP is the most popular networking protocol in existence. Not only is it the primary protocol suite of the Internet, it's something that you can find on just about any device that supports network connectivity in one form or another. Your computer understands this suite very well, but nowadays your phone, TV, and perhaps even a kitchen appliance or two supports this technology. It really is everywhere. Although TCP/IP is often referred to as a protocol, it's actually a **protocol suite** made up of several individual protocols. From the name, I'm sure you can gather that two of them are the TCP and IP protocols. In addition, there is also a third, UDP, which is part of this protocol suite as well.

TCP is an acronym for **Transmission Control Protocol**. It's responsible for breaking down network transmissions into sequences (also known as packets or segments), which are then sent to the target node and reassembled back into the original message by TCP on the other end. In addition to managing packets, TCP also ensures that they were properly received (to the best of its ability). It does this via **error correction**. If a packet is not received by the target, TCP will resend it. It knows to do this because of the **retransmission time**r.

Before we discuss error correction and retransmission, let's first take a look at the actual process that TCP uses to send data. When setting up a connection, TCP performs a **three-way handshake**, which consists of three special packets that are sent between the communicating nodes. The first packet, **SYN (synchronize)**, is sent to the receiver by the sender. Essentially, it's how the node announces that it wants to start a communication. On the receiving end, once (and if) the packet is received, a **SYN/ACK (synchronize acknowledgment)** packet is sent back to the sender. Finally, an **ACK (acknowledge)** packet is sent to the receiver from the sender, which is an overall verification that the transfer is all set to proceed. From that point forward, the connection is established and the two nodes are able to send information to each other. Further packets are then sent, which make up the remainder of the communication.

If we lived in a perfect world, this would be all that is needed. Packets would never get lost in transmission, bandwidth would be unlimited, and packets would never get corrupted during transmission. Unfortunately, we don't live in a perfect world and packets are lost and/or corrupted all the time. TCP has built-in features to deal with these types of things. Error correction helps ensure that the packet which was received is the same as the one that was sent. TCP packets contain a checksum, and an algorithm is used to verify it. If the verification fails, the packet is deemed incorrect and is then discarded. This verification isn't perfect, so it's still possible that the file you just downloaded may still have an error or two, but it's better than nothing. Most of the time, it works just fine.

The flow control feature of TCP handles the speed at which data is transferred. While most of us geeks have a very nice set of networking hardware that is able to handle a ton of bandwidth, the Internet is not a consistent place. Your uber high-end switch may be able to handle whatever you throw at it, but that really doesn't matter if there is a weak link somewhere upstream within the connection. A network transmission is only as fast as its slowest point. While you're sending a transmission to another node, you're only able to send as much data as its buffer is able to hold. At some point, its buffer will fill up and then be unable to receive any additional packets until it deals with the ones it already has. Any additional packets sent to the receiver at this time are dropped. The sender sees that it is no longer receiving ACK replies, and then backs off and slows down its rate of transfer. This is the method that TCP uses in order to adjust the transfer speed according to what receiving nodes are able to handle.

Flow control works by utilizing what is known as a **sliding window**. The receiving node specifies what is known as a **receive window**, which tells the sender how much data it's able to receive before it becomes overwhelmed. Once this receive window runs dry, the sender waits for the receiver to clarify that it's ready to receive data again. Of course, if the receiving end sends an update to the sender that it is ready to receive data and the sender never gets the memo, we could run into a real problem if the sender waited forever for an all-clear message that was lost in transmission. Thankfully, we have a **persist timer** in place to help deal with this. Essentially, the persist timer represents how long the sender is willing to wait before it needs to verify that the connection is still active. Once the persist timer elapses, the sender transmits another packet to the receiver, to see whether it is able to deal with it. If a reply is sent, the reply packet will contain another receive window, which identifies that it is indeed ready to continue the conversation.

The **IP** (short for **Internet Protocol**) handles the actual sending and receiving of the packets that TCP wants to send or receive. Within each packet, there is a destination known as an **IP address** (which we'll discuss further in this chapter). Each connected network interface will have its own IP address, which the IP protocol will use to figure out where a packet needs to go, or which device it is from. Together, TCP and IP make up a powerful team. TCP splits up a communication into packets, and IP handles routing them to their destination.

Of course, there's also **UDP** (short for **User Datagram Protocol**), which is part of the suite as well. It's very similar to TCP in that it breaks up a transmission into packets. The main difference, however, is that UDP is **connectionless**. This means that UDP does not verify anything. It sends the packets, but does not guarantee delivery. If a packet isn't received by the target, it will not be resent.

Those learning about UDP for the first time may question why such an untrustworthy protocol would even be considered. The fact is, in some cases, a connection-oriented protocol such as TCP may add unwanted overhead to certain types of transmissions. One example of this is contacting a colleague via Skype, which offers audio calls over the Internet as well as video calls. If a packet was lost by either end during a communication, it wouldn't make much sense to resend it. You would just hear a bit of static for a second or so, and retransmitting a packet certainly wouldn't change the fact that you had difficulty hearing a word or two. Adding error correction to such a transmission would be pointless and add overhead.

Discussing TCP/IP in its entirety would be a book in and of itself. In Linux, this protocol is handled in much the same way as other platforms, the real difference is in regards to how the protocol is managed. Throughout this book, we'll talk about ways we can manage this protocol and tweak our network.

Naming the network device

Nowadays, it's not uncommon for a computer to have multiple network interfaces. For example, if you're using a laptop (other than an Ultrabook), it's likely that you have a wired, as well as a wireless, network interface. Each network interface will have its own IP address and they operate independently of each other. In fact, you can even route traffic between multiple interfaces, though this is typically disabled by default in most Linux distributions. Just like each interface has its own IP address, each will also be identified by the system by its own device name. Before we discuss this further, go ahead and take a look at the device names on your system. Open up a terminal and type the following command:

```
ip addr show
```

Your output will look like this:

```
root@localhost:~                                          _  +  ×
[jlacroix@trinity:~]$ ip addr show
1: lo: <LOOPBACK,UP,LOWER_UP> mtu 16436 qdisc noqueue state UNKNOWN
    link/loopback 00:00:00:00:00:00 brd 00:00:00:00:00:00
    inet 127.0.0.1/8 scope host lo
    inet6 ::1/128 scope host
       valid_lft forever preferred_lft forever
2: eth0: <BROADCAST,MULTICAST,UP,LOWER_UP> mtu 1500 qdisc pfifo_fast state UP qlen 1000
    link/ether 54:ee:75:00:19:57 brd ff:ff:ff:ff:ff:ff
    inet 10.10.97.3/22 brd 10.10.99.255 scope global eth0
    inet6 fe80::56ee:75ff:fe00:1957/64 scope link
       valid_lft forever preferred_lft forever
14: wlan0: <BROADCAST,MULTICAST> mtu 1500 qdisc mq state DOWN qlen 1000
    link/ether e0:9d:31:60:42:dc brd ff:ff:ff:ff:ff:ff
[jlacroix@trinity:~]$
```

The output of the ip command, showing network interfaces and address assignments

In this example, we see three network interfaces listed. The first, lo, is the local loopback adapter. The second listing, eth0, is the wired interface. Finally, wlan0 represents the wireless interface. Given this output, you can deduce that there is a network cable plugged in (eth0 has an IP address) and it is not currently utilizing its wireless interface (there is no IP address listed for wlan0).

The output shown previously was taken from a system running Debian. Now, let's take a look at the output of the same command when run on a CentOS system:

```
                              jlacroix@localhost:~                          _ + x
[jlacroix@localhost ~]$ ip addr show
1: lo: <LOOPBACK,UP,LOWER_UP> mtu 65536 qdisc noqueue state UNKNOWN
    link/loopback 00:00:00:00:00:00 brd 00:00:00:00:00:00
    inet 127.0.0.1/8 scope host lo
        valid_lft forever preferred_lft forever
    inet6 ::1/128 scope host
        valid_lft forever preferred_lft forever
2: enp0s3: <BROADCAST,MULTICAST,UP,LOWER_UP> mtu 1500 qdisc pfifo_fast state UP qlen 100
0
    link/ether 08:00:27:97:fe:8a brd ff:ff:ff:ff:ff:ff
    inet 10.10.99.253/22 brd 10.10.99.255 scope global dynamic enp0s3
        valid_lft 85775sec preferred_lft 85775sec
    inet6 fe80::a00:27ff:fe97:fe8a/64 scope link
        valid_lft forever preferred_lft forever
[jlacroix@localhost ~]$
```

The output of the ip command, this time run from a CentOS system

Do you see the difference? If you look at the wired connection, you can tell that it's named quite differently than the wired connection from the Debian example. With Debian, it was named eth0. But on CentOS, it was named enp0s3. This brings us to the point of this section: network devices are named differently in CentOS and Debian.

In the past, wired ethernet devices were named beginning with the prefix of eth, and wireless devices were prefixed with wlan. For example, the first wired ethernet adapter would be labeled eth0; the second would be eth1, and so on. Wireless devices were handled similarly as well, with the first device being wlan0, the second would be wlan1, and so on. With Debian, this is still the case (even in newer releases). However, some distributions that utilize **systemd** feature a different naming scheme for network devices. In fact, Debian 9 will change its naming scheme for interfaces once it's released.

The reason for this change is because the previous naming scheme was at times unpredictable. It was possible to have network device names cross when a machine was rebooted, causing confusion as to which interface is which. The various distributions deal with this problem in their own way, but systemd has a built in naming scheme that is based on the position of the card in the system's bus, rather than just using the names eth0, eth1, and so on as the devices are probed. As mentioned before, Debian still utilizes the older naming scheme, despite the fact that Debian 8 also utilizes systemd. Throughout this book, we will practice systemd commands; however, systemd will be explained more thoroughly in *Chapter 5, Monitoring System Resources*, so don't worry too much if you aren't aware of how it works just yet.

For the CentOS machine used in the second example, the wired network card was given the designation of enp0s3. So, what exactly does this mean? First of all, we know that en represents ethernet, and this part of the designation is given to wired network cards. The rest of the given name represents the position of the network card on the bus of the system. Since each wired card, if you had more than one, would reside in its own physical position, the name given to the device would be predictable. If you were to write startup scripts for a specific network interface, you can be reasonably certain that you'd be writing the script to reference the appropriate device.

Understanding Linux hostname resolution

On a network, it's much more convenient to look up other resources by name, rather than remembering the IP address of every resource we connect to. By default, looking up hosts by name may not function without a little configuration. For example, you can try the ping command against the name of one of your Linux machines, and you may or may not get a response. This is because a DNS entry for the resource you're connecting to might not exist. If it doesn't, you'll see an error similar to the following:

```
ping: unknown host potato
```

However, if you ping the device by its IP, it would more than likely respond:

```
64 bytes from 10.10.96.10: icmp_seq=2 ttl=64 time=0.356 ms
```

 Press *Ctrl* + *C* on your keyboard to break out of your ping command, as it will ping forever if it finds a connection.

The reason for this is in order for a network host to be able to contact another, it needs to know its IP address. If you type in a name instead of an IP address, the machine will attempt hostname resolution, and if there is a valid entry in **Domain Name System** (**DNS**) for the machine you're attempting to contact, you'll be able to receive a reply. In Microsoft networks with Windows-based **Dynamic Host Configuration Protocol** (**DHCP**) and DNS servers, it's very typical for the server to register a **dynamic DNS** entry whenever it assigns an IP address to a host. Linux-based DHCP and DNS servers are capable of dynamic DNS as well, but it's not configured by default and it's rarely enabled by the administrator. In an all Linux network or any network that doesn't assign DNS dynamically, this ping would most likely fail. We discuss DNS in more detail in chapter *Chapter 6, Configuring Network Services*.

In most cases, DNS is not the first place that a Linux host will look in order to resolve hostnames. There is also a file saved locally on the system (/etc/hosts) that your machine will check first. If an entry for the host you're contacting isn't included there, your machine will then contact its configured primary DNS server in order to find an IP address for the name that you entered. Here's an example of a host file:

```
127.0.0.1     localhost
127.0.1.1     trinity-debian

# The following lines are desirable for IPv6 capable hosts
::1     localhost ip6-localhost ip6-loopback
ff02::1 ip6-allnodes
ff02::2 ip6-allrouters
```

In the hosts file presented, we can see an entry for localhost and an entry for trinity-debian. Both of these entries, which begin with a 127.0.x.x IP address, represent the machine itself. To test this, try pinging localhost as well as the name of your machine (in this case, trinity-debian). Either way, you'll get a reply. This is because the machine is aware of its hostname, and localhost uses the loopback adapter to reach itself. If you desired to do so, you could create additional name to IP address matches within this file. For example, if you had a computer named potato at IP address 10.10.96.10, you could add it to the end of the hosts file as follows:

```
10.10.96.10 potato
```

From now on, you'd be able to reach IP address 10.10.96.10 by typing in potato. You could ping it, or even enter it into the address bar of your browser (providing the machine was serving web content). In fact, the host entry doesn't even need to be a local resource in your network. You could even enter an IP address for an external website, and reach it by a different name. However, this only works in theory—a well-designed website may not operate under such circumstances.

While `/etc/hosts` is checked first, your Linux installation includes a file, `/etc/nsswitch.conf` that it uses to make the ultimate determination on the order in which host resolution occurs. The line in question begins with `hosts`, and you can easily check the host resolution order on your machine with the following command:

```
cat /etc/nsswitch.conf |grep hosts
```

You'll get the following output:

```
hosts:          files mdns4_minimal [NOTFOUND=return] dns
```

Here, we can see the system is set up to check `files` first, which represents local files, which includes `/etc/hosts`. If the search is for a local domain and it is not found, the `NOTFOUND=return` entry causes the remainder of the search to abort. If you're searching for anything else, the next resource that will be used is DNS, as shown with `dns` being the last entry. Unless you changed this file, chances are that your distribution will also be set up to look within local hosts files first, and then DNS if the resource is not found locally.

Understanding the net-tools and iproute2 suites

For quite some time, **net-tools** has been the suite of tools used to manage network connections on Linux systems. The net-tools suite includes commands such as `ifconfig`, `route`, `netstat`, and others (which we'll discuss shortly). The problem with net-tools is that it hasn't been updated by its developers in well over a decade, making many distributions opt to abandon it in favor of the **iproute2** suite, which offers the same functionality (but with different commands to achieve the same goals). Even though net-tools are being deprecated, quite a few distributions still include it. For example, Debian includes both iproute2 and net-tools, so you can use commands from either suite. In CentOS, iproute2 is present though net-tools is not installed by default. If you would like to utilize the older net-tools, you can install it in CentOS with the following command:

```
# yum install net-tools
```

So, why would you want to install `net-tools` if it's being abandoned? Many systems still have scripts that use commands from the net-tools suite, so it's not something that will disappear from the Linux community any time soon. Learning net-tools, as well as the newer iproute2, will enable you to easily adapt to any environment. This is especially the case for older data centers that are using older distributions.

Let's see these suites in action. First, to report basic information about your network connections, type the following:

`/sbin/ifconfig`

You should see the following output:

```
jlacroix@trinity-vm-debian-testing: ~                              — ✕

jlacroix@trinity-vm-debian-testing:~$ /sbin/ifconfig
eth0      Link encap:Ethernet  HWaddr 08:00:27:6a:2a:00
          inet addr:10.10.99.254  Bcast:10.10.99.255  Mask:255.255.252.0
          inet6 addr: fe80::a00:27ff:fe6a:2a00/64 Scope:Link
          UP BROADCAST RUNNING MULTICAST  MTU:1500  Metric:1
          RX packets:394 errors:0 dropped:0 overruns:0 frame:0
          TX packets:212 errors:0 dropped:0 overruns:0 carrier:0
          collisions:0 txqueuelen:1000
          RX bytes:37456 (36.5 KiB)  TX bytes:28759 (28.0 KiB)

lo        Link encap:Local Loopback
          inet addr:127.0.0.1  Mask:255.0.0.0
          inet6 addr: ::1/128 Scope:Host
          UP LOOPBACK RUNNING  MTU:65536  Metric:1
          RX packets:29 errors:0 dropped:0 overruns:0 frame:0
          TX packets:29 errors:0 dropped:0 overruns:0 carrier:0
          collisions:0 txqueuelen:0
          RX bytes:3251 (3.1 KiB)  TX bytes:3251 (3.1 KiB)

jlacroix@trinity-vm-debian-testing:~$ ▌
```

The output of the ifconfig command

Here, we can see statistics from both the internal wired connection (eth0) as well as the loopback adapter (lo). We see HWaddr, which is the **MAC address** of the network card. We also have inet addr, which is the IP address that the card was provided by the **DHCP server**. In addition, we can see the subnet mask, Mask, which is 255.255.252.0 in this case. While troubleshooting networking issues, we would use this tool to check these basic things, such as ensuring we have an IP address and we are on the appropriate subnet. In addition, we can also see the number of packets sent and received on the interface, as well as the number of errors.

With the iproute2 suite, we can find most of the same information with the following command:

```
ip addr show
```

Here's the output from a reference machine:

```
jlacroix@trinity-vm-debian-testing:~$ ip addr show
1: lo: <LOOPBACK,UP,LOWER_UP> mtu 65536 qdisc noqueue state UNKNOWN group defau
lt
    link/loopback 00:00:00:00:00:00 brd 00:00:00:00:00:00
    inet 127.0.0.1/8 scope host lo
       valid_lft forever preferred_lft forever
    inet6 ::1/128 scope host
       valid_lft forever preferred_lft forever
2: eth0: <BROADCAST,MULTICAST,UP,LOWER_UP> mtu 1500 qdisc pfifo_fast state UP g
roup default qlen 1000
    link/ether 08:00:27:6a:2a:00 brd ff:ff:ff:ff:ff:ff
    inet 10.10.99.254/22 brd 10.10.99.255 scope global dynamic eth0
       valid_lft 84786sec preferred_lft 84786sec
    inet6 fe80::a00:27ff:fe6a:2a00/64 scope link
       valid_lft forever preferred_lft forever
jlacroix@trinity-vm-debian-testing:~$
```

The output from the ip addr show command

As you can see, the information reported is mostly the same, though the layout is a bit different. For example, one difference is that you don't see the number of packets sent and received, nor an error count (by default). In the past, the following command would show the IP addresses in use as well as sent and received packets:

```
ip -s addr show
```

```
:: ▭                          jlacroix@pandora:~                            – ✕
[jlacroix@pandora:~]$ ip -s addr show
1: lo: <LOOPBACK,UP,LOWER_UP> mtu 65536 qdisc noqueue state UNKNOWN group default
    link/loopback 00:00:00:00:00:00 brd 00:00:00:00:00:00
    inet 127.0.0.1/8 scope host lo
       valid_lft forever preferred_lft forever
    inet6 ::1/128 scope host
       valid_lft forever preferred_lft forever
    RX: bytes   packets  errors  dropped overrun mcast
    877835333   4653892  0       0       0       0
    TX: bytes   packets  errors  dropped carrier collsns
    877835333   4653892  0       0       0       0
2: enp0s25: <BROADCAST,MULTICAST,UP,LOWER_UP> mtu 1500 qdisc pfifo_fast state UP group default qlen 1000
    link/ether bc:5f:f4:bb:d5:27 brd ff:ff:ff:ff:ff:ff
    inet 10.10.97.1/22 brd 10.10.99.255 scope global dynamic enp0s25
       valid_lft 59615sec preferred_lft 59615sec
    inet6 fe80::be5f:f4ff:febb:d527/64 scope link
       valid_lft forever preferred_lft forever
    RX: bytes   packets  errors  dropped overrun mcast
    101634669099 74918615 0      1818    0       148097
    TX: bytes   packets  errors  dropped carrier collsns
    39365828160 45318610 0       0       0       0
[jlacroix@pandora:~]$ █
```

The output of the ip addr show command with the -s flag added

Unfortunately, recent versions of the iproute2 suite don't seem to show this information anymore (despite adding the -s switch), but we'll look at additional tools later on in this book.

> Instead of addr in the previous commands, you can also type out the entire string (address) such as:
>
> ```
> ip address show
> ```
>
> The output will be the same. The commands shown in these examples were condensed, which save typing time.

The iproute2 suite features many more commands than just these, and we'll discuss them as the book continues. For now, it's important to understand the difference between the two command suites and to note that net-tools won't be available forever. In the time period in which this book was written, both are common. However, iproute2 is the name of the game going forward.

Before closing out this section, there's a really easy command in the iproute2 suite that might prove useful:

```
hostname
```

This simple command just prints the hostname of the machine on which your shell is attached. If you're using your default bash prompt, chances are you are already aware of your machine's hostname. However, the hostname command can at least help you verify that your device is reporting the hostname you think it should be; this can be useful when you're dealing with name resolution issues.

Manually managing network interfaces

In most cases, after you install your desired distribution of Linux, it receives an IP address via DHCP and away it goes. Whether you're using a graphical desktop environment or a shell environment with no GUI, the magic mostly happens in the background. While there are GUI tools to manage your network connections, anything you can do via a graphical tool, you can do via the shell. In the case of servers, there may not be a graphical environment at all, so learning how to manage your network connection via the shell is very important. In this section, we'll discuss the method for manually configuring an interface in Debian, and then discuss how to do the same thing with CentOS.

In the previous section, two methods were discussed for finding your current IP address. Depending on whether your distribution ships net-tools or iproute2, you can use one method or the other (or both). Of course, that's the first step. Do you have a connection? Checking to see whether or not you have an IP address is a logical place to start. You can also utilize a simple ping test:

```
ping www.yahoo.com
```

If you do get a response, chances are that you have a network connection. However, if you don't get a response, it doesn't necessarily mean that there's something wrong with your network. Some sites are configured to not respond to ping tests. Whenever possible, ping against local resources instead (such as your local DNS or DHCP server).

In Linux, ping works a bit differently than in Windows. For starters, the `ping` command in Linux will run virtually forever by default. To break out of it, press *Ctrl + C* on your keyboard. If you prefer to have `ping` stop after a certain number of tries, add the `-c` flag accompanied by the number of times you'd like it to attempt. In this case, our `ping` command will be like this:

```
ping -c 4 www.yahoo.com
```

In this case, `ping` will attempt four times, stop, and then report some basic statistics to you.

Knowing how to check whether or not you're connected is one thing, but what do you do when you're not? Or what if your network connection is active, but reports invalid information and you need to reconfigure it?

First, let's explore how to check our current configuration. In Debian, the file that controls the network devices by default is the following:

`/etc/network/interfaces`

Depending on several variables, which include how you configured your Debian installation, this file may be created differently. First, you may see several interfaces listed, such as your loopback adapter, wired Ethernet, and wireless. If you have more than one wired interface, you'll see any additional adapters here as well. This file is, simply put, a **configuration file**. It's a text file that contains information that the underlying Linux system understands, and causes a device to be configured as designated in the file.

To edit files such as these, there are many Linux text editors available, both GUI and terminal based. My personal favorite is **vim**, though many administrators typically start off with **nano**. The nano text editor is fairly easy to use, though very light on features. Alternatively, vim has many more features than nano but is a bit harder to get used to. Take your pick. To open a file in nano, all you need to do is type `nano` along with the name of a text file you would like to edit. If the file doesn't exist, the command will create it if you save the file. In the case of our `/etc/network/interfaces` file, the command will be similar to this:

`# nano /etc/network/interfaces`

Using nano is simply a matter of opening a file, using the arrow keys on your keyboard to move the insertion point to where you want to type, pressing *Ctrl + O* to save the file, and pressing *Ctrl + X* to exit. There are more features, but for the purposes of editing our configuration files, that's all we need for now. A tutorial for vim is beyond the scope of this book, but feel free to play around with it if you wish.

Now, back to the subject of our `/etc/network/interfaces` file. It's important to note that this file is not required for the purposes of ethernet and wireless adapters. If you see nothing in this file at all (other than the loopback device) it means that the network connections are being managed by **Network Manager**. Network Manager is a graphical tool for managing client-side network connections (which we'll discuss later in this chapter). For our purposes in this section, Network Manager is typically installed when you decide to include a graphical desktop environment when setting up Debian for the first time. If you did opt for a graphical environment (such as GNOME, Xfce, and so on), then Network Manager was more than likely set up for you and is handling the job of configuring your interfaces. If your `interfaces` file is blank other than the entry for the loopback adapter, then that means Network Manager is handling this task.

With Debian, it's extremely common to see installations in the wild with no graphical environment installed at all. A GUI is usually not necessary for the server to fulfill its purpose. A typical Linux administrator will configure a server with the minimum required packages for it to do its job, which often will not include a desktop environment. In this case, Network Manager may not be installed at all. If it's not, the `/etc/network/interfaces` file will then be responsible for setting up the connection. In other cases, perhaps Network Manager is installed, but was disabled by the administrator whom configured the network connections in this file instead.

So, when should you use Network Manager, and when should you just configure your connections in the `interfaces` file? In the case of end-user workstations (desktops and laptops), Network Manager is almost always preferred. In the case of servers, setting up the configuration in `/etc/network/interfaces` is preferred, especially when setting up a static IP address.

We've discussed what the `interfaces` file is, and when you'd want to use it. Now, let's take a look at some various types of configurations you can expect to see. First, let's gander at the `interfaces` file when only the local loopback adapter is listed:

```
cat /etc/network/interfaces
```

```
# The loopback network interface
auto lo
iface lo inet loopback
```

Comments are declared with the first character #, which is ignored when the configuration file is parsed. In the previous example, the first line is ignored and it just serves as information.

In this example, the machine most likely has Network Manager in use, as neither the wired (typically `eth0`) or wireless (typically `wlan0`) interfaces are shown. To verify this, we can check to see if Network Manager is running via the following command:

```
ps ax |grep NetworkManager
```

If Network Manager is running, you might see an output like this:

```
446 ?        Ssl    0:00 /usr/sbin/NetworkManager --no-daemon
```

That mystery is solved; the machine uses Network Manager, so there is no configuration for `eth0` or `wlan0` stored in `/etc/network/interfaces`. Now, let's take a look at an example from a machine where Network Manager is not being used. To configure `eth0` in such an installation, the `interfaces` file would look similar to this:

```
# The loopback network interface
auto lo
iface lo inet loopback

# Wired connection eth0
auto eth0
iface eth0 inet dhcp
```

As we can see, we still have the loopback entry as we did before, but at the end of the file, configuration details were included for `eth0`. Just as in our loopback entry, we declare `auto` and then an interface name `eth0`, which means that we would like interface `eth0` to automatically come up. In the next line, we clarify that we'd like to utilize `dhcp` for interface `eth0` so that it will obtain an IP address automatically from a DHCP server.

In the real world, there's no good reason to abandon Network Manager in favor of manually configuring the connection when all we're going to do is use DHCP. However, this example was included here because it's actually fairly common in situations where a server receives a **static lease** from a DHCP server, rather than a dynamic one. With a static lease, the DHCP server will provide the same IP address for a particular MAC address each time. So in such a scenario, a server could have a designated IP address for it, but the IP address is still provided by a DHCP server. This is also known as a **DHCP reservation**.

Of course, it's also possible (and perhaps more common) to simply declare a static IP in the interfaces file. We'll even explore that method next. But a static lease is worth pointing out because it does carry with it an additional benefit. With a static lease, the node's IP configuration is not tied to its configuration with its installed distribution. If it's booted from live media, or even if the distribution is reinstalled, the node will still receive the same IP address each time its interface comes up. An additional benefit of a static lease is that you can configure the static IPs of all your nodes in one central place (on the DHCP server), rather than keep track of individual configuration files from machine to machine.

It's important to note that seeing dhcp listed in the interfaces file for an interface does not always mean that a static lease is in use. For Debian, it's common for an administrator to simply not install Network Manager, and then manually type the interfaces file when bringing up a server.

Now, let's look at an example interfaces file where a static IP has been manually configured:

```
# The loopback network interface
auto lo
iface lo inet loopback

# Wired connection eth0
auto eth0
iface eth0 inet static
    address 10.10.10.12
    netmask 255.255.248.0
    network 10.10.10.0
    broadcast 10.10.10.255
    gateway 10.10.10.1
```

First, notice the change in the following line:

```
iface eth0 inet static
```

At the end, we declare static instead of dhcp. If we had forgotten to change this, all the remaining lines of the configuration file would then be ignored.

Then, we declare the statistics for interface eth0. We set the IP address to 10.10.10.12, the subnet mask to 255.255.248.0, the network we're joining to 10.10.10.0, the broadcast ID as 10.10.10.255, and the gateway as 10.10.10.1. We'll discuss what each of these values actually mean later on in this book, but for now the important thing to note is the syntax for this file.

So now you may be wondering how we make these changes take effect, now that we went through the trouble of configuring our interface. To do so, you would use the following command:

```
# systemctl restart networking.service
```

With CentOS, the process of manually configuring network interfaces is a bit different to Debian systems. First, we'll need to know which interfaces are installed on our machine. Running the following command will list them, along with any IP addresses that are currently assigned:

```
ip addr show
```

In this section, I'll use enp0s3, which is the default on the test machine used for this book. If yours differs, change these example commands accordingly. Anyway, now that we know what interface we're working with, let's configure it. Next, navigate to the following directory:

```
cd /etc/sysconfig/network-scripts
```

If you list the storage for the files within that directory (the ls command), you should see a configuration file with a name that matches the name of your interface. In our example of enp0s3, you should see a file named ifcfg-enp0s3.

Open this file with your chosen text editor and you'll see the configuration looks similar to the following:

```
HWADDR="08:00:27:97:FE:8A"
TYPE="Ethernet"
BOOTPROTO="dhcp"
DEFROUTE="yes"
PEERDNS="yes"
PEERROUTES="yes"
IPV4_FAILURE_FATAL="no"
IPV6INIT="yes"
IPV6_AUTOCONF="yes"
IPV6_DEFROUTE="yes"
IPV6_PEERDNS="yes"
IPV6_PEERROUTES="yes"
IPV6_FAILURE_FATAL="no"
NAME="enp0s3"
UUID="a5e581c4-7843-46d3-b8d5-157dfb2e32a2"
ONBOOT="yes"
```

As you can see, this default file is using dhcp, which is listed on the third line. To configure this connection to utilize a static address, we'll need to change the file accordingly. Changes to the file are marked in bold:

```
HWADDR="08:00:27:97:FE:8A"
TYPE="Ethernet"
BOOTPROTO="static"
IPADDR=10.10.10.52
NETMASK=255.255.255.0
NM_CONTROLLED=no
DEFROUTE="yes"
PEERDNS="yes"
PEERROUTES="yes"
IPV4_FAILURE_FATAL="no"
IPV6INIT="yes"
IPV6_AUTOCONF="yes"
IPV6_DEFROUTE="yes"
IPV6_PEERDNS="yes"
IPV6_PEERROUTES="yes"
IPV6_FAILURE_FATAL="no"
NAME="enp0s3"
UUID="a5e581c4-7843-46d3-b8d5-157dfb2e32a2"
ONBOOT="yes"
```

Here, we made just four changes to the file. First, we changed BOOTPROTO to static. Then, we added the following brand new lines just underneath it:

```
IPADDR=10.10.10.52
NETMASK=255.255.255.0
NM_CONTROLLED=no
```

I'm sure you can gather what the first two lines are responsible for. The fourth line we added may be obvious too, but just in case it isn't, we're basically telling our system that we would rather not manage our connection via Network Manager, and would like to take care of that ourselves with this configuration file.

Of course, we need to restart networking in order for these changes to take effect. Since CentOS uses systemd (just like Debian 8), the command is very similar:

```
# systemctl restart network.service
```

And, there you have it. We took care of manually setting up our network interfaces in both Debian and CentOS.

Managing connections with Network Manager

While we just went through the trouble of manually configuring our network interfaces, it's not always the case that this is desirable. End user workstations, for example, would benefit from Network Manager handling this job for us. For laptops and their wireless interfaces, Network Manager does the job better than most of us would.

Network Manager is usually installed by default in most distributions of Linux. For Debian, it is typically installed whenever you opt for a graphical desktop environment. If you opted for a shell-only install (you unchecked the options for a desktop environment during installation), you probably don't have it installed. To be sure, execute the following command (works on both Debian and CentOS):

```
ps ax |grep NetworkManager
```

If you see that Network Manager is running, then it is installed. But to be double-sure, you can execute this command in Debian:

```
aptitude search network-manager
```

If Network Manager is installed, you'll see it listed as follows (there will be an i designation to the left of it):

In CentOS, you can check whether Network Manager is installed or not using the following command:

```
yum list installed |grep NetworkManager
```

If you're running a desktop environment, you may have an implementation of Network Manager running within your system tray. If so, feel free to manage your connection via the available GUI tools. Depending on which desktop environment you're using, the instructions for doing so will be different. In this section, we discuss a more universal approach to utilizing Network Manager to configure connections. This method is to use the following command:

```
nmtui
```

The nmtui command allows you to configure Network Manager within a shell environment, but with GUI-like controls.

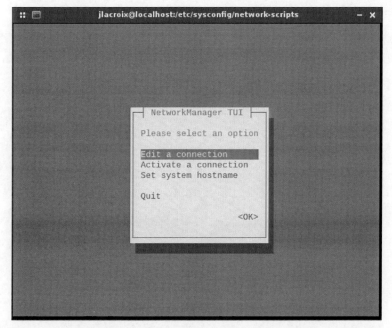

Configuring a system's network connection via nmtui

If we click on **Edit a connection**, we will see a list of interfaces available on our machine:

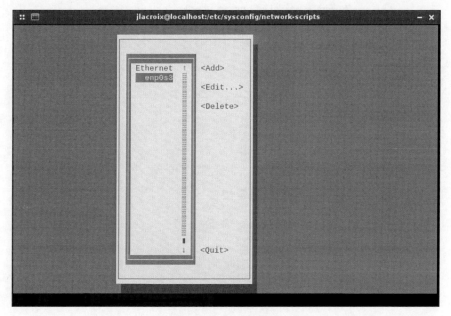

nmtui interface selection

When we select an interface, we'll first see some basic information.

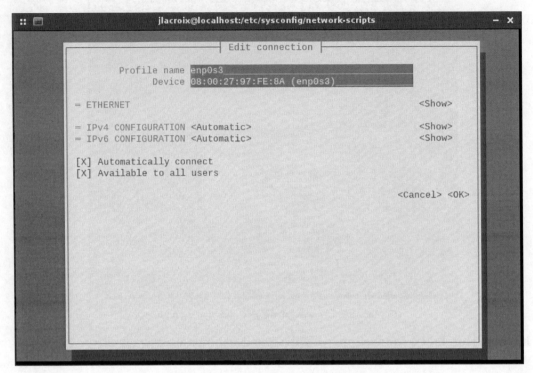

First screen of editing a connection in nmtui

To edit the IP address for this interface, press the down arrow key to select **<AUTOMATIC>** on the left-hand side of **IPv4 CONFIGURATION** and press *Enter*. Then, press the right arrow key to select the **<Show>** option and expand the remaining fields.

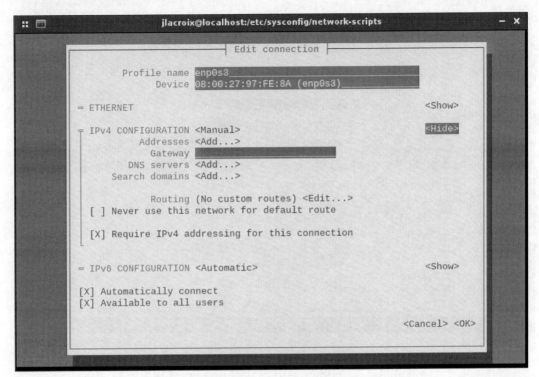

Editing a connection with nmtui

To edit an item, press the down arrow key to the **<Add...>** option next to the field. It will expand a textbox to allow you to edit the item.

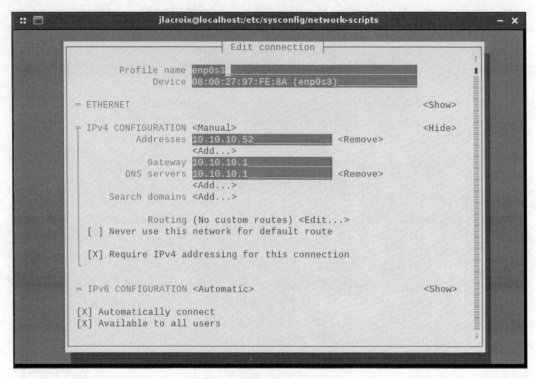

Editing a connection with nmtui

When finished, scroll all the way down and press *Enter* on **<OK>** to save your changes. There you have it; you should be able to manage your connections via Network Manager, should you choose to do so.

Summary

In this chapter, we discussed the basics of TCP/IP networking in Linux and even configured our interfaces manually. We explored how to edit the configuration files associated with Debian and CentOS, as well as how to restart networking on both platforms. We briefly talked about the systemd method, though we'll explore systemd in more depth in *Chapter 5, Monitoring System Resources*. We finished the chapter by utilizing the nmtui tool to configure Network Manager for our system.

In the next chapter, we'll take a look at how to use **Secure Shell (SSH)** to remotely manage our systems.

3

Communicating Between Nodes via SSH

SSH is one of the most important tools for a Linux network administrator. It allows you to connect to servers and other workstations remotely, and work on them from within your favorite terminal emulator—all from the comfort of your desk. While SSH might not be the perfect tool for every situation, it's one of those that you won't be able to imagine life without, once you start using it.

In this chapter, we explore SSH and cover the following topics:

- Using OpenSSH
- Installing and configuring OpenSSH
- Connecting to network hosts via openssh-client
- The OpenSSH config file
- Understanding and utilizing scp
- Transferring files to another node via scp
- Tunneling traffic via SSH
- Generating public keys
- Keeping SSH connections alive
- Exploring an alternative to SSH – utilizing Mosh (mobile shell)

Using OpenSSH

SSH, or **Secure Shell**, is a very handy utility. SSH is not an absolute requirement for performing tasks in your server room, but it is one of those things that will make your life a lot easier. With SSH, you are able to execute commands on a different Linux machine as though you were sitting right there in front of it. Sure, you could always walk into your server room, grab the keyboard, and start working, but nowadays remote administration is the name of the game. This is especially true if it's your turn to be on call and an issue comes up at the office. Depending on the nature of the issue, SSH may allow you to fix the problem from home (or even on your smart phone) without having to make the trek all the way to your company's server room. That's not all; SSH also allows you to copy files from one machine to another and set up an actual storage mount to a directory on a server, which can be treated, on your workstation, like the directory were a local part of your filesystem.

The concept of connecting to a remote host and opening a command shell is not new, and SSH is not the first to do it. Other solutions, such as telnet or rlogin, have existed for quite a while. What makes SSH desirable is that it is more secure than earlier technologies, as communication is encrypted. There are two protocols for SSH, protocol 1 and protocol 2. Protocol 1 should not be used under any circumstances, as it is no longer secure. Traffic sent between two hosts utilizing protocol 1 could be intercepted by an attacker. We will discuss this aspect of SSH in *Chapter 9, Securing Your Network*, but for now I want to make sure that you understand that you shouldn't use an SSH connection with protocol 1. You should not offer protocol 1 to any of your hosts. Nowadays, protocol 2 is the default.

By default, SSH uses port 22 to communicate. If this port is blocked by a firewall, you will not be able to connect. This is extremely common in Windows-centric businesses, since SSH is more common in the Linux/UNIX world. By changing the configuration of the SSH server, you can configure it to listen on any port you like. While we won't get into how to configure this just yet (we'll discuss this in *Chapter 9, Securing Your Network*), it's mentioned here because it's important to note that you may run into a situation where you aren't able to connect to an SSH server, for example, when the port is either closed or has been changed to a different one.

Although I mentioned that learning SSH isn't actually required to perform tasks on a server or workstation, it is highly recommended that you spend time to learn it. Not only do companies that utilize Linux servers expect you to know it, you won't want to miss out on its advantages. Thankfully, as useful as SSH is, it's by no means difficult to learn. You could easily learn the most basic functionality in five minutes, or advanced usage within a week.

Installing and configuring OpenSSH

OpenSSH comes in two pieces, the client application and the server application. It's likely that the client application is installed by default in your distribution. The client allows you to connect to other nodes via SSH, but having the client alone doesn't allow others to connect to you. If you want to access a machine via SSH, that machine must also have the SSH server application installed. Your chosen distribution may have the server application installed by default, but most don't. This is due to security—unless you absolutely need to have an application running and listening for connections, it should be absent. The fewer applications, the smaller the attack surface someone could use against you.

In Debian, SSH server is an option during the installation process. If selected, the server application of SSH will be present and will start by default. To check whether the SSH server package is installed on a Debian system, execute the following command:

```
aptitude search openssh-server
```

In the output, if the first character is i, then the package is installed. You can check whether the **sshd** service is running with the following command:

```
ps ax | grep sshd
```

If the service isn't running, you can start it by executing the following command on Debian:

```
# systemctl start ssh.service
```

On Debian, you can check the status of the SSH service by executing the following command:

```
# systemctl status ssh.service
```

If it's running, the output should include active (running):

If your system doesn't have the SSH server package installed, you can install it with the following command:

```
# apt-get install openssh-server
```

After you've installed the package, check the status of the service with the following command to see if it's enabled:

```
systemctl status ssh.service
```

Otherwise, it won't start automatically the next time you boot the machine.

In CentOS, you also use the `systemctl` command in order to check the status of the SSH service, though the daemon is named a bit differently:

```
systemctl status sshd.service
```

In the previous command in Debian, the service was named `ssh.service`. In CentOS, it's named `sshd.service`. In CentOS, both the client and server packages for SSH are installed by default, so you should already have them as soon as your CentOS system finishes installation. If you don't have the package installed for some reason, you can install it via `yum`:

```
# yum install openssh-server
```

After installation, ensure that the service is enabled by checking the status:

```
systemctl status sshd.service
```

If the SSH service is not in an enabled state (start on boot), execute the following command:

```
# systemctl enable sshd.service
```

Now that SSH is installed on your machines, we're ready to start using it.

Connecting to network hosts via openssh-client

For this experiment, you'll need at least one Linux installation with the SSH server active, and another with at least the SSH client installed. For the client, you'll need to either install the `openssh-clients` package in CentOS, or the `openssh-client` package in Debian. The client package for SSH is installed by default on both, so you shouldn't need to install it unless the package was removed. For this activity, it doesn't matter which distribution is on the server or the client end of the connection. Feel free to mix it up.

Next, all we need is to record the IP addresses of the node we wish to connect to. Regardless of the distribution, you should be able to discover the IP address by executing the following command:

```
ip addr show
```

To connect to that machine via SSH, execute the `ssh` command against the IP address of the host. For example, if the host you want to connect to has an IP address `192.168.1.201`, execute the following command:

```
ssh 192.168.1.201
```

As long as your username is the same on both sides, that command should ask for your password and then let you in. If your username is different on the host you're attempting to connect to, add the appropriate username to the command like this:

```
ssh jdoe@192.168.1.201
```

With SSH, you can connect to another Linux installation using any username that exists there, as long as you know the password for it. In fact, depending on how the distribution was configured by the vendor, you may even be able to log in directly as root. In CentOS, root login is enabled by default. In Debian, root login via SSH is not allowed unless you're using an RSA key (we'll discuss this in *Chapter 9*, *Securing Your Network*). Although we'll discuss more about security (including how to allow/disallow users) in that chapter, for now it's important to understand that allowing root access to a system via SSH is a very bad idea; I hope that you'll keep this disabled on production servers and workstations. If you wish to disable root access now, go to the relevant section of *Chapter 9*, *Securing Your Network*, and then come back here.

SSH also allows you to specify a host name rather than an IP address. In fact, host names are the preferred method since it's difficult to memorize IP addresses if you have a great number of machines in your network. SSH itself doesn't resolve host names; it relies on DNS for that. If the DNS server on your network has an A (address) record for the machine you wish to connect to, you should be able to use the host name instead of the IP address:

```
ssh jdoe@chupacabra
```

 If the machine doesn't have a DNS entry in your network, or if you have yet to set up a DNS server, don't worry. We'll discuss setting up our very own DNS (bind) server in *Chapter 6*, *Configuring Network Services*.

Another important aspect of connecting to a host is specifying a port. As mentioned earlier, the default port is 22. If you don't specify a port, then port 22 is assumed. If you need to specify a different port, you can do so with the -p flag, as follows:

```
ssh -p 6022 jdoe@chupacabra
```

After a successful connection, you should have a command prompt to a shell on the target machine. From here, you can install packages, manage users, configure the network, or do anything else that you'd be able to do if you were able to log in to the machine in person. Your only limit is whatever permissions your user has to the system. If it's a machine that belongs to you, or one that you set up yourself and you know the root password for, you can literally do anything you want. If the machine belongs to someone else, you might have permission to modify your local home folder only. Either way, you successfully connected to a machine using SSH. The remaining sections of this chapter, as well as *Chapter 9, Securing Your Network*, will expand on this basic knowledge.

The OpenSSH config file

When utilizing SSH for the first time, the .ssh directory will be created in your home directory. This directory contains useful files for your SSH client, which include known_hosts, id_rsa, and id_rsa.pub once you generate your keys (which we will do later). While we will discuss those files later on in this chapter, there is another file that the SSH client recognizes: config. This file is not created by default. If you create it yourself (following the proper syntax), then SSH will recognize it. So, what does this config file do? If you have one or more hosts that you connect to frequently, you can fill this file with the specifics for each host without having to enter the details each time. Let's look at an example ~/.ssh/config file.

```
Host icarus
Hostname 10.10.10.76
Port 22
User jdoe


Host daedalus
Hostname 10.10.10.88
Port 65000
User duser


Host dragon
Hostname 10.10.10.99
Port 22
User jdoe
```

For this file, SSH will recognize three hosts straight away: Icarus, Daedalus, and dragon. This is regardless of whether or not these machines are listed in DNS. If we were to type ssh icarus and the previous config file was used, SSH would know not only how to get to it (the IP address is given in the file) but SSH would also know which user and port to use. Even if our username is not jdoe, it will be used for this connection (since it's listed in the file)—unless we give the ssh command a different user in the command string.

In the second entry in our sample file (daedalus), you'll notice that it is a bit different from the others. First, the port is different. For all the other hosts in this file, the default of 22 is used. But with daedalus, we issue a different port. If we connect to daedalus via SSH, it will automatically try the referenced port. Next, you'll also notice that the username is different for this host. Even if our local user was jdoe and we didn't supply a different username, user duser would be automatically used instead. We can override this by providing user@ before the host name, if we wished to.

Since this file doesn't exist by default, all we need to do is create it using any text editor and save it to the following:

`~/.ssh/config`

As long as we typed it out correctly, SSH should see the file and allow us to use it. Then, we can create our own list of hosts in this file to easily provide the required parameters for each, and allow easier access. Go ahead and give it a try in your lab.

Understanding and utilizing scp

SSH actually has several uses; it's not just for connecting one machine to another, though that is the most popular use case. SSH also allows you to transfer files to another machine, or even transfer files from a remote machine to your local one. The utility that allows you to do this is the scp (**secure copy**) command, which is part of the SSH suite of utilities. Of course, you can also transfer files via network shares, but the beauty of scp is that it offers an on-the-fly file transfer, with no share configuration being necessary. The scp command is simple and fast. You can transfer a file from your machine to anywhere on the filesystem of a target machine that you have permission to access.

The scp utility is primarily meant for those who need a quick transfer of a file, as it is not a long-term solution for file access and storage. In a situation where you need to create a storage repository that others need to access, you would typically set up an **NFS** or **Samba** share to accomplish the goal. However, scp is a great utility that will prove very useful to you, whenever you want to simply send a file to another machine without configuring anything.

Transferring files to another node via scp

Let's give scp a try. As with our previous SSH activity, you'll need at least two machines: one with the SSH server installed and running, and another with at least the client. In this case, the distribution shouldn't matter as long as you meet this simple requirements. In addition, we'll need a file to test with. The file can be something small (such as a text file or image) or large (such as an ISO file for a Linux distribution). The goal is to transfer this file to another machine using scp. Let's see how to do this.

For the sake of this tutorial, I'll outline the procedure for a machine named foo to transfer a file to a machine named bar.

First, let's take a look at a simple example of scp:

```
scp my-image.jpg 192.168.1.200:/home/jdoe/
```

In that example, we've executed the scp command against a file named my-image. jpg. Next, we outline the target. In this case, a machine with the IP address of 192.168.1.200. Then, we type a colon and the path where we'd like the file to be stored. In this case, we are going to copy the file into the home directory for jdoe.

Since we know the name of the target machine (bar), we could use the name of the machine instead of the IP address, assuming that it is recognized by the DNS server. It was configured in ~/.ssh/config, or is an entry on foo's /etc/hosts file. The command is as follows:

```
scp my-image.jpg bar:/home/jdoe
```

We simplified the command a bit, since we know the name of the machine. Additionally, we don't have to type out the name of the directory if we're intending to copy to a user's home directory. We could have simplified the command to the following:

```
scp my-image.jpg bar:.
```

In the example, instead of typing out /home/jdoe, we replaced the path with a period. This works because the home directory is assumed, unless you give the command a separate path. We'd also get the same result if we used a tilde (~) instead:

```
scp my-image.jpg bar:~
```

What if the data we wish to copy is an entire directory, instead of just a single file? If we try to use the scp command against a directory, it will fail. In order to copy an entire directory, we need to add the -r flag that performs a recursive copy:

```
scp -r my_dir bar:~
```

Now, the my_dir directory and its contents will be transferred over. Another useful flag when copying files is -p, which preserves the modification times when the file is copied. If we combine that with the previous command, we get:

```
scp -rp my_dir bar:~
```

However, each of these commands will fail if the user name is different on the two machines. For example, if the logged-on user on foo is dlong and the user doesn't exist on bar, the command would fail because the sending computer would default to using dlong, the currently logged-on user. In this case, the other computer would ask you for the password three times, and then give you a message that access is denied. This is because you would essentially be typing a password for a user that doesn't exist. If we need to specify the username for the target, the command would become similar to the following:

```
scp my-image.jpg jdoe@bar:~
```

With the new version of the command, you'll be prompted for the jdoe password and then the file would be copied to /home/jdoe on the receiving end.

As mentioned previously in this chapter, the default port for SSH (port 22) may not be open on the target, as perhaps it is listening on a different port. With scp, we can specify a different port. To do so, use the -P flag. Note that this is an uppercase P, unlike the ssh command that uses a lowercase -p for specifying the port (this can be somewhat confusing at first when switching between ssh and scp). For example, this flag is appended to the previous command:

```
scp -P 6022 my-image.jpg jdoe@bar:~
```

Go ahead and give it a try in your lab. Find a file of any type and attempt to transfer it to another Linux machine. If you do this a few times, you should be able to get the hang of it fairly quickly. Another point of interest in regards to scp is that you can use it to copy a file or directory from a remote machine to your local one, if you already know the path of the file you wish to download. In the last example of this section, I'm copying myimage.jpg from remote host bar to my current working directory (which I designate with a period):

```
scp jdoe@bar:~/myimage.jpg .
```

Tunneling traffic via SSH

One of the most useful features of SSH is creating an **SSH tunnel**. An SSH tunnel allows you to access services locally that originate from another computer or server. This allows you to do such things as bypass local DNS filtering, or even access an IRC server that is segregated within your company, from home.

Be very careful when utilizing SSH tunnels. If you aren't able to access a resource while at work, or a work resource is blocked from being accessible from outside the network, chances are the network administrator (if that person is not you) set it up this way for a reason. When bypassing restrictions or accessing work resources from outside the network, always ensure you have permission to do so.

In order for an SSH tunnel to be effective, you first need to be able to access SSH where the service you'd like to access is hosted. If you're able to initiate a normal SSH connection to a network containing the service, chances are that you'll have no problem creating a tunnel.

While utilizing SSH to create a tunnel, the command changes a bit. Instead of just executing the ssh command against a host name or IP address, there are a few more flags added. First, we add the -L flag. This sets up what is known as a bind address, which basically means we are taking a local port and forwarding it to a specific port on the other end.

The syntax for such a command string would be something like this:

```
ssh -L <local-port>:localhost:<remote-port> <username>@10.10.10.101
```

Basically, we execute SSH with the -L flag and use localhost since we intend to forward a local service to a remote one. However, we sandwich the command with a port and a colon on either side. The port on the left-hand side is our local port and on the right-hand side of the IP address, we have a colon and then the remote port. We then finish off the command with our usual syntax, that is, we type our user name and then the IP address of the gateway we will use for the connection.

Confused yet? Let's break this down further and use an example.

By default, VNC (a graphical remote access program) utilizes ports 5900-5902. If you wanted to access a desktop environment on a remote host with an IP address of 10.10.10.101, use the following command:

```
ssh -L 5900:localhost:5901 jdoe@10.10.10.101
```

Here, we're forwarding port 5900 on our local machine to port 5901 on 10.10.10.101. As soon as the session connects and is established, we can then use the following in our VNC viewing application on our local machine to connect to the VNC service on the remote end:

```
localhost:5900
```

Anytime localhost:5900 is used, we'll be forwarded to our remote machine. To end the session, exit from the SSH connection. For VNC, we need to specify which VNC session to use. In order to use the VNC Viewer application to open a VNC session to 10.10.10.101, we would execute the following command:

```
vncviewer localhost:1
```

However, what if the machine or service we wish to connect to is behind a different gateway? The previous example only works if the IP address, 10.10.10.101, is routable through the Internet, or we are actually on the same network as the resource we wish to connect to. This is not always the case, and generally useful services are not exposed directly to the Internet. For example, if you're at home and you wish to connect to the remote desktop protocol on a computer in your work network, the previous example wouldn't work.

In this example, at the office, we have a computer with a remote desktop exposed with an IP address 10.10.10.60. We can't get to this machine directly from home, because it is not routable through the Internet. However, we just so happen to have a server at work that actually, is exposed to the Internet with an outside IP address 66.238.170.50. We are able to SSH directly into that machine from home, but host 10.10.10.60 is further within that network.

Here, we can utilize host `66.238.170.50` to facilitate our connection to `10.10.10.60` inside our work network. Let's look at a command:

```
ssh -L 3388:10.10.10.60:3389 jdoe@66.238.170.50
```

In this example, `jdoe` has a user account on host `66.238.170.50` and wishes to connect to host `10.10.10.60`, which is inside her company network. In this example, `jdoe` is forwarding local port `3388` on `localhost` to port `3389` on host `10.10.10.60`, but establishing the connection through host `66.238.170.50`. Now, user `jdoe` is able to open a remote desktop client and use the following command for the connection address:

```
localhost:3388
```

As long as the SSH connection remains open, `jdoe` will then be able to utilize a remote desktop on the server from her local computer. If the shell is closed, then the connection will terminate.

Using SSH tunnels can be very useful. Feel free to give it a try and see which services you can forward through your network.

Generating public keys

SSH also supports **public key authentication**, in addition to traditional passwords, which is more secure. While the encryption that SSH employs using protocol 2 is strong, the greatest encryption in the world won't save you if your password is leaked or brute-forced. This is especially catastrophic on a mission-critical server.

Utilizing public key authentication allows you to connect to a host using a private and public key relationship, instead of using a password. By default, SSH will allow a user to log in via either the username/password combination or a username / key pair combination. The first method is only as secure as the password. By utilizing public key authentication, you can bypass the need for a password completely, and connect to a server without being prompted. But if a server still accepts your password as a means of authentication, then public key authentication is not at its strongest point.

On the server end of the SSH connection, it is possible to configure it to accept authentication only from a public key, rather than password. If password authentication is disabled, then no one would be able to brute force the password and get into the server, since the password would be ignored. If the attacker doesn't have access to the private key, then he or she would not be able to connect.

Generating a key pair is simple using the ssh-keygen command, which will guide you through the process of setting up your keys. During this process, you will be asked to create a passphrase. You could, if you wanted to, disregard this prompt and simply press *Enter* to create a key without a passphrase. Doing so, however, drastically lowers the security of that key. While it is certainly much more convenient to not have to type anything at all when connecting to a host via SSH, it's definitely recommended to use a passphrase and benefit from the added security.

With public key authentication, two files are created in the user's home directory: id_rsa and id_rsa.pub. These files are created when you run through the process while executing ssh-keygen, mentioned earlier. After the command completes, these two files should be located in the .ssh directory of your home directory. The id_rsa file is your private key. You should keep it local and not transmit it or share it in a public place. The id_rsa.pub file is your public key, which you can safely copy to other hosts that you connect to. From that point forward, you will be able to use public key authentication to connect to another host.

Let's summarize the entire process. First, while logged in to your local or main machine, execute ssh-keygen and walk through the steps. Make sure to create a passphrase for added security.

```
jlacroix@localhost:~
[jlacroix@localhost ~]$ ssh-keygen
Generating public/private rsa key pair.
Enter file in which to save the key (/home/jlacroix/.ssh/id_rsa):
Created directory '/home/jlacroix/.ssh'.
Enter passphrase (empty for no passphrase):
Enter same passphrase again:
Your identification has been saved in /home/jlacroix/.ssh/id_rsa.
Your public key has been saved in /home/jlacroix/.ssh/id_rsa.pub.
The key fingerprint is:
30:58:38:82:14:c1:d0:49:79:2a:29:90:d2:c0:ca:3d jlacroix@localhost.localdomain
The key's randomart image is:
+--[ RSA 2048]----+
|B@+o ..          |
|=o* +o           |
|=..+..o          |
|=..E   o         |
|..   . S         |
|                 |
|                 |
|                 |
|                 |
+-----------------+
[jlacroix@localhost ~]$
```

Creating a key pair for SSH using ssh-keygen

Next, utilize the ssh-copy-id command in order to copy your key to the remote server you wish to connect to. The command syntax is as follows.

```
ssh-copy-id -i ~/.ssh/id_rsa.pub <remote host IP or name>
```

This command will copy your public key into the `authorized_keys` file under your `~/.ssh` folder on the target machine. This file stores all the keys that the machine knows about. If you were to check before and after running through the `ssh-copy-id` process, you'd notice that the `authorized_keys` file on the target either didn't exist, or didn't include your key until after you executed the command.

```
jlacroix@localhost:~                                                    _ + x
[jlacroix@localhost ~]$ ssh-copy-id -i ~/.ssh/id_rsa.pub 10.10.11.232
The authenticity of host '10.10.11.232 (10.10.11.232)' can't be established.
ECDSA key fingerprint is fd:fd:20:6d:c8:7f:f2:5f:02:bc:a5:fe:fa:2d:1c:4b.
Are you sure you want to continue connecting (yes/no)? yes
/usr/bin/ssh-copy-id: INFO: attempting to log in with the new key(s), to filter out any that are al
ready installed
/usr/bin/ssh-copy-id: INFO: 1 key(s) remain to be installed -- if you are prompted now it is to ins
tall the new keys
jlacroix@10.10.11.232's password:

Number of key(s) added: 1

Now try logging into the machine, with:   "ssh '10.10.11.232'"
and check to make sure that only the key(s) you wanted were added.

[jlacroix@localhost ~]$
```

Copying a public key to a remote host using ssh-copy-id

As mentioned earlier, it is possible to configure your computer or server to disallow authentication via password, only allowing public key authentication instead. This portion will be discussed further in *Chapter 9, Securing Your Network*. For now, it's important to get in the habit of generating, copying, and using keys. Feel free to create a key pair on your local machine and copy the public key to a server that you frequently connect to.

Keeping SSH connections alive

Depending on how your SSH server or internal firewalls are configured, your SSH session may automatically disconnect after some time. It's possible to configure SSH to send a special packet every certain number of seconds, to keep the connection from idling and becoming a candidate for disconnection. This is useful if you have a service that utilizes SSH, that you do not want to be disconnected. To employ this tweak, we must configure the `ServerAliveInterval` setting.

There are two ways of configuring this, one that affects your user account and another that will deploy the setting system wide. First, let's explore how to configure this for your user account.

Remember the ~/.ssh/config file that we configured earlier in this chapter? Open it up again in your text editor. Here's a sample of this file for your convenience:

```
Host icarus
Hostname 10.10.10.76
Port 22
User jdoe


Host daedalus
Hostname 10.10.10.88
Port 65000
User duser


Host dragon
Hostname 10.10.10.99
Port 22
User jdoe
```

As before, we have three systems. If we wish to configure a host, for example icarus, to send an alive packet once every 60 seconds, we can add the following setting to it:

```
Host icarus
ServerAliveInterval 60
Hostname 10.10.10.76
Port 22
User jdoe
```

If we wish to set the ServerAliveInterval setting for all hosts we connect to, we could add this option as a wildcard instead by adding the following to the top of the file:

```
Host *
ServerAliveInterval 60
```

With this, the setting takes effect for all systems we initiate a connection to. Although we haven't discussed them (yet), there are two system-wide (global) configuration files for SSH. We'll discuss these files later in this book, but the subject of this section is an opportunity to give you a quick introduction:

- `/etc/ssh/ssh_config`: This file will impact all users whom make outbound connections. Think of this as the client configuration file.
- `/etc/ssh/sshd_config`: This is the global config file for the server.

Anything you configure in one of these two files will impact anyone. The `ssh_config` file impacts all outbound connections, and the `sshd_config` impacts all the incoming connections. For this section, the file we're interested in is the `ssh_config` file, since we can set the `ServerAliveInterval` setting for all users by including it there. In fact, regardless of whether we're configuring `/etc/ssh/ssh_config` or the local `~/.ssh/config` file, the option is the same. Simply add it to the end of the file:

```
ServerAliveInterval 60
```

Of course, we'll explore configuring these options further later on in this book. For now, just remember the purpose of these two files and where they're located.

Exploring an alternative to SSH – utilizing Mosh (mobile shell)

While starting out with SSH, you might notice one quirk right away: if your network connection drops, it can be difficult to regain control of what you were doing on the machine you were connected to. This is especially common with laptops, as your connection state on such a device will change depending on where you are or what network you're connected to. While running commands within a terminal multiplexer such as tmux or screen, can keep your workflow alive even after disconnecting, there is an alternative to SSH that may work for you. **Mosh (mobile shell)** is an alternative to SSH that will keep your remote session alive, even if you disconnect from the network where the resource resides. When you reconnect to the network, Mosh will allow you to pick up where you left off.

Installing Mosh in Debian is extremely easy. Simply install the `mosh` package, as it is available from within the default repositories:

```
# apt-get install mosh
```

In CentOS, Mosh is not available from that distribution's default repositories, so you'll first need to add an additional repository in order to make it available. First, enable the EPEL repository with the following command:

```
# yum install epel-release
```

Then, you should be able to install the `mosh` package:

```
# yum install mosh
```

In order for Mosh to be effective, you will need to install it not only on your local machine, but also any machines you wish to connect to. The syntax is similar to SSH:

```
mosh jdoe@10.10.10.101
```

Like SSH, we can supply the `-p` flag to specify a different port to use:

```
mosh -p 2222 jdoe@10.10.10.101
```

In fact, Mosh actually utilizes SSH to initiate the connection, and then the mosh program takes over from there. After you connect, you can simulate a disconnect by removing your network cable or disconnecting from your wireless access point. You will notice that the next time you connect using mosh, your session should be just as you left it. To see the magic in all its glory, consider starting a process (such as running the `top` command) before disconnecting.

While there are many ways to keep processes running on a remote server even when your session is disconnected, Mosh is one of the newer and more unique solutions. Give it a try!

Summary

In this chapter, we discussed SSH in all its glory. We started off with a discussion of what SSH is and why it's useful, and then we ensured it was installed on our systems. Using SSH, we were able to connect to other Linux machines and execute commands. We also took a look at configuring hosts in the `~/.ssh/config` file and transferring files from one host to another using `scp`. In addition, SSH tunneling was discussed, as well as an introduction to public key authentication. We finished the chapter with a look at Mosh, which is a neat alternative to SSH.

In the next chapter, we'll tackle file sharing by setting up our very own file server. We'll set up file shares via Samba as well as NFS, as well as the individual quirks of each solution. See you there!

Setting up a File Server

4

In the previous chapter, we covered SSH and discussed SCP. While SCP is a great method to manually transfer individual files from one place to another, having one or more central locations to store shared files adds a lot of value to a network. Whether you're sharing important files on a business network or family photo albums on a home network, a central file storage location on your network is a convenient asset. In this chapter, we'll discuss three ways of accomplishing this goal. We'll first talk about some considerations while designing your file server, and then we'll cover NFS, Samba, and SSHFS.

In this chapter, we will cover:

- File server considerations
- NFS v3 versus NFS v4
- Setting up an NFS server
- Learning the basics of Samba
- Setting up a Samba server
- Mounting network shares
- Automatically mounting network shares via fstab and systemd
- Creating networked filesystems with SSHFS

File server considerations

As with most things in the Linux world, there is more than one way of accomplishing any goal. With each method, there are a multitude of best practices and caveats to understand before implementing a solution. As mentioned earlier, the three most common methods of sharing files from one Linux system to another are **Network File System (NFS)**, **Samba**, and **Secure Shell File System (SSHFS)**. Each of these three primarily serve different needs, and your network layout will determine which you should use.

The first consideration while designing a network file server is what types of platforms will need to access its files. NFS is often a great choice within a Linux-based environment; however, it doesn't handle mixed environments as well, so you may not want to choose it if you have Windows machines on your network that you need to share files with. It's not that you can't access NFS shares on Windows systems (you certainly can), but Microsoft limits NFS availability (called **Services for NFS)** to the most expensive edition of each version of Windows. Services for NFS is fine if you utilize versions of Windows that support it, but due to the extra licensing hurdle you'd need to overcome, it may make more sense to avoid it. Generally speaking, NFS is a great choice only when your network consists primarily of UNIX and Linux nodes.

Next up for consideration is Samba. Samba allows you to share files between all three major platforms (Windows, Linux, and Mac OSX) and is a great choice within a mixed environment. Since Samba uses the **SMB** protocol, Windows systems are able to access your Samba shares regardless of the version you have installed, so licensing isn't as much of an issue. In fact, even the standard or home editions of Windows are able to access these shares natively, with no added plugins required for you to install. The downside to Samba is in the way that it handles permissions. When saving files between Windows and Linux nodes, some extra work is required to handle permissions, such that it's not always the best choice when dealing with UNIX or Linux nodes that need to retain specific permissions.

Finally, SSHFS is another method that is primarily geared toward sharing files between Linux nodes. It's certainly possible to connect and access SSHFS from Windows, but only with third-party utilities, as no built-in method exists in Windows (at least at the time this chapter is being written). Where SSHFS shines is its ease of use and the fact that file transfers are encrypted. While encryption certainly helps you to avoid eavesdropping, keep in mind that SSHFS (just like any other solution) is only as secure as the policies you have in place. But in good hands, SSH (and SSHFS) is a secure method of transferring files from one node to another. In addition, SSHFS is the easiest of the three methods listed here to get running. All you need is access to another node and permissions to access one or more directories. That's all you need, and then you're automatically able to create an SSHFS connection to any directory you have access to. Another benefit to SSHFS is that there's nothing to configure on the server other than SSH itself, which most servers have available anyway. SSHFS connections can also be created and disconnected on-demand very quickly. We'll discuss SSHFS later on in this chapter.

NFS v3 versus NFS v4

Another consideration regarding NFS is the version you'll be using. Nowadays, most (if not all) Linux distributions default to NFS v4. However, there are some cases where you may have older servers on your network, and you'll need to be able to connect to their shares. While NFS v4 is definitely the preferred version going forward, you might need to connect to a node using the older protocol.

In both cases, directories on a file server can be shared via NFS by editing the /etc/ exports file, which is where you'll list your shares (exports), one per line. We'll go over this file in more detail in the next section. But for now, keep in mind that the /etc/exports file is where you declare which directories on your filesystem are available for use with NFS. Different versions of NFS have different techniques of handling file locks and they differ in terms of the introduction of **idmapd**, performance, and security. Also, there are other differences such as NFS v4 moving to TCP-only (previous versions of the protocol allowed either UDP or TCP) and the fact that it is **stateful**, while previous versions were **stateless**.

By being stateful, NFS v4 includes file locking as part of the protocol itself, rather than relying on **Network Lock Manager** (**NLM**) to provide that function as NFS v3 did. If an NFS server were to crash or become unavailable, one or more nodes that were connected to it may have had open files, which would have been locked to those nodes. When the NFS server starts to back up, it re-establishes these locks and tries to recover from the crash. Although NFS servers do a fairly good job of recovering, they aren't perfect, and at times file locking can become a nightmare for administrators to deal with. With NFS v4, NLM is decommissioned and file locking is a part of the protocol itself, so locks are dealt with much more efficiently. However, it's still not perfect.

So, which version should you use? It's recommended to always use NFS v4 on all of your nodes and servers, unless you're dealing with an older server with older protocols that you still need to support.

Setting up an NFS server

Configuring an NFS server is relatively straightforward. Essentially, all you need to do is install the required packages, create your /etc/exports file, and ensure the required daemons (services) are running. In this activity, we'll set up an NFS server and also connect to it from a different node. In order to do so, it's recommended that you have at least two Linux machines to work with. It doesn't matter if these machines are physical or virtual machines, or any combination of those. If you've already followed through with *Chapter 1*, *Setting up Your Environment*, you should already have several nodes to work with; hopefully, a mix of Debian and CentOS, since this procedure differs a bit between them.

First, let's set up our NFS server. Pick a machine to act as the NFS server and install the required packages. It doesn't matter which distribution you choose as your server and which you choose as your client, I'll go over the configuration process for both CentOS and Debian. Since quite a few distributions are either based on Debian or use the same configuration as CentOS, this should work for most distributions out there. If you're using a distribution that doesn't follow either package naming convention, all you have to do is look up which package or meta-package to install on your server for your specific distribution. The rest of the configuration should be the same, since NFS is fairly standard.

To install the required packages on a CentOS system, we would execute the following command:

```
# yum install nfs-utils
```

And for Debian, we install `nfs-kernel-server`:

```
# apt-get install nfs-kernel-server
```

> During installation of these packages, you may receive an error that NFS hasn't been started, due to /etc/exports not being present on the file system. When you install the required NFS packages on some distributions, this file may not be automatically created. Even if it does get created automatically, the file will just be a skeleton. If you do receive such an error, ignore it. We'll create this file shortly.

Next, we'll want to make sure that the services related to NFS are enabled so that they will start as soon as the server starts up. For CentOS systems, we'll use the following command:

```
# systemctl enable nfs-server
```

And for Debian, we can enable NFS via:

```
# systemctl enable nfs-kernel-server
```

Keep in mind that we simply enabled the NFS daemon on our server, which means that when the system is restarted, NFS will also be started (providing we configured it properly). However, we don't have to restart our entire server in order to start NFS; we can start that any time after we create our configuration files. Since we haven't actually configured NFS yet, we won't need to start the daemon yet. We'll do that later. In fact, until we actually create our configuration, your distribution probably won't let you start NFS anyway.

The next step is to determine which directories on our server we wish to make available on our network. Which directories you share is pretty much up to you. Anything on the Linux filesystem is a candidate for an NFS export. However, some directories, such as /etc (which contains your systems configuration) or any other system directory, are probably best left private. While you can share any directory on your system, it's actually a common practice to create a single directory to house all of your shares, and then create subdirectories underneath, that you would then share to your clients.

For example, perhaps you would create a directory called exports at the root of your filesystem (mkdir /exports) and then create directories such as docs and images that would be accessible to others. The beauty of this is that your shares could be managed from one place (the /exports directory) and NFS itself has the ability to classify this directory as your export root (we'll discuss this later). Before moving on, create some directories on your filesystem that you'll use to share, as we'll be placing these directories in a configuration file in the next section.

Once you've determined which directories in the file system you'd like to share and created them, you're ready to begin the actual configuration. Each NFS share, referred to as an export, is configured by adding one line per directory we wish to share in the /etc/exports file. Since you've already installed the required packages in order to get NFS on your system, this file may or may not already exist. In my experience, CentOS doesn't create this file during installation while Debian does. But even if you did get a default exports file, it would only contain commented out lines of code that don't have any practical purpose. In fact, you may have even received a warning or error during installation that the NFS daemon wasn't started as /etc/exports was not found. That's fine because we'll create this file soon.

While the default exports file is different from distribution to distribution (if it even gets created by default at all), the format for creating new exports is the same regardless of your chosen distribution, as NFS is fairly standard. The process for adding an export is to open the /etc/exports file in your favorite text editor and add each export to its own line. Any actual text editor will do, as long as it is a text editor and not a word processor. For example, if you're a fan of vim, you can execute the following command:

```
# vim /etc/exports
```

If you prefer nano, you can execute the following command:

```
# nano /etc/exports
```

In fact, you can even use graphical text editors such as Gedit, Kate, Pluma, or Geany if you would prefer to use GUI tools. These packages are available in the repositories of most distributions.

 It probably goes without saying, but to edit files within the /etc directory or any others that are owned by root, you'll need to prefix such commands with sudo in order to edit them if you aren't logged in as root. As a best practice, it's recommended to not log in as root unless you absolutely have to. If you're logged in as a normal user, execute the following command:

```
sudo vim /etc/exports
```

In Debian, you'll see that the default /etc/exports file contains a list of comments, which may be helpful to you in viewing how exports are formatted. We can create new exports by simply adding them to the end of the file, preserving the contents. If you'd prefer to start off with a blank file, you may want to back up the original in case you want to refer to it later.

```
# mv /etc/exports /etc/exports.default
```

Once you have the file open in your favorite text editor, you should be ready to go. All of the directories you wish to share or *export* should be placed in this file, one on each line. Then, you append parameters to the share to control how it can be accessed and by whom. Here's an example exports file with some example directories and some basic configuration parameters for each:

```
/exports/docs 10.10.10.0/24(ro,no_subtree_check)
/exports/images 10.10.10.0/24(rw,no_subtree_check)
/exports/downloads 10.10.10.0/24(rw,no_subtree_check)
```

As you can see with those example exports, the format of each basically includes the directory we'd like to export, a network address we'd like to allow access to, followed by some additional options in parenthesis. There are many options you can append here, and we'll go over some of them later in this chapter. But if you would like to view all of the options you can set here, refer to the following man command:

```
man exports
```

Let's discuss each section of the example exports file that was used previously:

- /exports/docs: The first section contains the directory we're exporting to other nodes on the network. As mentioned before, you can share pretty much any directory you'd like. But just because you *can* share a directory doesn't mean you *should*. Share only the directories that you wouldn't mind others having access to.

- 10.10.10.0/24: Here, we're limiting access to nodes within the 10.10.10.0/24 network. A node outside of that network will not be able to mount any of these exports. In this example, we could have used 10.10.10.0/255.255.255.0 and we would have achieved the same result. In our example, /24 was used, which is known as the **Classless Inter-Domain Routing (CIDR)** notation that is a shorthand for typing out the subnet mask. Of course, there is much more to CIDR than that, but for now, just keep in mind that the CIDR notation was used instead of the subnet mask to keep the example shorter (plus, it looks cooler).

- ro: In the first export (docs), I've set it to read-only for no reason other than to show you that you can. This is probably self-explanatory, but a directory exported as read-only would allow others to mount the export and access the files within it, but not make any changes to anything.

- rw: A read-write export allows nodes that mount it, to create new files and modify existing ones (as long as the user has the required permissions set on the files themselves).

- no_subtree_check: While this option is default and we don't actually need to explicitly make a request, not including it may make NFS complain when it restarts. This option is the opposite of subtree_check, which is largely avoided nowadays. This option in particular, controls whether or not the server scans the underlying filesystem when processing actions within exports, which can increase security a bit but lower reliability. As disabling this option is known to increase reliability, it's been made the default in recent versions of NFS.

Although I didn't use it in any of my examples, a common export option you'll see set in /etc/exports is no_root_squash. Setting this option allows the root user on end-user devices to have root access to the files contained within the export. In most cases, this is a bad idea, but you will see this from time to time in the wild. This is the opposite of root_squash, which maps the root user to nobody instead. Unless you have a very good reason to do otherwise, no_root_squash is what you want.

In addition to classifying options for a single network, you can make your exports available to additional networks by adding configuration for them to the same line. Here's an example of our docs mount shared with an additional network:

```
/exports/docs 10.10.10.0/24(ro,no_subtree_check),192.168.1.0/24(ro,no_
subtree_check)
```

With this example, we're exporting `/exports/docs` so that it can be accessed by nodes within the `10.10.10.0/24` network and the `192.168.1.0/24` network. While I used the same options for both, you don't have to. You could even configure the export to be read-only for one network and read-write for another if you so desired.

So far, we've been sharing our exports with entire networks. This is done by making the last octet of the allowed IP address a `0`. With the last example, any node with an IP address of `10.10.10.x` or `192.168.1.x` and a subnet mask of `255.255.255.0` would qualify for access to the export. However, you may not always want to give access to an entire network. Perhaps you may want to allow access to a single node instead. You can classify an individual node just as easily:

```
/exports/docs 10.10.10.191/24(ro,no_subtree_check)
```

In the previous example, we allowed a node with an IP address of `10.10.10.191` access to our export. Specifying an IP address or network enhances security, though it is not a 100 percent catch-all. However, limiting access to only the hosts that absolutely need it is a very good place to start when building your security policy. We'll cover security in greater detail in *Chapter 9, Securing Your Network*. But for now, keep in mind that you can limit access to the export by specific networks or individual IPs.

Earlier, we touched on the fact that starting with Version 4, NFS can use a directory to serve as its export root, also known as the NFS pseudo filesystem. In the `/etc/exports` file, this is identified by placing either `fsid=0` or `fsid=root` as an option while exporting this directory. In this chapter, we've been using `/exports` to serve as the base of our NFS exports. If we wanted to identify this directory as our export root, we would change the `/etc/exports` file like this:

```
/exports *(ro,fsid=0)
/exports/docs 10.10.10.0/24(ro,no_subtree_check)
/exports/images 10.10.10.0/24(rw,no_subtree_check)
/exports/downloads 10.10.10.0/24(rw,no_subtree_check)
```

At first, this concept might be a big confusing, so let's break this down a bit. In the first line, we identify our export root:

```
/exports *(ro,fsid=0)
```

Here, we declare /exports as our export root. This is now the root of the NFS filesystem. Sure, you have a complete filesystem beginning with / in terms of Linux itself, but as far as NFS is concerned, its filesystem now begins here at /exports. In this line, we also declared /exports as read-only. We don't want anyone to make changes to this directory, as it is the NFS root. It's also shared with everyone (notice the *) but that shouldn't matter, as we set more granular permissions for each individual export. With the NFS root in place, clients can now mount these exports without needing to know the full path to get to it.

For example, a user might type the following to mount our downloads export to his or her local filesystem:

```
# mount 10.10.10.100:/exports/downloads /mnt/downloads
```

This is how you mount an NFS export from a local file server (10.10.10.100 in this case), which is *not* using an NFS root. This requires the user to know that the directory is located at /exports/downloads on that server. But with the NFS root in place, we can have the user simplify the mount command as follows:

```
# mount 10.10.10.100:/downloads /mnt/downloads
```

Notice that we left out /exports in the previous command. While this may not seem like much, we're basically asking the server to give us the downloads export, wherever it may be on the file system. It doesn't matter if the downloads directory is located at /exports/downloads, /srv/nfs/downloads, or wherever else. We simply ask for the downloads export and the server knows where it is, because we set the NFS root.

Now that we've configured our /etc/exports file, it's a good idea that we edit the /etc/idmapd.conf configuration file to configure some additional options. This isn't absolutely required but it's definitely recommended. The default idmapd.conf file is different from distribution to distribution, but each contains the options we would need to configure in this section. First, look for a line such as the following (or very similar):

```
# Domain = local.domain
```

First, we'll need to uncomment that line. Remove the # symbol and the trailing space so that the line begins with Domain. Then, set your domain so that it is the same as other nodes on your network. This domain would most likely have been chosen during installation. If you don't remember what yours is, running the hostname command should give you your domain name, which is immediately after your hostname. Do this for every node you'd like to be able to access NFS exports.

You might be wondering why this is necessary. When user and group accounts are created on a Linux system, they're assigned a **UID (User ID)** and **GID (Group ID)**. Unless you created your user accounts on all of your systems in the same exact order, the UID and GID will most likely be different on each node. Even if you did create your user and group accounts in the same order, they could still be different. The idmapd file helps us by mapping these UIDs from one system to another. In order for idmapd to work, the idmapd daemon must be running on each node, and the file should also be configured with the same domain name. On both CentOS and Debian, this daemon runs under /usr/sbin/rpc.idmapd and is started along with the NFS server.

So, you might be wondering; what's the purpose of the Nobody-User and Nobody-Group? The nobody user runs scripts or commands that would be dangerous if run by a privileged user. Typically, the nobody user cannot log in to the system and does not have a home directory. If you run a process as nobody, its scope is limited if ever the account should be compromised. In the case of NFS, the nobody user and nobody group serve a special purpose. If the files are owned by a specific user on one system that doesn't exist on another, the permissions for the file will be displayed as being owned by the nobody user and group. This is also true of accessing files via the root user, when no_root_squash is not set. Depending on which distribution you're using, these accounts may have different names. In Debian, both Nobody-User and Nobody-Group default to simply nobody. In CentOS, these are both nobody. You can see in your idmapd.conf file which account is used for the nobody user and nobody group. You shouldn't need to rename these accounts, but if for some reason you do, you'll need to ensure that the idmapd.conf file has the correct names for them.

Now that we have NFS configured and ready to go, how do we start using it? If you've been following along, you may have caught the fact that we enabled the NFS daemon but have yet to start it. Now that the configuration is in place, nothing is stopping us from doing so.

On Debian we can start the NFS daemons by executing the following command:

```
# systemctl start nfs-kernel-server
```

On CentOS, we can execute the following command:

```
# systemctl start nfs-server
```

From this point onwards, our NFS exports should be shared and ready to go. Later on in this chapter, I'll explain how to mount these exports (as well as Samba shares) on other systems.

There is one more thing in NFS that is worth mentioning. The `/etc/exports` file is read whenever the NFS daemon starts, which means you can activate new exports after you add them by restarting the server or the NFS daemon. However, in production, it's not practical to restart NFS or the server itself. This would interrupt users that are currently using it and possibly cause stale mounts, which are invalidated connections to network shares (not a good situation to be in). Thankfully, activating new exports without restarting NFS itself is easy. Simply execute the following command and you'll be good to go:

```
# exportfs -a
```

Learning the basics of Samba

Samba, like NFS, allows you to share directories on your server with other computers within your network. Although both serve the same purpose, they fit different environments and use cases.

NFS is the oldest method and is widely used in the Linux and UNIX world. While we certainly have newer solutions (such as SSHFS), NFS is tried and true. But it's perhaps not the best solution in a mixed environment. These days, it's possible that not every computer on your network runs a particular operating system, so you may have nodes where NFS access isn't available or is not practical.

As mentioned earlier, only the more expensive editions of Windows support NFS. If you have a large network of Windows machines, it would be quite expensive to update them all to a higher edition if you wouldn't otherwise need to. This is the area where Samba shines the most. Windows, Linux, and Mac computers can access directories shared via Samba. In the case of Windows, even the lower end editions can access Samba shares (such as Windows 7 Home Professional or Windows 10 core) without any new installations or purchases.

The downside to Samba is that it doesn't handle permissions as well as NFS does, so you need to manage the configuration file in special ways to respect permissions. However, it's not foolproof. For example, Windows and Linux/UNIX systems adopt very different schemes of permissions, so they are not inherently compatible. In Samba's configuration file, you can tell it to use certain user and group permissions on newly created files, and you can even force Samba to treat ownership as something other than what is actually stored with the file. So there are certainly ways to make Samba handle permissions better, but not inherently as good as a Linux or UNIX native solution such as NFS.

As far as how as Samba server might fit within your network, the basic rule of thumb is to use Samba in a mixed environment and NFS whenever cross-platform compatibility is not necessary.

Setting up a Samba server

In this section, we'll go ahead and set up a Samba server. In the next section, I'll explain how to mount Samba shares. First, we'll need to install Samba. On both CentOS and Debian systems, the package is simply referred to as samba. So, install that package via apt-get or yum and you should have everything you need:

```
# yum install samba
```

The command using apt-get is as follows:

```
# apt-get install samba
```

On Debian systems, Samba is started as soon as it is installed. In fact, it's enabled as well, so it will automatically start each time you bring up your system. In the case of CentOS though, it is not enabled nor started after installation. If you chose CentOS to be your Samba server, you'll need to enable and start the daemon:

```
# systemctl start smb
# systemctl enable smb
```

Now, Samba is installed, enabled, but not configured. To configure Samba, we'll need to edit the /etc/samba/smb.conf file. By default, this file is created as soon as you install the required packages. However, the default file mainly exists to provide you with configuration examples. It's quite massive, but you may want to take a look at it to see some syntax examples you may want to use later. You can either open the file in a text editor or simply cat the file to view it on your terminal:

```
cat /etc/samba/smb.conf
```

To simplify things, I recommend that you start with a fresh file. While the configuration examples are definitely good, we should probably use a shorter file for production purposes. Since the original file may be useful later, create a backup:

```
# mv /etc/samba/smb.conf /etc/samba/smb.conf.default
```

Next, simply open the smb.conf file in a text editor, which will create a new/empty file since we moved the original file to a backup:

```
# vim /etc/samba/smb.conf
```

We can start with the following basic configuration:

```
[global]
server string = File Server
workgroup = HOME-NET
security = user
map to guest = Bad User
name resolve order = bcast hosts wins
include = /etc/samba/smbshared.conf
```

Let's go through this configuration file line by line. First, we start with the [global] section, which is where we're configuring options that will take effect for the entire server. In fact, this is the only section in this particular file.

Next, we have server string. The server string is the description you'll see if browsing the network shares on a Windows system. For example, you may see a share named Documents and with a description beneath that reads; File Server. This section isn't required, but it's nice to have. In a business network, this can be useful for outlining a note about the system, such as where it is, or what it's used for.

Following that, we set our `workgroup`. Those of you who have been administrators of Windows systems probably know this very well. The workgroup serves as a namespace to contain all systems of a particular purpose. In practice, this is typically the name of your LAN. Each computer within your LAN would have the same workgroup name, so they would show up as existing within the same network. When browsing shares on a Windows system, you'll likely see a list of workgroups and double-clicking on one of them would take you to a listing of systems that are sharing resources underneath that workspace. In most cases, you'll probably want to have the same workgroup name on each system, unless you'd like to separate resources. To view the workgroup name on an existing system, right-click on **My Computer** or **This PC** (depending on your version) and click on **Properties**. Your workgroup name should be listed within the window that appears.

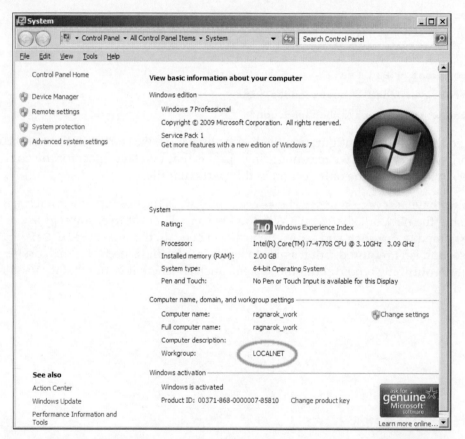

Viewing properties of a Windows system to gather the workgroup name, which is LOCALNET in this case

The setting `security = user` tells Samba to use the user's username and password for authentication. If this matches, the user won't be prompted for a password to access the resource.

The `map to guest = Bad User` tells Samba that if the username and password that's provided does not match a local user account, treat the connecting user as if he or she connected via a guest account. If you'd rather such mapping not take place, remove this section.

Next, `name resolve order = bcast hosts wins` determines the order in which name resolution happens. Here, we're using whatever name is broadcast first, followed by any hostname mappings in our `/etc/hosts file`, followed by `wins` (`wins` has largely been replaced by DNS, it's only included here for compatibility). In most networks, this order should work fine.

Finally we've `include = /etc/samba/smbshared.conf` at the end of our configuration file. Basically, this allows us to include another configuration file as if it were part of the existing one. In this case, we're including the contents of `/etc/samba/smbshared.conf`, which would be read by Samba once it reads this particular line. We'll create this file next. Essentially, this allows us to designate our shares in a separate configuration file. This isn't required, but I think it makes things much easier to manage. If you'd prefer, you could include the contents of the `smbshared.conf` file in your `smb.conf` file so that everything is in a single file.

Here's an example `smbshared.conf` I've created for the purposes of this activity. In your case, all you would need to do is to ensure that the values match your system and the directories you've chosen to share:

```
[Music]
## My music collection
        path = /share/music
        public = yes
        writable = no


[Public]
## Public files
        path = /share/public
        create mask = 0664
        force create mode = 0664
        directory mask = 0777
        force directory mode = 0777
        public = yes
        writable = yes
```

Here, I've created two shares. Each share begins with a name in brackets (which will be displayed on other systems while browsing shares on this machine) and then the configuration for that share. As you can see, I have a shared directory called `Music` and another called `Public`.

To declare the path to a share, use `path` = and then the path to the directory that the share corresponds to. In my example, you can see that I have the following directories shared:

```
/share/music
/share/public
```

Next, I also declare the shares as public by adding `public` = `yes`. This means that it's okay for guests to be able to access this share. If I would prefer guests not to be able to access it, I could set this to `no`.

In my music share, I have `writable` = `no`. As the name suggests, this disables the ability for other computers to change files within this share. In my case, I share my music collection with other computers on my network, but I wouldn't want to accidentally delete music files.

In my public share, I have added a few extra options:

```
create mask = 0664
force create mode = 0664
directory mask = 0777
force directory mode = 0777
```

These options all correspond to the permissions that are defaulted to when a new file is created within that share. For example, if I mounted my public share and then created a directory there, it would obtain permissions of `777`. If I created a file, its permissions would be `664`. Of course, you may not want to allow your files to be wide open, so you can change these permissions as you see fit. This option ensures consistency with permissions on newly created directories and files. This can be essential on a network where you may have automated processes running that need to access these files, and you'd want to make sure that you wouldn't need to manually correct the permissions each time such a process is run.

Now that you've created your own Samba configuration, it's a good idea to test your configuration. Thankfully, Samba itself includes a special command that allows you to do this. If you run `testparm` on your system, it will display any errors in syntax that you may have in your file. Then, it will display your configuration. Go ahead and run `testparm` on your system. If there are any errors, go back and ensure that there are no issues with what you typed in. If everything proceeds normally, you should see no errors, and then you'll get a summary of your configuration. Once you've verified your configuration, restart the Samba daemon so that the changes take effect. To do that, simply run the following command on your Debian system:

```
# systemctl restart smbd
```

For CentOS, use the following command:

```
# systemctl restart smb
```

Now, you should be able to access your Samba shares on Windows or Linux systems. On Linux, most GUI file managers should allow you to browse your network for Samba shares. On Windows, you should be able to open **My Computer** or **This PC** and then click on **Network** to browse local networked computers with active shares. Perhaps a simpler way to access the shares on a Windows machine is to press the Windows key on your keyboard followed by *R* to open a run dialog, and then simply type in the name of your Samba server beginning with two backslashes. For example, to access my Debian-based file server (Pluto) from a Windows system, I would type the following into the run dialog and press *Enter*:

```
\\pluto
```

I got a list of shares from that system, as shown in the following screenshot:

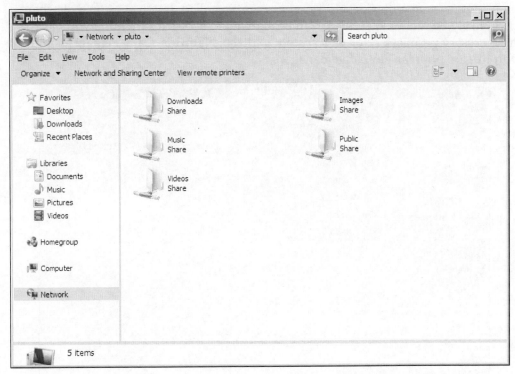

Viewing Samba shares (served from a Linux System) from a Windows 7 PC

Mounting network shares

So far in this chapter, we've worked through creating both NFS and Samba shares. But we haven't actually mounted any of those shares yet. In this section, we'll take care of that.

In Linux, the mount command works for mounting just about everything. Whether you connect an external hard drive, insert a CD, or wish to mount a network share, the mount command serves as a Swiss Army Knife to allow you to mount such resources to your system. The mount command allows you to mount a resource and attach it to a local directory on your system. In most cases, mount runs automatically on most Linux systems where a graphical desktop environment is used. You've probably seen this if you've inserted a flash drive or some sort of optical media. In network shares, these are not mounted automatically, though they can be configured to be.

Perhaps the easiest way to mount network shares is to use a GUI file manager if you are using a system with a desktop environment installed. If you click on a file share, it will likely be mounted and you will be allowed to access it providing you have the necessary permissions on that system to do so. **Nautilus**, **Caja**, **Pcmanfm**, and **Dolphin** are popular Linux file managers.

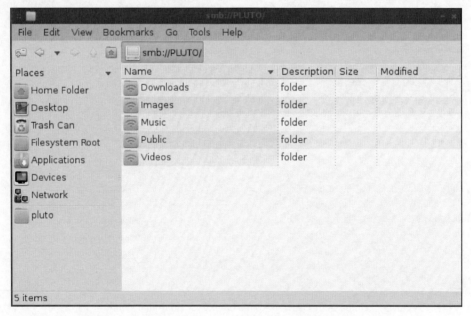

The pcmanfm file manager, viewing shares from a Samba file server

The `mount` command is most useful on systems without a graphical environment, or when you'd prefer to mount a resource somewhere other than the default. To use the `mount` command, give it the type of resource you'd like to mount, where it can find the resource, followed by which local directory to use for the mount. For example, to mount an NFS export, we might do something like this:

```
# mount -t nfs 10.10.10.101:/exports/docs /mnt/docs
```

Alternatively, use the following command if we set our NFS root, as I mentioned earlier:

```
# mount -t nfs 10.10.10.101:/docs /mnt/docs
```

In that example, we tell the mount command we'd like to mount an NFS export by providing it with the `-t` parameter followed by `nfs` for the type. In my lab, this share exists on a computer with an IP address `10.10.10.101`, which I provide next with a colon and the directory on that system I'm accessing. In this case, `/exports/docs` on `10.10.10.101` is being accessed. Finally, I have a local directory `/mnt/docs`, which exists on my local computer where I'd like for this share to be mounted. After executing this command, each time I access `/mnt/docs` on my local computer, I'm actually accessing `/exports/docs` on my file server. After using this export, I simply unmount it:

```
# umount /mnt/docs
```

Mounting a Samba share on a Linux machine is a bit more involved. I'll include an example command that can be used to mount a Samba share from that same server. But before we get to that, you'll first need to have the necessary packages installed on your system in order to be able to mount Samba shares. On CentOS, install `samba-client`. On Debian, the package is `smbclient`. After you install the required package, you should be able to mount Samba shares by executing the following command:

```
# mount -t cifs //10.10.10.101/Videos -o username=jay /mnt/samba/videos
```

If you need to access the resource via a password, use the following command:

```
# mount -t cifs //10.10.10.101/Videos -o username=jay,
password=mypassword /mnt/samba/videos
```

As you can see, the same basic idea is used to mount a Samba share. But in this case, we format our target path differently, we use `cifs` for the filesystem type and we also include the username (and password, if your Samba server requires it). As in previous examples, we end the command with a local directory we would like to attach the mount to. In this case, I've created a `/mnt/samba/Videos` directory for this share.

Automatically mounting network shares via fstab and systemd

As handy as mounting network shares via the `mount` command can be, you may not want to manually mount a share each time you wish to use it. In a network with a central file server, it makes sense to configure workstations to mount network shares automatically so that every time you boot your system, the share will automatically be mounted and ready to go.

The tried and tested approach to mounting resources automatically is the `/etc/fstab` file. Every Linux system has a `/etc/fstab` file, so go ahead and look at yours. By default, this file only contains configuration for mounting your local resources, such as partitions on your hard disk. It's standard practice to add additional lines of configuration to this file to mount anything from additional hard drives to network shares.

 Be careful while editing your `/etc/fstab` file. If you accidentally alter the configuration for your local hard disk, your system won't boot the next time you go to start it. Always use caution while editing this file.

Here's an example `/etc/fstab` file:

```
# root filesystem
UUID=4f60d247-2a46-4e72-a28a-52e3a044cebf          /                 ext4
errors=remount-ro            0 1
# swap
UUID=c9149e0a-26b0-4171-a86e-a5d0ee4f87a7          none              swap
sw                           0 0
```

In my file, the **Universally Unique Identifier (UUID)** reference my local hard disk partitions. These will be different on each system. Next, a mount point is listed for each. The / sign represents the root of the filesystem, and the swap partition doesn't need a mount point so it is set to `none`.

At the end of the `/etc/fstab` file, we can add additional mounts that we would like to be available each time we start the system. If we wish to add an NFS share, we could do the following:

```
10.10.10.101:/share/music/mnt/music  nfs  users,rw,auto,nolock,x-systemd.
automount,x-systemd.device-timeout=10 0 0
```

In the first section, we declare the IP address of the server followed by a colon and the path to the exported directory. In this case, I'm accessing `/share/music` on `10.10.10.101`. The next section is the mount point, so I'm attaching this export to `/home/jay/music` on my local system. Next, we designate that the share we're accessing is `nfs`. No surprises there. Finally, we end the configuration with some options for how we would like to mount this share. An easy mount option is `rw`, which stands for read-write. We could've used `ro` here if we wanted to prevent the files contained within from being changed.

Among the options in the previous example is `x-systemd.automount`. Basically, this tells systemd (the default `init` system on Debian and CentOS since version 8 and 7 respectively) that we would like to keep this mounted if possible. With this option, systemd will try its best to remount this share if for some reason it gets disconnected. Also, `x-systemd.device-timeout=10` can be added which tells the system to wait no longer than 10 seconds if the share isn't available on the network. We end the line with `0  0` because this isn't a local filesystem and doesn't need consistency check while booting.

If you're not using a distribution with systemd (such as CentOS 7 and Debian 8), do not include the `x-systemd` options because they won't be understood by distributions that use different `init` systems.

Similarly, Samba shares can also be added to your `/etc/fstab` file. Here's an example:

```
//10.10.10.9/Videos  /samba  cifs  username=jay  0  0
```

One final note regarding the `/etc/fstab` file before we move on. The examples in this section have all assumed that you want a network share to be available automatically. However, this may not always be the case. If you add the `noauto` mount option to a configuration line in your `fstab`, the share will not automatically be mounted at boot time. With `noauto` added to our Samba example, the `fstab` line would be changed as follows:

```
//10.10.10.101/Videos   /samba  cifs  noauto,username=jay  0  0
```

An NFS example would look like this:

```
10.10.10.101:/share/music
/mnt/music    nfs    users,rw,noauto,nolock,x-systemd.device-timeout=10 0
0
```

There are several situations where this might be useful. One example might be using a laptop, where you wouldn't always be connected to the same network. If that is the case, you wouldn't want your machine to try and automatically mount something unless you're actually connected to that network. With `noauto` added as a mount option, you can manually mount the resource any time you need it, without needing to memorize a long `mount` command to do so. For example, to mount an NFS export that's contained in your `fstab` file, you would execute the following:

```
# mount /mnt/music
```

By comparison, that's a lot easier than typing the following each time you wish to mount that export:

```
# mount -t nfs 10.10.10.101:/exports/music/ mnt/music
```

Since we added the export to the `fstab` file, the `mount` command looks for a relevant line when we type a simplified `mount` command as we have just done. If it finds a configuration for the mount point you're trying to access, it will let you access it without needing to type out the entire command. Even if you don't want to access remote shares automatically, it can still be quite handy to add them to your `fstab` file.

Creating networked filesystems with SSHFS

In the previous chapter, we worked through SSH, which is a crucial utility that is used multiple times per day by most Linux administrators. But while it's great for accessing other Linux systems on your network, it also allows you to access remote filesystems as if they were mounted locally. This is known as **SSHFS**. One of the great things about SSHFS is that there is no need to clarify any exported directories before hand. If you're able to connect to a remote Linux server and access a directory via SSH, then you're automatically able to mount it locally as if it were a network share.

On Debian systems, you can simply install the `sshfs` package. On CentOS, the `sshfs` package is not available by default. Before you can install `sshfs` on a CentOS system, you'll need to add a whole new repository, known as **Extra Packages for Enterprise Linux (EPEL)**. To do that, simply install the `epel-release` package:

```
# yum install epel-release
```

After installing the `epel` repository, you should be able to install `sshfs`:

```
# yum install sshfs
```

Once installed, you're able to mount directories on your local file system quite easily:

```
sshfs jay@10.10.10.101:/home/jay/docs /home/jay/mnt/docs
```

In order to work, your user account must have access not only to the remote system, but also to the local mount point. Once you initiate the command, you'll see prompts similar to those you'd normally see while connecting to the server via SSH. Essentially, that's exactly what you're doing. The difference is that the connection remains open in the background, maintaining the relationship between the remote directory and the local directory.

Using `sshfs` is a great idea for when you need to mount something on a remote filesystem, but you may not need to access it again or that often. But similar to NFS and Samba shares, you can actually use `/etc/fstab` to mount a resource via SSHFS. Consider the following `fstab` example:

```
jay@10.10.10.101:/home/jay/docs              /home/jay/mnt/docs
fuse.sshfs        defaults,noauto,users,_netdev    0 0
```

As we've done before, we set `noauto` so that we can establish this connection by simply typing:

```
mount /home/jay/docs
```

Summary

In this action-packed chapter, we worked through several ways of accessing and sharing files within a Linux-based network. We started off discussing NFS, which is an old but trusty method of sharing files within a Linux and UNIX network. We also covered Samba, a method of sharing resources within a mixed operating system environment. We also discussed how to mount such shares manually as well as automatically. We finished our discussion with SSHFS, which is a quite handy (yet not well-known) feature of SSH that allows us to mount directories from other systems on-demand.

Of course, with relying on our networked resources in our network, it's important to keep each node running in tip top shape. In the next chapter, we'll work through monitoring system resources and keeping our nodes happy and healthy.

5
Monitoring System Resources

As the needs of your organization expand, your network will grow and change in order to match the growth. Keeping track of the resources on each node is extremely important for stability. While Linux handles resources exceptionally well, it can only do so much. CPUs can be overutilized, disks become full, and excessive input/output can halt even the strongest of servers. Keeping an eye on these things is very important, especially when systems are used in production and depended upon by others.

In this chapter, we'll look at ways to inspect what's running on your Linux systems and manage their resources to help ensure your nodes are good citizens on your network.

In this chapter, we will cover:

- Inspecting and managing processes
- Understanding load average
- Checking available memory
- Using shell-based resource monitors
- Checking disk space
- Scanning used storage
- Introduction to logging
- Maintaining log size with logrotate
- Understanding the systemd init system
- Understanding the systemd journal

Inspecting and managing processes

In a typical troubleshooting scenario, you might have a process that is misbehaving or needs an action performed against it. If you're using a graphical desktop environment for a workstation, you might use a tool such as the GNOME System Monitor to investigate processes running on your system, and then kill the problem child. In most cases though, you probably won't have a desktop environment (at least not on servers), so you would use a command such as `kill` in order to get rid of whatever process is misbehaving. But before you can kill a process, you'll need to know its **process identifier (PID)**. One method that works on all Linux systems to find the PID of a process is to open a terminal and us the `ps` command. Here's an example of its usage:

```
ps aux
```

Along with `ps`, it's common to use `grep` if you happen to already know the name of the process. In that case, you can pipe the output of `ps aux` into `grep` and then search for a process.

```
ps aux |grep httpd
```

The `ps` command will give you a list of running processes. If you used `grep`, the output would be narrowed down to a list of processes matching the search term. You'll see the PID located for each process that comes up in the results within the second column. In the third column, you'll see how much CPU the process is consuming, followed by a column for memory usage immediately after that.

```
jay@packt-debian:~$ ps aux
USER       PID %CPU %MEM    VSZ   RSS TTY      STAT START   TIME COMMAND
root         1  0.0  0.8  28544  4504 ?        Ss   12:30   0:00 /sbin/init
root         2  0.0  0.0      0     0 ?        S    12:30   0:00 [kthreadd]
root         3  0.0  0.0      0     0 ?        S    12:30   0:00 [ksoftirqd/0]
root         5  0.0  0.0      0     0 ?        S<   12:30   0:00 [kworker/0:0H]
root         6  0.0  0.0      0     0 ?        S    12:30   0:00 [kworker/u2:0]
root         7  0.0  0.0      0     0 ?        S    12:30   0:00 [rcu_sched]
root         8  0.0  0.0      0     0 ?        S    12:30   0:00 [rcu_bh]
root         9  0.0  0.0      0     0 ?        S    12:30   0:00 [migration/0]
root        10  0.0  0.0      0     0 ?        S    12:30   0:00 [watchdog/0]
root        11  0.0  0.0      0     0 ?        S<   12:30   0:00 [khelper]
root        12  0.0  0.0      0     0 ?        S    12:30   0:00 [kdevtmpfs]
root        13  0.0  0.0      0     0 ?        S<   12:30   0:00 [netns]
root        14  0.0  0.0      0     0 ?        S    12:30   0:00 [khungtaskd]
root        15  0.0  0.0      0     0 ?        S<   12:30   0:00 [writeback]
root        16  0.0  0.0      0     0 ?        SN   12:30   0:00 [ksmd]
root        17  0.0  0.0      0     0 ?        S<   12:30   0:00 [crypto]
root        18  0.0  0.0      0     0 ?        S<   12:30   0:00 [kintegrityd]
root        19  0.0  0.0      0     0 ?        S<   12:30   0:00 [bioset]
root        20  0.0  0.0      0     0 ?        S<   12:30   0:00 [kblockd]
root        22  0.0  0.0      0     0 ?        S    12:30   0:00 [kswapd0]
root        23  0.0  0.0      0     0 ?        S    12:30   0:00 [fsnotify_mark]
root        29  0.0  0.0      0     0 ?        S<   12:30   0:00 [kthrotld]
root        30  0.0  0.0      0     0 ?        S<   12:30   0:00 [ipv6_addrconf]
root        31  0.0  0.0      0     0 ?        S<   12:30   0:00 [deferwq]
root        64  0.0  0.0      0     0 ?        S    12:30   0:00 [khubd]
root        66  0.0  0.0      0     0 ?        S<   12:30   0:00 [ata_sff]
root        67  0.0  0.0      0     0 ?        S    12:30   0:00 [scsi_eh_0]
```

Output of ps aux on a Debian system

USER, STAT, START, TIME, and COMMAND are additional columns we can see from this output. While USER is self-explanatory, here's a short description of the other column headers:

- STAT: This field identifies the state of the program, with a one or two-character code representing the state the program is currently in. For example, S means that the process is waiting for some event to complete, while D is an uninterruptible sleep state, typically related to IO. To view a complete list, check out the manual page on ps.

- START: This field refers to the time at which the process began running.

- TIME: This indicates the total time the process has been utilizing the CPU. Every time a process hits the CPU and needs work done, time is logged against the CPU.

- COMMAND: This displays the command that the current process is running.

Now that you know how to find the PID of a process, we can take a look at the kill command, which is a command that's useful in case you need to close a program that otherwise won't close by normal means. For example, if you are running a script with a process ID 25787, you could kill it by executing the following command:

```
# kill 25787
```

The kill command works by sending a specific signal to a PID. Signal 15, for example, is known as **SIGTERM**. If you execute the kill against a process without any parameters (as we did in our last example), you're sending signal 15 by default, which basically asks politely for the process to close down. There are 18 different signals you can send to a process, which you can read about in the manual pages. For the sake of our discussion here, SIGINT, SIGTERM, and SIGKILL are the ones you'll likely use the most. You can view a list of these signals, as well as their meanings, by executing the following command:

```
man 7 signal
```

To send a specific signal, type a hyphen after the kill command followed by the signal you wish to send. Since kill by itself sends signal 15, you can do the same thing by executing the following command:

```
# kill -15 25787
```

To send a different signal, such as 2 (**SIGINT**), type the following command:

```
# kill -2 25787
```

If you're *very* desperate, you could send signal 9 (**SIGKILL**) to the process:

```
# kill -9 25787
```

However, SIGKILL should be used only if you've already exhausted all your other options, and you cannot get the process to close despite your best efforts. SIGKILL closes the process immediately, but unfortunately it does not give it a chance to clean up after itself. This may cause unclean temporary files and open socket connections to remain on your system. Worse, it can actually damage databases and configuration. Therefore, I cannot stress this enough, kill -9 should definitely be the very last thing you try if you can't get a process to close out gracefully. Try every method you know to first close a process gracefully, and then make several more attempts before considering using it.

Another command that can be used to kill processes is the killall command. The killall command allows you to kill all the processes on your system which match a specific name. For example, let's say you have multiple Firefox windows open and the program stops responding. To kill all instances of Firefox running on your system instantly, simply execute the following command:

```
killall firefox
```

And just like that, every Firefox window on your system will instantly vanish. The killall command can be used to close down multiple processes that all share the same name, and it can be very useful on servers which run multiple instances of a single unresponsive program or script.

That's pretty much all there is to using the kill and killall commands. Sure, there are more options and the man pages will give you more information. But in a nutshell, those are the variations you'll actually use. In a perfect world, you should never need to use kill and all processes running on your servers will obey you without question. Unfortunately, we don't live in a perfect world and you'll probably use these commands more often than you'd like.

Understanding load average

For a Linux administrator, **load average** is one of the most important concepts you'll ever learn. While you may know already that this number represents how much load your system is experiencing, it also represents trending performance as well. Using this number, you'll be able to determine whether your system is being overwhelmed or it's recovering and calming down. Essentially, the load average consists of three numbers, each representing the average load of the system over a specific time frame. The first number represents one minute, the second represents five minutes, and the third represents 15 minutes. There are many ways in which you can view your load average, and it will also be displayed in most system monitors available for Linux. One way to view your load average in a snap is to execute the following command:

```
cat /proc/loadavg
```

Viewing the load average

A simpler technique is to use the uptime command. Though the main purpose of the uptime command is to view how long your system has been up, it displays the system's load average as well.

The output of the uptime command

So, how does one properly interpret this information? With the screenshot of the uptime command shown in this section, we see the following numbers:

```
0.63 0.72 0.71
```

As mentioned, the first three numbers represent the system's load during a period of 1, 5, and 15 minutes respectively. The load that's being referred to represents the number of processes that are waiting on, or currently utilizing, the CPU during each timeframe. On the system used in this example, we can see that the load on it is relatively low. We can also see trends with load average as well. On the example system, the load is trending upward but just by a bit.

Generally speaking, the lower the load averages, the better. But that's not always the case; lower numbers can be disturbing too. For example, if you have a server that's supposed to be doing a lot of work and its load average drops down to being less than one, that may be a cause for alarm. If the load is that low, the server clearly isn't busy. This might represent that a process which is supposed to be running has failed. For example, if you have a MySQL server that normally sees hundreds of queries at a time, it would definitely be odd to see that the server was suddenly bored. On the flipside, a server with load average in the hundreds would be so busy it would be unlikely that it could even process a login request for you to even access the system!

Let's take a look at another load average. Here's one from a busier system on a network that I help manage:

```
9.75 8.96 5.94
```

Here, we can see that the load on this system is much higher than the previous example. This might be something I'll want to look into. But one confusing thing about a system's load average is that the number itself isn't enough to justify cause for alarm. If that system had ten cores, I wouldn't be so worried. Despite the load average being over nine, there would be plenty of CPU's to handle the workload in that case. However, the system I took that output from has only four cores, so it's a cause for alarm. It means that during each of the three time windows, there were more processes waiting for CPU time than the system actually has in cores. That's not good. But thankfully, I can see that the system is recovering since the load is trending downward. In this case, I won't panic but I'll certainly want to keep my eye on it to ensure that it continues to recover. I may also investigate the system to find out what exactly caused the load to spike up so high. Perhaps the server just finished a really big job, but it's worth looking into.

As a general rule of thumb, it's a good idea to record a baseline of your systems when they are under their normal, expected load. Each system on your network will have a designated purpose and each will have a certain load you can reasonably expect your system to face at any one time. If the systems load average dips too far below or climbs higher than the baseline, then you would want to take a look and find out what's going on. If the load reaches a level where there are more processes than you have cores to handle, that's cause for alarm.

Checking available memory

Linux systems handle memory exceptionally well, though it's always possible for things to get out of hand if a process misbehaves or not enough memory was allocated. In such a situation where a system starts to perform sluggish, checking your available memory will probably be one of the first things you look into. To do this, we use the `free` command. To make the output even more readable, you can add the `-m` option, which shows your memory usage in terms of megabytes, which can make it much easier to read. Reading this output may be confusing at first, though I'm sure you'll find it straightforward after we go through the output.

```
11:05:51 [bahamut:~]$ free -m
              total       used       free     shared    buffers     cached
Mem:           7923       6995        927        120        441       2367
-/+ buffers/cache:        4186       3736
Swap:          1906        118       1788
11:05:56 [bahamut:~]$
```

The output of the free command

When running the `free` command, we're presented with three rows and six columns of information. The first row shows us our actual RAM usage, while the second row declares buffers and the third our swap usage. Under `total`, we see that this system has 7923 MB of RAM installed. Technically, this system has 8 GB of RAM, though some is reserved for the kernel or some kind of hardware and may not show here. In the next column (`used`) we see how much of our system's RAM has been consumed, followed by `free` where it shows us how much of the system's RAM is unused. In our preceding example, it would appear as though we only have 927 MB free of our 8 GB, but that's not exactly correct. So, how exactly does one interpret how much memory is actually free?

First, `used` on the first line corresponds to how much memory is actually being used, including what has been cached. Essentially, memory management in Linux declares what is known as a **disk cache**, which is a chunk of memory set aside for data that has yet to be written to disk. You can see this in our output of the `free -m` command; it's the number on the far right underneath `cached`. This memory is not necessarily being used by a process; it's declared in order to make your system run faster. If a process is started and it requires more RAM than what shows in the first line under `free`, the Linux kernel will happily give up memory from the disk cache to other processes as needed.

The disk cache helps increase performance. When you read something from the disk, it is stored in the disk cache, and then read from there instead of from the disk each time. For example, say you take a look at a text file saved in your /home directory several times each day. The first time you read it, you're reading it from the disk. From that point on, it's stored in disk cache, and accessed from there each time you wish to read the file from that point forward. Since RAM is faster than your disk, this file will open each additional time because it only has to read it from disk one time, then going forward its read from the disk cache.

The information stored within the disk cache ages out over time. As disk cache fills up, the oldest information stored there drops off to make room for other things. In addition, when memory is needed for processes, memory from the cache can be taken back at any time. This is why that even though it may appear that an excessive amount of RAM is being used up by the cache at times, it's not a big issue — applications are never prevented access to this memory when they need it.

Going back to our example, the number we want to look at when determining how much memory we have free is the amount shown in the second column, on the second row. In the case of this example, 3736 MB is considered free. This is plenty of free memory in regards to this particular system. You should worry when this number decreases and swap starts to increase to compensate. As long as your system has enough RAM for its designated purpose, swap should barely be used. A small amount will almost always be used, but it is a problem when a large amount is being used. When your system actually does start to run out of memory, it will start to use your swap partition. Since your hard drive is many times slower than your RAM, you do not want this. If you see your swap space being abused, you should run some sort of resource monitor (a few of which we discuss in this chapter) to identify what is using it up.

To make sure we have a well-rounded understanding of the free command output, let's go over all of the sections it contains, starting with the very first row. We already covered total, which is the amount of memory your system has physically installed (minus whatever your kernel or hardware has reserved). Next in the first row, we have used, which refers to the amount of memory which is being used by anything at all, including the cache. The free column is the exact opposite and refers to memory that is not being used by anything whatsoever.

The last two items on the first row are `buffers` and `cache`. While these two sections aren't being used by any process, the kernel uses them to cache data for performance optimization. But if a process needs more memory, it's welcome to take from these two numbers. We already covered the disk cache, which is the last number. The `buffers` refer to data that hasn't yet been written to disk. Linux will, at various intervals, run a `sync` to write this information to the disk. You can even run the `sync` command yourself if you want, though this is rarely necessary. The concept of a buffer is also a key indicator on why you don't want to abruptly remove external media from your computer without unmounting first. If your system hasn't yet synced the data to the disk, you may lose it if you eject the media prematurely.

On the second row, we have `-/+ buffers cache` (which in our example above is 4186 MB and 3736 MB, respectively). The first number on this row (4186 MB) is a number calculated by subtracting the total of buffers and cache (2808 MB) from the used column of the first row (6995 MB). This gives us a total of 4187 MB, which is a bit off due to rounding (we're viewing the output in MB since we used the `-m` flag, so we're off by a small amount), but close enough. If we followed the same math but without the `-m` flag in our `free` command, the result would've been exact. The next number on the second row is 3736 MB. As mentioned earlier, this is the amount of memory that is actually free for the system to use. To get this number, we subtract the used memory (4186 MB) from our total memory (7923 MB).

Again, the amount of memory under `free` on the second row is the number you care about when wondering how much memory you have left. However, it's also important to understand how we arrived at this number and how Linux manages memory for us.

Using shell-based resource monitors

When you install any Linux distribution with a desktop environment, chances are there will be a graphical system monitor bundled along with it. Popular among these are **KSysGuard** and the **GNOME System Monitor**, but there are many others. For the most part, these are fine and do the job well. The GNOME System Monitor is capable of showing you your load average, currently running processes (as well as their PID, CPU percent, memory, and more), and how much of your disks are being used. Many graphical system monitors also show this information and more. While these tools are great, nodes within a typical Linux-based network don't always have a graphical user interface available. Thankfully, there are many different resource monitoring tools available via the shell and they don't require that you're running a desktop environment at all. Some of these are so great that you'll, at some point, forego the graphical tools for the shell tools. Popular tools in this category include `top`, `htop`, `iotop`, and `ncdu`.

First, we would need to make sure the aforementioned tools are installed on our system. In most cases, `top` is already installed for us but the others will need to be installed manually. You can verify that `top` is installed by running:

```
which top
```

You should see the following output:

```
/usr/bin/top
```

You can use your distribution's package manager to install the others. For Debian, you can install them all in one shot:

```
# apt-get install htop iotop ncdu
```

Unfortunately, on CentOS, not all of these packages are available in the default repositories. To install these tools on CentOS, you'll first need to add the `epel` repository, and then you can install all of the packages. The following outlines the commands to use:

```
# yum install epel-release
# yum install htop iotop ncdu
```

Feel free to give these tools a try. The `top` and `htop` commands will both run without root access. However, you'll need to run `iotop` with at least `sudo` for it to function. The `ncdu` command will function as a normal user, but would then be limited to viewing only the resources that user has access to. Let's take a closer look at these tools.

What do these tools do for us, anyway? First, `top` is tried and true; something that you've probably used before if you're not new to Linux. When it comes to seeing what's running on your system, `top` is quite common. With `top`, you'll see all kinds of information, such as uptime, load average, used memory, used swap, cache, and more. In the bottom section of the screen, you'll see a list of processes. When you're finished, simply press *Q* to exit.

```
                              jay@centos7:~
top - 14:35:30 up 11 min,   3 users,   load average: 0.00, 0.04, 0.05
Tasks:  86 total,   2 running,  84 sleeping,   0 stopped,   0 zombie
%Cpu(s):   0.0 us,   0.0 sy,   0.0 ni,100.0 id,   0.0 wa,   0.0 hi,   0.0 si,   0.0 st
KiB Mem :   501400 total,    101536 free,     91048 used,    308816 buff/cache
KiB Swap:   839676 total,    839668 free,         8 used.    305932 avail Mem

  PID USER      PR  NI    VIRT    RES    SHR S %CPU %MEM     TIME+ COMMAND
11902 jay       20   0  129892   1660   1204 R  0.3  0.3   0:00.05 top
    1 root      20   0   56632   6684   3912 S  0.0  1.3   0:00.56 systemd
    2 root      20   0       0      0      0 S  0.0  0.0   0:00.00 kthreadd
    3 root      20   0       0      0      0 S  0.0  0.0   0:00.21 ksoftirqd/0
    5 root       0 -20       0      0      0 S  0.0  0.0   0:00.00 kworker/0:0H
    6 root      20   0       0      0      0 S  0.0  0.0   0:00.02 kworker/u2:0
    7 root      rt   0       0      0      0 S  0.0  0.0   0:00.00 migration/0
    8 root      20   0       0      0      0 S  0.0  0.0   0:00.00 rcu_bh
    9 root      20   0       0      0      0 S  0.0  0.0   0:00.00 rcuob/0
   10 root      20   0       0      0      0 S  0.0  0.0   0:00.53 rcu_sched
   11 root      20   0       0      0      0 R  0.0  0.0   0:00.37 rcuos/0
   12 root      rt   0       0      0      0 S  0.0  0.0   0:00.00 watchdog/0
   13 root       0 -20       0      0      0 S  0.0  0.0   0:00.00 khelper
   14 root      20   0       0      0      0 S  0.0  0.0   0:00.00 kdevtmpfs
   15 root       0 -20       0      0      0 S  0.0  0.0   0:00.00 netns
   16 root       0 -20       0      0      0 S  0.0  0.0   0:00.00 writeback
   17 root       0 -20       0      0      0 S  0.0  0.0   0:00.00 kintegrityd
   18 root       0 -20       0      0      0 S  0.0  0.0   0:00.00 bioset
   19 root       0 -20       0      0      0 S  0.0  0.0   0:00.00 kblockd
```

The top command running on a CentOS system

There are several ways in which you can run `top`. By running `top` with no parameters, you'll see a screen similar to what was shown earlier in this section. You will see a summary of system performance in the upper section and various processes in the bottom. However, if you already know which process you want to monitor, you can use the `-p` flag coupled with a PID to watch only that process. For example, we could use the following to monitor a process with a PID of `12844`:

```
top -p 12844
```

By default, the output within the `top` command updates every three seconds. To change this, you can use the `-d` flag to choose a different frequency (in seconds):

```
top -d 2
```

If you prefer, frequency can be less than a second:

```
top -d 0.5
```

If `top` is already running and you would like to change how frequently it updates, you don't have to close it and start it up again. You can type s while it is running and you'll be prompted to designate a new frequency.

Within `top`, you can change how the process list is sorted by pressing a key on your keyboard. If you type P, you'll sort by CPU usage; using M, you can sort by memory usage (capitalization matters here). You can even kill a process from here if you wish, by pressing k, which will then prompt you for a PID to kill. Be careful though; this defaults to whatever happens to be at the top of your process list at the time you press it, so make sure that you don't press Enter until you've actually typed the PID or you may kill a process you didn't mean to.

So, why use `top` anyway? The main purpose that administrators use `top` for is to help determine what is causing a system to become CPU or memory bound. Most often, `top` is never the solution, but rather the beginning of a root cause analysis. You can immediately see which process is consuming your CPU or RAM, but depending on the context you may not have an idea yet on how to correct the problem. With `top`, you're only able to discover the culprit. Unfortunately, `top` may not always show you the root cause process, but it's definitely a very easy first place to look when you have a system that's running sluggish.

To begin your troubleshooting, the information at the top would give you a starting point to see which resource is being used up. On the `%Cpu(s)` line, we can tell immediately if the system is suffering from excessive **I/O wait** (the `%wa` field), which would basically mean there is more being thrown at the CPU than it's capable of handling. In this situation, tasks would back up and the load average would increase. Idle time (or `%id`) is a number that's better the higher it gets, which means your system would have CPU time to spare.

In some cases, you may find excessive CPU usage but not a lot in the process list to show for it. In such a case, you may bring up `iotop` in order to determine if your system is I/O bound. Using `iotop` (requires root) you can see just how much data is being written to or read from your disks. Using the left and right arrows, you can change focus from one column to another, which sorts the process list by that column.

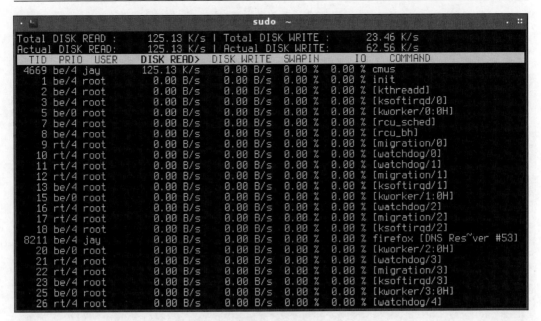

TID	PRIO	USER	DISK READ>	DISK WRITE	SWAPIN	IO	COMMAND

Running iotop on a Debian system

By default, the list of processes within `iotop` is quite crowded. You can slim it down by executing:

```
# iotop --only
```

By appending -only, you'll only see processes that have actual read and write operations occurring. In the `iotop` screenshot in this section, you can see that there are quite a few processes with no activity happening at all. But with -only, it may be easier to read since it cleans up the output. You can actually activate -only while `iotop` is running, by simply pressing *O* on your keyboard. In addition, another useful keyboard shortcut is the ability to change the sort order of any column with r.

Next in this section, we have `htop`. While `top` is the the tried and true standard for viewing system resources on a Linux system, `htop` is increasing in popularity very quickly.

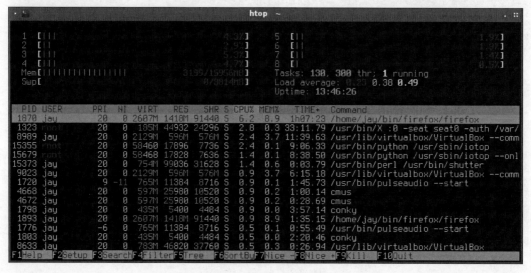

The htop command in action

The basic idea of `htop` is the same as `top` — the `top` area shows current CPU and memory usage and the bottom section provides a list of processes. But where `htop` differs is how it presents this information, which is easier to read and offers an area for graphs of your CPU's usage. In addition to that, it allows you to easily send a specific signal to a process. Earlier, we covered various signals you can use to end a process. Here, we can see that same concept illustrated graphically. To send a signal to a process, use the up and down arrows on your keyboard to highlight a process, and then press *F9* to choose a specific signal. SIGTERM is selected by default, but you can send any of the other signals to a process as well.

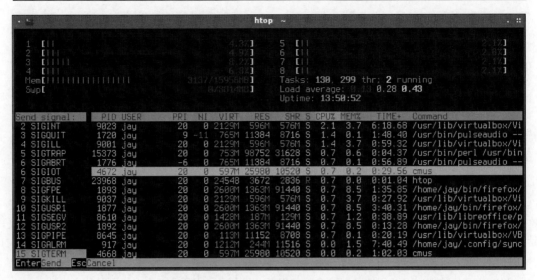

Preparing to send a signal to a process in htop

The process list in htop can be sorted similar to iotop. One thing that may not be apparent at first is that htop supports mouse input. While you can select columns with arrow keys, you can also click on them.

Another benefit to htop is how customizable it is. Although the default layout is decent for most use cases, you can add additional meters. To do so, press *F2* or click on **Setup** and you'll be brought to a menu where you can add or remove meters from the current view. Under Available Meters, highlight one that you want to add and press *F5* to add it to the left column or *F6* to add it to the right column. One meter you may find useful is the CPU average. Once you've added a new meter, you can reposition it by highlighting it and pressing *F7* to move it up or *F8* to move it down. When finished, press *Esc* to return to the main screen. These changes are saved automatically, so the next time you open htop, your custom layout will be intact.

Scanning used storage

Almost everyone experiences a situation where disk space seems to vanish, with no clear indication as to what is taking up all the space. There are multiple ways in which you can troubleshoot what in particular is eating your hard drive space for breakfast. In order to see an overview of your mounted filesystems as well as their used and free space, execute the `df` command. Using `-h` with `df` is easier to read for most people, as it will show used space in MB and GB:

```
df -h
```

Armed with that information, you'll know exactly what device is being used up and what volumes to focus your attention on. But the `df` command doesn't actually tell you what is using up all the space; it only gives you an overview of the current situation.

Next up is `du`. The `du` command, which can also be paired with `-h` for the same reason, shows you how much space is being used in a directory. All you would need to do is to `cd` into the directory you wish to check, and then run `du -h`. For even easier to read output, run the following in a directory:

```
du -hsc *
```

Breaking down that command, we have `-h` parameter that we already know makes the output easier to read. The `-s` parameter shows only a total and `-c` will present you with a grand total at the end. Since we used an asterisk with the command, it will run `du -hsc` against each subdirectory contained within the current one. With this command, you can determine which directories in your current working directory are using up the most space.

However, it gets even better than that. As useful as `du -hsc *` is, you still have to run it manually for each subdirectory. There are ways to use it to scan deeper, but `du` is only useful for an overview summary. An even better way is to install `ncdu`. The `ncdu` command is not a graphical utility in that it doesn't require a graphical desktop environment. But it's so easy to use; you may think that it actually was a graphical utility. Once kicked off against a particular directory, it does a deep dive and allows you to actually traverse the filesystem tree from that point and follow what is using up all your space straight down to the culprit.

You don't need to be the root user or have `sudo` permission to utilize `ncdu`, but keep in mind `ncdu` can only scan directories that its calling user has permission to access. In some cases, you may need to run it as root to get around that. The basic usage of `ncdu` is simple; call `ncdu` along with a path for it to scan. For example, you can scan your entire filesystem or a section of it:

```
ncdu /
```

Scanning the root filesystem of a CentOS system with ncdu

It's important to note that by default ncdu will scan everything within the directory you give it, including anything that may be mounted. An example of this can be mounted NFS shares or external disks, but you may not want external mounts to factor into the results. Thankfully, this is as easy as presenting the -x option to ncdu, which tells it to ignore anything you have mounted when you run your scan:

```
ncdu -x /
```

Once the scan is finished, you can traverse the results by pressing up and down keys on your keyboard, and press *Enter* to change into a directory. From within ncdu itself, you can even delete files without having to run any extra commands by simply pressing *D*. This way, you can do your auditing and cleanup from the same tool.

Feel free to run ncdu on your own systems and interrogate where your free space is going. Unless you actually start deleting things, it's harmless and can show you some potential items you may want to clean up. On actual servers, ncdu is quite useful in troubleshooting where your disk space is going.

Introduction to logging

By default, Linux logs almost everything. This is important for developing a root cause analysis when things go wrong. When you're faced with a problem on a production server, all you should need to do is determine the time in which the problem started and then read the log files for the types of things that happened on the system during that time. Linux logging is very informative.

But nowadays, the way that Linux handles logging is changing. With the rise of systemd, which is now the default init system on most Linux distributions, it's taken over almost everything, including logging. In the past, you would venture into /var/log whenever you wanted to read your logs, which is a directory containing various log files in plain text format. On both Debian and CentOS, you can still find logs in /var/log, so you'll still be able to utilize them for troubleshooting the same as we always have. But it's not yet certain how much longer this will be kept around.

Many might think that systemd taking over logging is a bad thing. After all, having the init system take care of so much of the system's upkeep gives it more work to perform, which may stretch it too thin. But one issue with syslog (the previous approach) is that there was no consistency from one distribution to another in how the logs were created or named. For example, Debian systems include an auth.log, which CentOS doesn't. Both have dmesg and only CentOS has a boot.log file. This makes troubleshooting a mixed environment, a beast.

The systemd approach (which we'll discuss later) offers a more consistent approach between distributions. So while it may be true that systemd is being spread thin with the multitude of responsibilities it has on the system, consistency is definitely welcome.

Both Debian and CentOS have a log file that is used whenever a user logs into the system, even if she or he does so via SSH. On CentOS, this log is located in /var/log/secure. Debian uses /var/log/auth.log for this purpose. If you need to know who is logging into your system and when, you would want to look at these logs in order to find out. On both, you can find /var/log/messages, which includes a smorgasbord of useful information, such as output from processes, network activation, services starting up, and more. When it comes to troubleshooting hardware, /var/log/dmesg is a great place to look. In fact, /var/log/dmesg has its own command. Typing dmesg from anywhere on the system (even if your current working directory isn't /var/log) will present you with the same log.

The log files in `/var/log` are very easy to follow in near real time by using `tail -f`. The `-f` flag of `tail` isn't specifically limited to log files. It allows you to display the output of a log file, as it's being written to. When you're troubleshooting a system, `tail -f` is indispensable. For example, if you have a user that cannot log in to the system, you could run the following on a Debian system to watch the `auth.log` file as they make their attempt. That way, you can see what error message the system is registering for their failed attempts at logging in:

```
# tail -f /var/log/auth.log
```

From there, as the `auth.log` gets updated, the results will show in your terminal immediately. To end, simply press *Ctrl + C* to stop following the output. You can do this with any log, or any text file on your system. This is very useful for a multitude of troubleshooting tactics, as most processes you may want to investigate will log its activities to at least one log.

Maintaining log size with logrotate

As you know, logs are crucial when it comes to troubleshooting. Linux generally does a very good job of logging almost everything you would want to know, but over time these logs can really add up. On a production server, a log file growing out of control and taking up literally all of your server's free space is a very real issue if left unchecked. In addition to disk space being consumed, a gigantic log file is very hard to open in a text editor in order to view the contents, which makes troubleshooting even harder. A log file of over 500 GB would not only take up a ridiculous amount of space; it would likely cause the system to hang if you try to open it, and transferring a log file to another server for analysis once it reaches a very large size isn't practical either.

For the most part, excessive log files are not as much of an issue on newer Linux distributions than those of the past. With syslog, there was no automatic maintenance. If you didn't either clean the logs yourself or set up something to rotate them for you, you would definitely need to keep an eye on them. Nowadays, **journald** handles this for us. But with Debian and CentOS, this can be somewhat of a mixed bag. This is because although the systemd journald takes care of logging for us on newer releases of most popular Linux distributions, syslog is still used for compatibility. Therefore, we still have to deal with log rotation even though all the pieces are in place for journald. The journald is the future, though syslog is still used on Enterprise Linux distributions today for compatibility.

Log rotation is the process of taking an existing log file, renaming it, and having the process write to a brand-new empty log file. The previous log files can all be kept, or you can keep only a few of them if you wish. It's not uncommon for Enterprise systems to have a specific retention policy. It's a common practice to compress previous logs, which saves a great amount of disk space. This is where logrotate comes in. It's a process that we can run on our server to automatically swap out our log files and (as an option) compress the backup copies.

While designing a Linux network, it's important to understand which processes each server needs to run and to take into account the logging requirements of those processes from the start. Having logrotate installed and configured before a server enters production is a good practice. Having a server run out of free space in the middle of production is never a good experience, and knowing first what log files a running process creates, and being prepared to handle them is a good idea. While configuring your logging, it's important to take into consideration the retention requirements of your company, if there are any.

On the CentOS system used in my lab, `logrotate` was installed by default. Debian had it installed out of the box as well. To verify this on your system, simply run the following command:

```
which logrotate
```

On CentOS, the `logrotate` binary is located in /usr/sbin, while Debian stores theirs in /usr/sbin. If the `which` command shows no output, you may need to use your distribution's package manager to install the `logrotate` package.

With the default installations of both Debian and CentOS, `logrotate` is already configured to run each day. When it does, it checks the /etc/logrotate.d directory for instructions and then executes them. The configuration for setting up `logrotate` rules is fairly straightforward. If you need example syntax, refer to your own system. By default, several `logrotate` scripts are created for you. An example of this is Debian's package manager `apt`. Whenever you install packages on a Debian system, it's logged in the following place:

```
/var/log/apt/history.log
```

If you view this file, you should see results of recent package installations that you or another user has performed. By default, the following file exists on Debian systems to handle the rotation of this log:

```
/etc/logrotate.d/apt
```

On Debian 8, this file contains the following:

```
/var/log/apt/term.log {
    rotate 12
    monthly
    compress
    missingok
    notifempty
}

/var/log/apt/history.log {
    rotate 12
    monthly
    compress
    missingok
    notifempty
}
```

As you can see, this configuration file for logrotate handles not only the history.log we mentioned earlier, but also term.log as well. Each section of this configuration begins with a path for logrotate to check, followed by individual options within brackets.

 The term.log file shows the actual terminal output that would've been seen while running an apt instance.

Among the options, we can see rotate 12, which means that up to 12 backup log files will be kept. Next, we see monthly, which details how often the log will actually be rotated. Despite the fact that logrotate is configured by default to run daily, it will follow the instructions contained within the individual configurations and only rotate if it meets that criteria. The compress option tells logrotate to compress the backed up file, which is probably what you want in most cases. Compressed log files use up very little space compared to the uncompressed live log, so it's definitely something to consider. missingok tells logrotate to keep running even if it encounters a missing log file. Otherwise, it would've displayed an error. Finally, we have notifempty, which simply tells logrotate to not bother with a log file if it is empty.

You can see a complete list of `logrotate` configuration options by perusing its man page:
`man logrotate`

While `logrotate` has some fairly decent default configuration for some of the services that ship with CentOS and Debian, you'll want to consider creating configuration for any new services that you set up. To do so, it's easiest to follow the format shown in example files that you'll already have stored in `/etc/logrotate.d`. It's as simple as beginning your configuration block with the path to a file you want `logrotate` to handle for you, followed by options within curly brackets. There's no service to restart or special command to make your new configuration active. The next time that `logrotate` runs, it will check the `/etc/logrotate.d` directory for new configurations and run them if there are no errors.

Understanding the systemd init system

On quite a few Linux distributions these days, the init system has been switched to systemd. This is true of Debian and CentOS starting with Version 8 and 7, respectively, but other distributions such as Fedora, Ubuntu, Arch Linux, and others have switched as well. Although some administrators prefer sysvinit, which was the previous dominant init system, systemd offers quite a few advancements over older systems.

With systemd, commands you would use to start processes are now different, though the majority of the older commands still work (for now). With sysvinit on a Debian 7 system, you would use the following command to restart Samba:

```
/etc/init.d/samba restart
```

However, with systemd, we now use `systemctl` to start, stop, or restart a process:

```
# systemctl restart samba
```

The sysvinit style of managing processes was the same in CentOS and Debian, and it is still the same now. At the time of this writing, both have switched to systemd. But the older /etc/init.d/<process-name> restart|stop|start commands still work in both Debian and CentOS with current releases, but instead of using sysvinit (which is gone) the commands are just translated to systemd commands instead. If you were to run the older sysvinit style commands, you'll likely see some text in the output informing you that the system is using systemctl instead. While this is great for the sake of compatibility (scripts relying on sysvinit style commands will likely still work), this won't be around forever. Learning systemd is important as once the sysvinit compatibility layer is removed, you'll no longer be able to rely on the older method. Thankfully, the basics of systemd are quick to learn.

To start a process with systemd, execute systemctl followed by the action you want to perform, followed by the process you would like to perform the action on. As we've done earlier with Samba, we executed systemctl restart samba. But we can also stop samba using systemctl stop samba, or we can start it by executing systemctl start samba as root.

The systemd init system also allows you to enable or disable a process. A process which is enabled will be started as the system is booted. A disabled process will only start if you do so manually. Depending on the distribution, processes (or units, as systemd calls them) may not be enabled by default. On CentOS, for example, you can install Samba, but it won't start automatically unless you tell it to do so. On Debian systems, it's largely assumed that since you installed something, you probably want it to run, so it will enable the newly installed process by default. Either way, it's not a good idea to assume that a process will automatically start with systemd. To find out, use the following command:

```
systemctl status <process>
```

Checking the status of a unit with systemctl

Checking the status with `systemctl` gives you a great deal of useful information, typically more than checking the status of processes with sysvinit. First, you can see whether or not a unit is running. In the previous screenshot, we can see that `nfs-kernel-server` is running. In addition, status gives us a few lines of log output as well, so if there are any problems starting a unit we may find the error right there.

You might be wondering how to find out whether or not a unit is configured to come up automatically when the system is booted. Systemd makes that easy as well. We can use `is-enabled` with `systemctl` in order to find out if the unit is enabled. For example, to ensure the `ssh` daemon is configured to automatically start, we would issue the following command on a Debian system:

```
systemctl is-enabled ssh
```

To show all the units on your system and how they're configured, run the following command:

```
systemctl list-unit-files
```

To enable a unit, pass `enable` as a parameter to `systemctl`. Similarly, you can do the same with `disable` to ensure a unit does not start at boot. Therefore, on a Debian system, `systemctl enable ssh` would configure the `ssh` daemon to start at boot, while `systemctl disable ssh` would ensure that it doesn't. CentOS would be the same, but substitute `sshd` for `ssh`. While the differing unit names can be annoying between Linux systems, always remember that you can use `systemctl list-unit-files` as mentioned earlier to see a list of the units registered to your system and what they're named.

In a nutshell, that's pretty much all the knowledge required to use `systemctl` to manage processes (units) on your Linux system. For the most part, starting, stopping, enabling, and disabling units covers most use cases. For more advanced usage, see the man page for `systemctl`.

Systemd handles power management as well. You can use options such as `reboot`, `poweroff`, and `suspend` with `systemctl` to power on, shut down, or suspend the entire system.

Understanding the systemd journal

Another component of systemd is journald, which handles logging. The systemd method of journald enables binary logs, which is quite a different approach to simple text files as used before. Due to the fact that many distributions which have adopted systemd are still in a transitional phase, you're likely to still see text file logs in /var/log in much the same way as you still may see init scripts in /etc/init.d. It's always recommended to use the systemd approach whenever possible, as that is the current solution that distributions are moving toward.

You can view journald logs with the `journalctl` command. In addition, various options can be used with the `journalctl` command in order to narrow down the output or perform certain actions. For example, you can use `journalctl -f` to follow new log output on your system, similar to how you could do the same with `tail -f` against log files stored in /var/log. Additionally, you can use `journalctl` to show output from a particular PID. To do so, simply use `journalctl` with PID= along with a PID. For example, to view output from PID 11753, you would execute the following command:

```
journalctl PID=11753
```

In addition, you can use the name of the unit to show its output:

```
journalctl -u sshd
```

While `journalctl` is relatively simple to use, for those of you that are accustomed to the pervious syslog style of logging will be happy to know that you can (at least for now) still navigate to /var/log and peruse the logs there. For example, the dmesg command and log is still alive and well. But while `journalctl` and the concept of binary logs may take a while to get used to, I'm sure you'll find with practice that it is actually very handy.

Summary

In this chapter, we covered various ways in which you can manage your system's resources and look at logs. We started with an overview of managing processes and discussed load averages. Then, we covered monitoring a system's memory. In addition, we looked at shell-based system monitors such as top and htop. We also covered investigating disk usage and ncdu, which is a neat tool that allows you to scan a filesystem and view its usage in an easy to use way. We also covered logrotate and systemd.

In the next chapter, we'll take a look at managing our Linux-based network. This will include things such as configuring DHCP, DNS, NTP, as well as using exim to send e-mail and advertising shared services over the network.

Configuring Network Services

6

So far, we've configured our nodes and allowed them to actually talk to one another. We can access our nodes to administer them remotely, transfer files between them, monitor their resources, and perform basic networking. In this chapter, we'll design the IP address scheme we'll use for our network, as well as set up the required services for putting the plan into action. This will include a discussion on setting up and configuring **Dynamic Host Control Protocol (DHCP)**, **Domain Name Service**, as well as **Network Time Protocol (NTP)**.

In this chapter, we will cover:

- Planning your IP address layout
- Installing and configuring a DHCP server
- Installing and configuring a DNS server
- Setting up an internal NTP server

Planning your IP address layout

Taking the time to come up with a great plan before implementing anything on your network is a great idea, but your IP address scheme is especially important. It's all too easy to accept defaults and get everyone up and running quickly. For some small companies, the default IP address layout that ships with your router (or whichever device handles DHCP by default) may suffice. But further down the road, it needs to change as companies grow. Being prepared for potential growth is critical. Implementing an IP address scheme is easy, but changing this scheme on a network that's already been rolled out is a great challenge. Always take the time to plan accordingly.

The first consideration for determining your IP address scheme is what types of machines you'll need to provide addresses to. Often, you'll have servers, workstations, and printers to deal with. But nowadays, we also have other devices on our network such as IP phones, company-issued phones, conference systems, tablets, and more. When you start to add all these devices together, a typical 24-bit network with 254 usable addresses doesn't seem to be all that large, even for a small company. Worse, some devices (such as laptops) have multiple network interface cards. If you put all that together, you'll find that those 254 addresses can get used up really quickly.

Having multiple subnets would certainly help. With subnetting, you can create individual networks for each type of service, each with their own set of IP addresses. You can, for example, have your servers on one subnet, printers on another, and end-user workstations on their own. Instead of having to split a single 24-bit subnet between these three types of devices, you can spread them out over several networks. We will cover subnetting in more detail in *Chapter 8, Understanding Advanced Networking Concepts*, but for now segregating your network is almost always a good idea, for reasons even beyond IP addressing.

Another factor to take into consideration is limiting your **broadcast domain**. A single 24-bit network (which is often the default on network devices out of the box) is a single broadcast domain. In a nutshell, one device can talk to another device on your network without being routed first and share the same broadcast domain. If you only have a few devices, this doesn't really matter (unless one device handles a ridiculously large amount of traffic). But in most networks, breaking up your broadcast domain enhances performance. If you have a router separating your subnets, you are effectively breaking up your broadcast domain. Thus, it would be more difficult for a single node to saturate your network if it is on its own subnet. However, no solution is perfect and individual broadcast domains can become saturated.

One useful tool that you can use when planning your IP scheme is the `ipcalc` utility. The `ipcalc` utility can help you understand how many IP addresses you will be able to have available with each scheme. This utility is available via `apt-get` in Debian, and it doesn't need any extra repositories. While there is an `ipcalc` command built into CentOS, it's not the same thing and it's not useful. If possible, I would stick to the Debian version. To use it, simply execute `ipcalc` along with a network you are thinking about using. For example, you could run the following as a test:

```
ipcalc 10.10.96.0/22
```

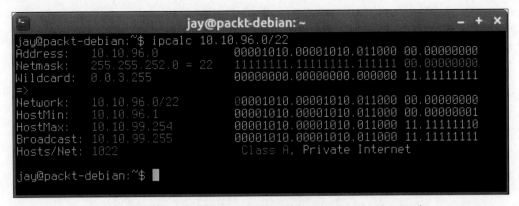

ipcalc showing subnet information for a 10.10.9.60/22 internal network

In the previous example, we can see that if we chose a `10.10.96.0/22` scheme, we would have `1022` allowable IP addresses, a subnet mask of `255.255.252.0` and this would be a class A private network. While you'll learn more about subnetting later in this book, the `ipcalc` utility will be handy for you to play around with and determine how specific IP layouts would look.

Another topic that's worth bringing up in IP addressing is IPv4 versus IPv6. For quite a long time, IPv4 has been sufficient for everyone's needs. Unfortunately, the time has come where IPv4 addresses on the public Internet are starting to run out (and in many situations, already has). The benefit of IPv6 is that there are so many IP addresses available; it's completely inconceivable that we would ever run out again. There is also a security benefit to IPv6, since the address space is so large that targets are abstracted (in essence, security through obscurity).

With this in mind, you might be tempted to roll-out IPv6 addresses over IPv4 within your network. However, my suggestion is unless you have a very good reason to do so, don't bother. The depletion of IPv4 addresses only affects the public Internet, not your internal network. While you can certainly roll-out IPv6 internally, there's no benefit to doing so. Given that IPv4 has over 4 billion addresses available, you would need quite a few devices in order to justify IPv6. On the other hand, IPv6 is certainly useful (and will eventually be required) for telecoms. It's also useful for those of you who are studying Cisco exams, as understanding of this topic is required. But for the purposes of this book and setting up Linux networks, IPv6 doesn't justify the administration overhead.

In summary, it's important to plan ahead. IPv4 is good enough for our needs and splitting our network into subnets is a good idea (even if you think your network will never surpass 254 addresses). Plan big; even in the worst-case scenario, you may never use all the IP addresses you configured. But even if you don't plan on using a large number of IP addresses, having them available in case you wish to grow your network is a good idea and much easier to implement later. In my experience, I've actually had the task of reconfiguring a company network that wasn't designed for growth. While it was definitely a learning experience, it wasn't an enjoyable one.

Installing and configuring a DHCP server

So far in this chapter, we talked about creating a layout for your network. In this section, we'll put that plan in action. Here, we'll set up a DHCP server on either a Debian or CentOS machine, and configure it to serve IPv4 addresses to our network. So, let's get started!

First, decide on which distribution will run your DHCP server. It doesn't matter if you choose Debian, CentOS, or a derivative. The configuration is the same on each, with the main difference being the name of the package that you'll need to install and the daemon to start up. With Debian, you'll install the `isc-dhcp-server` package, and you'll install `dhcp` for CentOS. Debian will enable the DHCP daemon (`isc-dhcp-server`) for you, but it won't start up because we haven't configured it yet. CentOS will not attempt to start or enable its DHCP daemon (`dhcpd`).

For both Debian and CentOS, the configuration file we'll need to edit is located at `/etc/dhcp/dhcpd.conf`. In order to set up our DHCP server, we'll need to edit this file and then start or restart the daemon. Go ahead and open this file with your favorite text editor. If you installed your DHCP server on Debian, you'll notice you're provided with a default `/etc/dhcp/dhcpd.conf` file that contains a fair amount of example configuration. CentOS, on the other hand, pretty much gives you a blank file to work with. For our purposes, we'll create some configuration from scratch. You can either remove or back up the default configuration file in the case of Debian.

What follows is an example configuration `/etc/dhcp/dhcpd.conf` file for DHCP. In this example, we're using the same network as identified earlier while demonstrating the `ipcalc` utility (`10.10.96.0/22`). This network gives us several subnets to use, but you don't have to go ahead with this scheme; feel free to adjust accordingly to fit your environment.

```
default-lease-time 86400;
max-lease-time 86400;
option subnet-mask 255.255.252.0;
option broadcast-address 10.10.99.255;
```

```
option domain-name "local.lan";
authoritative;
subnet 10.10.96.0 netmask 255.255.252.0 {
    range 10.10.99.100 10.10.99.254;
    option routers 10.10.96.1;
    option domain-name-servers 10.10.96.1;
}
```

So, let's go through this configuration line by line.

First, we have the following two lines:

```
default-lease-time 86400;
max-lease-time 86400;
```

Here, we're identifying how long we would like a DHCP lease to last for. In practice, when a node requests an IP address, its client will be given a lease along with the IP address. This means that the IP address is only valid for a particular period of time. Here, we're setting a lease time of 86400, which means our lease time is one day since this is referenced in seconds. We have this number listed twice, in the default and maximum lease times. The `default-lease-time` is given to any client if it doesn't specify a particular amount of time it is requesting the hold onto the IP address for. The `max-lease-time` means that if the client requests to hold onto the IP address for longer than this period, it won't be allowed to do so. We're basically setting the default and the maximum lease time to the same number. If we wanted to, we could have also included `min-lease-time` to enforce a minimum lease time in case a client asks for less.

Consider the following two lines:

```
option subnet-mask 255.255.252.0;
option broadcast-address 10.10.99.255;
```

With this section, we're setting the subnet mask that will be given to clients as well as the broadcast address. As you probably already know, the subnet mask identifies the network that each connecting node will be a part of. When clients check their IP info after being provided an address, the subnet mask we identify will be shown. The broadcast address is an address on which all nodes within this subnet would be able to receive packets.

Consider the following two lines:

```
option domain-name "local.lan";
authoritative;
```

Here, we're appending the domain name of local.lan to the hostnames of each node that connect to our DHCP server. This step isn't required by any means, but can be useful if normalizing domain names within your network. We also include authoritative in our configuration to establish that our DHCP server is the primary one for this subnet.

Consider the following lines:

```
subnet 10.10.96.0 netmask 255.255.252.0 {
    range 10.10.99.1 10.10.99.254;
    option routers 10.10.96.1;
    option domain-name-servers 10.10.96.1;
}
```

Finally, we have a very important block of code at the end. Here, we identify the network address for our subnet, its subnet mask, the range of IP addresses we're issuing, the default gateway, and our DNS server. In this example, we're starting our first DHCP-issued address at 10.10.99.100 and ending our pool at 10.10.99.254. If you recall the output of ipcalc earlier, you'd notice that the first address in this subnet begins at 10.10.96.1. Instead of starting our pool there, we're starting our pool much later. For the sake of reference, we used the 10.10.96.0/22 network, which gives us the following subnets:

```
10.10.96.0
10.10.97.0
10.10.98.0
10.10.99.0
```

If we wanted to, we could set our DHCP range to begin at 10.10.96.1 and end at 10.10.99.254. We would have 1,022 DHCP addresses in that case. However, the reason I didn't do that in my configuration is because the first three networks have been reserved for several purposes. I use the first (10.10.96.0/22) for servers, the next for DHCP reservations, and the third for network appliances. Since the first three subnets are outside the DHCP range, the DHCP server will never offer any of those addresses to clients, so I don't have to worry about a DHCP lease tackling a static address I may have set up. It's a very common practice to ensure that static IP addresses are outside the DHCP range.

To be fair, this configuration is fairly complicated, as I'm showing you how to use multiple subnets with DHCP rather than focusing on just one network. To simplify a bit, if we were setting up a default 24-bit network, our configuration would look like the following (if we were using a `10.10.10.0/24` network):

```
default-lease-time 86400;
max-lease-time 86400;
option subnet-mask 255.255.255.0;
option broadcast-address 10.10.10.255;
option domain-name "local.lan";
authoritative;
subnet 10.10.10.0 netmask 255.255.255.0 {
    range 10.10.10.10 10.10.10.254;
    option routers 10.10.96.1;
    option domain-name-servers 10.10.96.1;
}
```

With this configuration, I'm setting the DHCP range to start at `10.10.10.10` and end at `10.10.10.254`. This gives me nine IP addresses (`10.10.10.1 − 10.10.10.9`) that will never be assigned, so I have room to set up a few static IP addresses.

So, I mentioned *static IP addresses* a few times here. You probably already know what that means, but it's important to elaborate that static IP addresses are a great idea for servers. These are addresses that are reserved for certain servers or nodes, where you expect them to have the same IP address each time. This is probably a no-brainer if you've ever configured a network before. There's also the concept of a static lease that's important as well. A static lease is also known as a **reservation**. With a static lease, the IP address is still provided by the DHCP server, and the client still uses DHCP to request an address. The difference is that the client will receive the same address, each and every time it connects.

Setting up static leases is very easy. Reservations can be placed at the end of your `/etc/dhcp/dhcpd.conf` file. Here's an example to show what the syntax looks like:

```
host bahamut {
    hardware ethernet 28:B2:BD:05:1E:00;
    fixed-address 10.10.97.4;
}
```

Here, we have a host named `bahamut` with a MAC address `28:B2:BD:05:1E:00`. The name is arbitrary; it has no actual meaning other than for us to remember which host the reservation is for. It doesn't have to match the hostname of the device that's requesting an IP. The two lines within the block of code simply mean that any time a network card connects to the DHCP server with a MAC address `28:B2:BD:05:1E:00`, it needs to be provided an IP address of `10.10.97.4`. We can add as many similar code blocks as we'd like for as many static leases we wish to assign.

You might be wondering, when should you use a static IP and when should you use a static lease? In my opinion, use static leases whenever it makes sense and fits the design of your network. With static leases, you only need to check the `/etc/dhcp/dhcpd.conf` file whenever you'd like to see an overview of all your reservations. In addition, the host will always receive the same IP address, even if you reinstall the OS or boot it from a live install image. There's nothing you need to configure on the host itself for a static lease. Generally, static leases are easier to manage. Of course, your own preferences will supersede this.

Finally, in order for our DHCP server to run properly, it must be started and configured to run at boot. Debian already took care of enabling the daemon, so you would just need to restart it for our configuration to take affect:

```
# systemctl restart isc-dhcp-server
```

For CentOS, we need to enable and start the service manually:

```
# systemctl enable dhcpd
# systemctl start dhcpd
```

As you can see, configuring a DHCP server on Linux is fairly easy and straightforward. Of course, there are advanced usage scenarios and a plethora of additional options. But for most purposes, a configuration such as the one outlined here should suffice.

Installing and configuring a DNS server

Domain Name System (DNS) makes navigating networked resources much easier. Unless you have a very small network, it's unlikely that you'll remember which IP addresses belong to which machines. DNS helps by mapping names to IP addresses, so you can refer to computers by their hostname and DNS will do the work of translating that back to the IP address.

DNS is one of those things that virtually everyone with a network connected device uses all the time, regardless of whether or not the user realizes it. Computers, servers, smart phones, tablets, smart appliances, and more all utilize DNS. Whenever you look up a service on the Internet, such as a website or a remote resource, DNS translates the name of the resource to the IP address.

Though the idea of DNS and what it does for us may be common knowledge, it's one of those things that are easy to take for granted. DNS is one of those mythical things that works in the background and makes our lives much easier. Most of us use it, but very few of us actually understand how it works. Whenever you connect to an **Internet Service Provider (ISP)**, you're typically assigned a DNS server or two that you will use for your connection. The cleverer users out there will often bypass the ISP assigned DNS servers, to third-party servers such as those used by Google or OpenDNS in an attempt to squeeze additional performance.

DNS can also prove useful within your internal network as well. Most companies with more than a handful of workstations will set up DNS, and rightfully so. It makes navigating your network a cinch. For example, it's easier to refer to your local color printer as `hp-color-01` than it would be to remember an IP address, such as `10.19.89.40`. In this case, adding the printer would be easy. Just have your operating system browse to it by name. Any resource on your network can be named and creating a consistent and predictable naming scheme for all your networked resources is a great idea. So, let's do exactly that.

As is typical, the naming of the required packages is a bit different on Debian-based distributions than CentOS. In Debian, the package you'll want to install is `bind9`. CentOS simply calls their `bind`. If you were wondering, **BIND** stands for **Berkeley Internet Name Domain** (named after where it was developed, namely the University of California at Berkeley). This is the most popular name server on the Internet, so you'll definitely want to familiarize yourself with it. While you're at it, I recommend installing `bind-utils` if you are running through this activity on a CentOS system. This gives us the `dig` command, which will be useful for our purposes.

The first step is to install the required package on your server, and then all you'll need to do is start it and ensure that it's enabled to run at startup. Debian already takes care of starting the daemon and enabling it for us. You can confirm this with the following command:

```
# systemctl status bind9
```

CentOS doesn't configure the `bind` daemon to autostart, and it does not start it up for you. If CentOS is your distribution of choice, you'll want to execute the following command to enable `bind` and start it up:

```
# systemctl enable named
# systemctl start named
```

With this done, you actually have a working DNS server. Of course, we didn't configure anything, so our DNS server is not actually doing much for us. But now that we have it installed, we can add records to it and build our configuration.

First, let's take a look at the default configuration file. Debian stores the default configuration file for bind at `/etc/bind/named.conf`. CentOS stores theirs at `/etc/named.conf` (it doesn't have its own directory). Go ahead and take a gander at this file to get a feel for how the configuration works. We're going to use our own configuration file, so I recommend you to back up the default files and we'll install our own.

First, let's create a fresh `named.conf` file in our distribution's default directory (`/etc/bind/named.conf` in Debian and `/etc/named.conf` in CentOS). Regardless of which distribution you're using, we'll make the file the same. If this file already has text in it, copy it to a backup or empty it, as the following two lines are the only text we need in this file:

```
include "/etc/bind/named.conf.options";
include "/etc/bind/named.conf.local";
```

Here, we're going to include two additional files (which we will create, very soon). As you can see, our `named.conf` file is simply calling these files and contains no other configuration. This way, we can create our own standard place to find these files. `/etc/bind` is already the default location in Debian, but by calling out this directory in CentOS, we can force it to look for the configuration in the same place. But with CentOS, you'll need to create the `/etc/bind` directory. The command is as follows:

```
# mkdir /etc/bind
```

Next, let's create our `/etc/bind/named.conf.options` file and customize it:

```
options {
    forwarders {
        8.8.8.8; 8.8.4.4;
    };
};
```

Here, we're creating an options block with some code sandwiched in between curly braces, which then includes an additional set of curly braces where we identify our forwarding addresses. Since this DNS server is for locating resources within our internal network, the forwarders block tells our DNS server where to send requests, should it be unable to find what it's looking for locally. Your DNS server will likely still function perfectly fine without this, as in most cases it will still attempt another DNS server further down the chain. But setting the forwarders here allows us to force where we would like DNS lookups to go, in case we're looking for something externally. In this sample, I'm using Google's public DNS servers. However, you can choose your own. Some additional DNS servers (which are typically better) can be found at www.opennicproject.org, which is also a good choice if you're concerned about privacy or tracking.

Our next file is /etc/bind/named.conf.local, which contains the following code:

```
zone "local.lan" IN {
    type master; file "/etc/bind/net.local.lan";
};

zone "96.10.10.in-appr.arpa" {
    type master; notify no; file "/etc/bind/revp.10.10.96";
};

zone "97.10.10.in-appr.arpa" {
    type master; notify no; file "/etc/bind/revp.10.10.97";
};

zone "98.10.10.in-appr.arpa" {
    type master; notify no; file "/etc/bind/revp.10.10.98";
};

zone "99.10.10.in-appr.arpa" {
    type master; notify no; file "/etc/bind/revp.10.10.99";
};
```

In this file, we start of by identifying our domain name. Here, I chose `local.lan`. As this server is not authoritative of anything on the Internet, this name works well. Within this block, we're calling out another file, `/etc/bind/net.local.lan`. In fact, as you can see, there are several files being called out here (five in total). The first is our main DNS zone, and it's the most important of these. Those that follow are where we configure reverse DNS lookups. Essentially, DNS allows us to not only map hostnames to IP addresses, but we can also do the reverse (look map IP addresses back to hostnames). You may not need all the files that I created in my example. With mine, I am creating a reverse lookup file for each of my four subnets. If you aren't creating multiple subnets, you'll only need to create one. The naming convention of these is `revp`, followed by the network portion of the IP address. So, for example, the reverse lookup file for my `10.10.99.0` network is `revp.10.10.99`. These files will also be stored in `/etc/bind` as well.

Now, let's take a look at our master record, the `/etc/bind/net.local.lan` file:

```
;
; dns zone for for local.lan
;

$TTL 1D

@ IN SOA local.lan. hostmaster.local.lan. (

201507261 ; serial

8H ; refresh
4H ; retry
4W ; expire
1D )  ; minimum
IN A 10.10.96.1
;
@ IN NS hermes.local.lan.
ceres            IN       A    10.10.98.1
euphoria         IN       A    10.10.97.4
galaxy           IN       A    10.10.96.4
hermes           IN       A    10.10.96.1
puppet        CNAME galaxy
;
; dns zone for for local.lan
;
```

First, I placed some generic comments, with lines beginning with a semicolon. If a line begins with a semicolon, it is ignored by bind. Comments can be a good method of leaving notes or facts regarding the configuration. However, comments aren't used very often in bind. Next, we set our **Time To Live (TTL)** to one day:

```
$TTL 1D
```

This value governs how long other DNS servers would be able to cache each record. After this period, any servers that have cached one of these records must discard them. For the purposes of setting up an internal DNS server, this value doesn't affect us a great deal. However, if you're setting up multiple DNS servers, this might be an important value to configure. One example of where the TTL value might prove useful is changing an address record to a different IP address. Suppose you're switching your e-mail host to another provider. In that case, you would change the address record accordingly. However, before you enact this change, you may lower your TTL to something much less, such as one hour, and do this before you make this change. Then, servers are forced to discard this zone and refresh it, causing it to see your change in e-mail providers much quicker. When you are done, you would change this back. With the following line, we are identifying a **Start of Authority (SOA)**:

```
@ IN SOA local.lan. hostmaster.local.lan. (
```

In this case, we are identifying that this DNS server has the authority for the local.lan domain. We also clarify that hostmaster.local.lan is responsible for it. Although it may not look like it, hostmaster.local.lan is actually an e-mail address in the format that bind prefers. However, this is obviously a fake address, which doesn't matter for our internal DNS server. At the end of this line, we are opening a configuration block, in this case with an opening parenthesis. The following line represents our serial, and it's a very important concept to understand in order for our DNS server to work properly:

```
201507261 ; serial
```

Each time our `bind` daemon is restarted, it will reload this file. But when it does, the serial number is the first thing it will look at. If it is the same, it will likely not load in any changes. Thus, every time you change a zone file in `bind`, you must change this serial number as well. In this example, the current date is being used without hyphens or spaces. The last digit is just a revision number for that day, if the file is changed multiple times in one day. You can use whatever scheme you'd like. But using the date is a very popular approach. Regardless of the format you use, always ensure you increment the serial by 1 with every change you make. You'll save yourself frustration wondering why newly created records aren't taking affect.

```
8H  ; refresh
4H  ; retry
4W  ; expire
1D ) ; minimum
```

These values dictate how often slave DNS servers will be told to check for updates. The first value will configure slaves to refresh zone records from the master (this server) every eight hours. In regards to retry, we're letting slaves know that should there be a problem connecting, check back in this amount of time. Finally, we're setting our minimum age of zone records to one day, and the maximum to four weeks. Configuring slave DNS servers is beyond the scope of this book, but having this configuration in place doesn't hurt anything in case you do decide to configure slave DNS servers later on.

```
@ IN NS hermes.local.lan.
```

Here, we're identifying this name server. In my case, I'm calling it `hermes` and its full domain name is `hermes.local.lan`.

```
galaxy      IN   A   10.10.96.4
hermes      IN   A   10.10.96.1
```

Finally, in this sample configuration, four address records are called out. This basically means that any time someone is looking for one of these hosts, the request is mapped to the listed domain name. These can be among multiple subnets or a single subnet. In my case, these hosts are on different subnets:

```
puppet      CNAME galaxy
```

The final line of this configuration contains a **Canonical Name (CNAME)** record. Basically, this allows us to refer to a server by another name. In this example, `galaxy` is also used for software known as `puppet`, so a CNAME record has been set up for it. This way, if someone were to try to access `galaxy.local.lan` or `puppet.local.lan`, their request would resolve to the same IP address (`10.10.96.4`). A CNAME records can be very useful if a single server provides more than one service to the network.

Earlier, I called out four reverse lookup records, /etc/bind/revp.10.10.96, /etc/bind/revp.10.10.97, /etc/bind/revp.10.10.98, and revp.10.10.99. Next, I'm going to demonstrate one of these files (in this case, for the 10.10.96.0 network):

```
$TTL 1D
@ IN SOA hermes.local.lan. hostmaster.local.lan. (
201507261 ; serial
28800 ; refresh (8 hours)
14400 ; retry (4 hours)
2419200 ; expire (4 weeks)
86400 ; minimum (1 day)
)
;
@ NS hermes.local.lan.
1    PTR    hermes.local.lan.
3    PTR    nagios.local.lan.
4    PTR    galaxy.local.lan.
```

With this configuration, you'll notice we have a *start of authority* record as with our master zone, and we also have a serial number. The same idea applies here. Whenever you update any record (including reverse lookup records), you should update the serial number of the file. The start of authority entry works the same as earlier, no surprises here. Where the file differs is how the hosts are called out. Rather than calling out an entire IP address, we only need to identify the last octet since the entire file is dedicated to reverse IP address lookups from the 10.10.96.0 network. For each of your subnets, you'll need to create a similar file. Again, in our sample configuration there are four subnets, but you don't need that many. It was only provided in this way in order to provide an example of how to handle separate subnets, should you need to do so.

With our configuration in place, feel free to restart the bind service on your DNS server and test it out. We can restart bind with the systemctl command, as before.

For Debian, use the following command:

```
# systemctl restart bind9
```

For CentOS, use the following command:

```
# systemctl restart named
```

One way we can test our DNS server is via the `dig` command. With Debian, you should already have this package installed. CentOS requires the installation of the `bind-utils` package. `dig` (domain information groper) is a utility that allows us to request information from a DNS server. To give it a shot, try it out with an internal hostname:

```
dig myhostname.local.lan
```

If your DNS server comes up under SERVER in the output, then your DNS server is functioning properly. If for some reason it doesn't, verify what you've typed, your serial number, and whether or not you have restarted `bind` since your last configuration change.

Feel free to practice setting up additional nodes and records within your DNS server. Setting up `bind` can be frustrating at first, but stick with it and you'll be a pro in no time. Using examples from this section, you should have a working skeleton you can use to set up a DNS server within your environment. Make sure that you change the hostnames and IP addresses contained within the configuration files to those that match your network. In addition, make sure you set up `bind` to match your subnets, or remove mentions of other subnets if you don't have any. To be safe, instead of copying the configuration directly from this book, it's usually better to type everything manually just in case.

Setting up an internal NTP server

Most Linux distributions offer a **Network Time Protocol** (**NTP**) client that can be used to keep your local time up to date. The idea is that with an NTP client configured, your computer or server will periodically check in with an NTP server somewhere on the Internet and synchronize its clock to ensure it is as exact as possible. This is really important; very strange things can happen on Linux machines if the clock is off. These oddities can include things such as a node being unable to associate with a DHCP server to obtain an IP address, files becoming unsynchronized between file servers, and more. The moral of the story is this: you'll want to have NTP set up and working in your environment.

Quite a few Linux distributions that are targeted toward end-user workstations (such as Ubuntu, Linux Mint, and so on) will often set up an NTP client for you. This means that out of the box, there's a good chance that your clock is probably synchronized already, assuming of course your installation has access to the Internet. By default, these clients will connect to a distribution-specific NTP server. This can be perfectly fine, but setting up your own NTP server instead has merit. One good reason for this is that by setting up your own NTP server, you're being a good network citizen. Think about it this way. If you have a company with a hundred Linux machines, each of those machines will be checking in with a public NTP server periodically if left with the default configuration. This causes unnecessary strain on that server. If you set up your own NTP server, only one of your servers will be checking in with the public server, which means you'd be absorbing fewer of its resources. In addition, some companies do not allow public access to **port 123** (the port NTP uses) for security reasons. However, perhaps a single NTP server would be allowed to access port 123, which you can then configure your clients to connect to and use NTP.

Before we get into setting up an NTP server, it's important to note that Debian and CentOS can often be the exception as to having an NTP client installed out of the box. Depending on the options and packages you selected during installation, the NTP client may or may not be functional yet. In my test environment, neither CentOS nor Debian had a working NTP client by default when I installed via a minimal installation and a net installation, respectively. However, setting up an NTP client is extremely easy. All you have to do is install NTP and enable it. This is actually one of those rare cases when both Debian and CentOS have the same name for the same package. The package is simply called `ntp`, so go ahead and install it if you don't already have it installed. Once installed, Debian will start the `ntp` daemon and enable it for you. With CentOS, execute the following commands to get it going:

```
# systemctl enable ntpd
# systemctl start ntpd
```

With both distributions, the file /etc/ntp.conf will be created once the package is installed, and this file will have a default configuration that will point your NTP client to your distribution's NTP server. Feel free to take a quick look at this file, if you're curious about what it looks like. To view which server your machine is synchronizing with, along with some stats regarding its synchronization, execute the ntpq -p command.

```
jay@debian8: ~
jay@debian8:~$ ntpq -p
     remote           refid      st t when poll reach   delay   offset  jitter
==============================================================================
+name1.glorb.com 128.10.19.24     2 u   67   64  377   28.261   -3.954   1.432
+pool-test.ntp.o 127.67.113.92     2 u   56   64  377   68.092   -0.991  23.683
*clock.team-cymr 204.123.2.72      2 u   52   64  377   18.962   -1.607   0.665
-helium.constant 192.5.41.40       2 u   29   64  377   58.779  -10.741  20.422
jay@debian8:~$
```

Viewing connected NTP servers

First, let's take a quick look at what these numbers mean. The first column remote includes a list of NTP servers we're connected to, no surprises there. Next is refid, which is where those servers are connected to. The st column refers to the **stratum** of that server, which is a number that refers to the layer on which that time server sits. Typically, the lower the number, the better it is; as it means that the server is reasonably close to the source that is providing it time. Each server down the chain has an increased stratum; lowest doesn't always mean that the server is better, but generally speaking, lower numbers are good. The t column refers to the type. This can be unicast, broadcast, multicast, or manycast. In this case, we have u for unicast.

The when column refers to how long ago the server was last polled. In the case of the sample screenshot, each server was polled 28, 24, 21 and 61 seconds ago, respectively. This can also be listed in hours or days as well. The poll column refers to the polling frequency, which here is set to poll every 64 seconds. The reach column is an octal number, which contains the results of the most recent eight NTP updates. If all eight were successful, this value will read 377, which is as high as it can get. This means that all eight attempts received a 1 (success) which in octal, totals 377.

Finishing up, the delay field references the delay (in milliseconds) to the NTP server. The offset field corresponds to the difference between the local clock and the clock of the server. Finally, jitter refers to the network latency between you and the server.

In order to set up an NTP server, you must first install the client as was mentioned earlier in this chapter. Install it, configure the daemon to automatically start, and then start it up. After performing those tasks, you're already most of the way there (the same client is used for the server as well). Essentially, if you point your other computers to a server which has NTP installed and configured, you essentially have everything you need.

However, there are a few things that should be configured first. Mainly, the `/etc/ntp.conf` configuration file. This file is located in the same place on both Debian and CentOS. If you look at the file, you'll see some lines that look similar to the following:

```
server 0.centos.pool.ntp.org iburst
server 1.centos.pool.ntp.org iburst
server 2.centos.pool.ntp.org iburst
server 3.centos.pool.ntp.org iburst
```

Here, you can see that by default, CentOS is identifying four NTP servers to synchronize with. These servers are generally fine for most use cases, but you may want to consider official NTP servers. To do so, check out the following website:

```
http://www.pool.ntp.org
```

That website will allow you to view official NTP servers from the NTP Pool Project. To navigate, select your continent on the right and then your country. You should then see a list of NTP servers you can use. In my case, I get the following details:

```
server 0.north-america.pool.ntp.org
server 1.north-america.pool.ntp.org
server 2.north-america.pool.ntp.org
server 3.north-america.pool.ntp.org
```

It's up to you whether you use the NTP servers provided by your distribution or those provided by the NTP pool project. Personally, I prefer the latter. Once you have your servers configured, there's one more change we should make. You should see a line in the configuration similar to the following in CentOS:

```
#restrict 192.168.1.0 mask 255.255.255.0 nomodify notrap
```

Alternatively, similar to the following in Debian:

```
#restrict 192.168.123.0 mask 255.255.255.0 notrust
```

On your NTP server, uncomment that line and change the network address to yours, as well as the subnet. Remove `notrust` if it is there. For reference, the line in my configuration appears as the following:

```
restrict 10.10.96.0 mask 255.255.252.0 nomodify notrap
```

With this configuration, we're restricting NTP access to local clients and also ensuring that they do not have access to change configuration on the NTP server (only read from it). Another change I like to make in NTP is to designate a log file. systemd takes care of logging with `journalctl`, but sometimes it's useful to have a text file to peruse in case of problems. If you'd like that, then add the following line somewhere near the top:

```
logfile /var/log/ntp.log
```

If you have any problems, check that file. Next, if you're using CentOS as your NTP server, you should enable NTP traffic through its firewall. To do that, run the following code:

```
firewall-cmd --add-service=ntp –permanent
firewall-cmd --reload
```

Now that we have that out of the way, restart your NTP server. We can do so via one of the following commands (as root).

Use the `systemctl restart ntpd` command on CentOS, or `systemctl restart ntp` on Debian.

At this point, you have an NTP server. On your clients, change the server that they are configured to synchronize with to the IP of the machine you've designated as your NTP server. In my case, the command is as follows:

```
server 10.10.99.133
```

After restarting NTP, give your systems some time to synchronize. In some cases, it can take over a half an hour for them to start synchronizing. Give it a bit of time and then check your configuration to ensure that it is syncing with the `ntpq -p` command.

```
:: 🗵                              jay@debian8: ~                              – ✕
jay@debian8:~$ ntpq -p
     remote           refid      st t when poll reach   delay   offset  jitter
==============================================================================
 10.10.99.133    198.60.22.240    2 u   40   64    7   0.258  5530434   0.328
jay@debian8:~$ █
```

Output from a machine synchronizing with a custom NTP server

As you can see in this output of my test environment, I started up an NTP server at 10.10.99.123 that this Debian machine is synchronizing with and currently the server has a reachability of 7, but this number is slowing going up. This is fine, as the server has only been running a few minutes.

If you have any issues, make sure that port 123 is open in any firewalls you may have in your network (with CentOS as the server, make sure you've run the firewall commands that were mentioned earlier). But before you get frustrated, give it time — it's not uncommon for an NTP server to take a bit to get going when first set up. Typically, everything should get going within 20 minutes, but I've seen it take longer.

Summary

In this chapter, we configured the layout of our network. We started off with a discussion on planning our network IP address layout, followed by putting that into action by creating our own DHCP server. This discussion included how to split this configuration into multiple subnets, without multiple subnets. We continued with setting up a DNS server so that we can resolve our network nodes by name. We wrapped up this chapter by setting up an NTP server, so we can ensure all of our nodes have the correct time.

In the next chapter, we'll look into hosting web content with Apache.

7

Hosting HTTP Content via Apache

Apache is the most common web server used on the Internet. While there are other web servers available, such as Microsoft's **Internet Information Services (IIS)**, Apache rules the kingdom when it comes to serving web content. Available in both Linux and UNIX platforms, Apache enables you to host content and share it over your local intranet, as well as the Internet. There are many uses for an Apache server, including (but certainly not limited to) hosting a blog or company website, or setting up an employee portal for your company.

In this chapter, you'll learn all about installing and configuring Apache. We will cover the following topics:

- Installing Apache
- Configuring Apache
- Adding modules
- Setting up virtual hosts

Installing Apache

As usual, installing Apache on your system is just a matter of installing the proper package from your package manager. On a CentOS system, you can obtain Apache by installing the `httpd` package, and on Debian systems with the `apache2` package (`yum install httpd` or `apt-get install apache2` respectively, as root). Once you install the package, Apache's daemon is now present with a default set of configuration files. You will be able to confirm the existence of the daemon on your system with `systemctl`, though the name of the daemon is different depending on your distribution.

Use the following command on Debian:

```
# systemctl status apache2
```

Use the following command on CentOS:

```
# systemctl status httpd
```

By default, Debian starts and enables the daemon for you. As is typical, CentOS makes no assumptions and does neither. You can start and enable the daemon easily with the `systemctl` command:

```
# systemctl enable httpd
# systemctl start httpd
```

Once you install and enable Apache, you technically already have a working web server on your network. It may not be particularly useful (we haven't configured it yet) but at this point it exists, and it is technically working. Both the CentOS and Debian builds of Apache look for web content in the same directory, `/var/www/html`. There, Debian creates a sample web page in the form of an `index.html` file, which you can view via a web browser on another computer (just point it to the IP address of your web server). CentOS, on the other hand, does not create a sample HTML page for you. This is easy to rectify; all you should have to do is manually create the `/var/www/html/index.html` file with some sample code. It doesn't need to be extravagant; we just want to make sure we have something to test with. For example, you could just put the following code in that file:

```
<html>
  <title>Apache test</title>
  <body>
    <p>Apache is awesome!</p>
  </body>
</html>
```

At this point, you should have Apache installed and its service started. You should also have an example `/var/www/html/index.html` file present on your system, whether you are using Debian's default or you manually created it on a CentOS system. Now, you should be able to browse to your web server and view this page via a web browser. If you know the IP address of your webserver, just type that in to the address bar in your web browser. You should see the sample page immediately. If you're using a web browser on your web server, you should be able to browse to the localhost (`http://127.0.0.1` or `http://localhost`) and view the same page.

If you chose CentOS for your web server, the default firewall may get in your way if you are trying to browse to it from another machine. Depending on your configuration, you may need to allow traffic to your web server through the firewall. To do this, execute the following commands:

```
# firewall-cmd --zone=public --add-port=80/tcp
--permanent
# firewall-cmd --reload
```

Be sure to add port 443 as well, if you plan on hosting a secure site. Just use the same `firewall-cmd` as before, but replace 80 with 443.

If for some reason you don't see the default page, make sure that Apache is running (remember the `systemctl status` commands I mentioned earlier). If the daemon isn't running, you'll likely get a **connection refused** error. Also, keep in mind that hardware-based firewalls can prevent access as well.

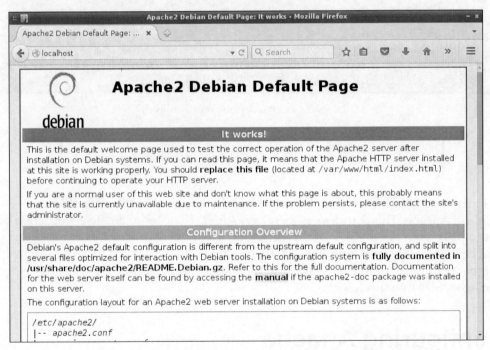

The default web page served from an unconfigured Apache, running on Debian

Another way of testing whether or not your server is serving web pages is via `lynx`, a text-based web browser you can use within a shell. This may be preferred in some situations, as it doesn't have the overhead of a graphical web browser and is very quick to launch. Once you install the lynx package on your machine, you can navigate to your web server from the server itself by executing `lynx http://localhost`, or `http://<ip address>` if you are coming from a different machine.

Using lynx to test web server functionality

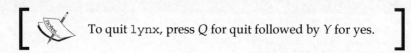

To quit `lynx`, press *Q* for quit followed by *Y* for yes.

As I mentioned, both Debian and CentOS look in the same directory for files to share via Apache. This directory is `/var/www/html`. In order to create a web site, you would place your site's files into this directory. The typical process of setting up an Apache server is by installing Apache, then testing whether or not it can be reached by other computers on the network, and then finally developing your site and placing its files into this folder.

Configuring Apache

Configuring Apache is done by editing its configuration file, which will be located in one of two places, depending on your distribution.

Use the following command on CentOS:

```
/etc/httpd/conf/httpd.conf
```

Use the following command on Debian:

```
/etc/apache/apache2.conf
```

The default web document directory, `/var/www/html`, can be changed. While `/var/www/html` is fairly standard, there's nothing stopping you from changing it should you decide to store your web files elsewhere. If you peruse the configuration file in CentOS, you'll see this directory called out within a configuration block that begins on line 131. If you take a look at the configuration file in Debian, you won't see this called out at all. Instead, you'll see a directory within `/etc/apache2` called `sites-available`. Within the directory, there will be two default files, `000-default.conf` and `default-ssl.conf`. Both of these files designate `/var/www/html` as the default path, but how they differ is that the `000-default.conf` file designates configuration for port 80, while `default-ssl.conf` is responsible for the configuration on port 443. As you probably know, port 80 references standard HTTP traffic, while port 443 corresponds to secure traffic. So essentially, each type of traffic has its own configuration file on Debian systems.

In all those cases, the **document root** is being set to `/var/www/html`. If you'd like to change that to a different directory, you would change the code to point to the new directory. For example, if you wanted to change the path to something like `/srv/html`, there are a few changes you would need to make to the file.

First, look for the following line:

```
DocumentRoot /var/www/html
```

Change it to point to the new directory:

```
DocumentRoot /srv/html
```

On my test systems, I found the `DocumentRoot` callout in the following configuration file on Debian:

```
/etc/apache2/sites-available/000-default
```

On CentOS, I found that on line 119 in the default configuration file:

```
/etc/httpd/conf/httpd.conf
```

After you change that, we have to set our options for the new directory. On Debian, we need to make these changes in the following file:

```
/etc/apache2/apache2.conf
```

On CentOS, we need to make these changes in the following file:

```
/etc/httpd/conf/httpd.conf
```

Open up one of those files, depending on which distribution you're using. The code we need to change looks like this:

```
<Directory "/var/www/html">
    Options Indexes FollowSymLinks
    AllowOverride None
    Require all granted
</Directory>
```

Change the following accordingly:

```
<Directory "/srv/html">
    Options Indexes FollowSymLinks
    AllowOverride None
    Require all granted
</Directory>
```

> There may be some comments intermixed with the code shown in the previous example, but the basic idea is the same. Find the line that starts with <Directory "/var/www/html"> and ensure the uncommented code within that block matches the example. As long as you do that, you should be fine.

Finally, it probably goes without saying, but to save you a headache you should make sure that you have set the permissions to /srv/html such that the directory and contents are readable by everyone. Also, ensure you created or copied an example HTML file (such as index.html) into this directory. Once you restart Apache, you should be able to serve web content from this new directory.

In addition to setting up the document root, the Apache configuration file also allows you to configure a few very important security settings as well. For example, access to the entirety of the server's file system is disabled by default. This is a good thing. The following code is an example taken from a CentOS system, and it is responsible for preventing filesystem-wide access. The code is as follows:

```
<Directory />
    AllowOverride none
    Require all denied
</Directory>
```

Remotely viewing the `.htaccess` files are also disabled by default with the following configuration block:

```
<Files ".ht*">
    Require all denied
</Files>
```

Other options, such as the default location of Apache's log files, can also be set. By default, the following default line of configuration directs the log files to `/etc/httpd/logs`:

ErrorLog "logs/error_log"

However, this may be misleading, as the `/etc/httpd/logs` directory on CentOS systems is actually a symbolic link to `/var/log/httpd`, which is where you would actually find the log files should you need to view them. By default, the logging is set to `warn`, and this can also be changed within the Apache configuration file and set to any one of `debug`, `info`, `notice`, `warn`, `error`, and `crit`.

It's important to note that for any change you make to Apache, you will need to reload or restart the daemon. If you restart the daemon, it will shut down Apache and start it back up again. Reload simply causes Apache to reread its configuration file. In most cases, reload is the better option. By doing this, you can apply new configuration without disrupting access to your website. As with most systemd units, Apache uses the following commands to manage the running state of the daemon:

1. Start the Apache daemon with the following command:

   # systemctl start apache2

2. Stop the Apache daemon with the following command:

   # systemctl stop apache2

3. Enable the Apache daemon at boot time with the following command:

   # systemctl enable apache2

4. Reload the Apache daemon while attempting to maintain its running state:

   # systemctl reload apache2

5. Restart the Apache daemon with the following command:

   # systemctl restart apache2

If you're using CentOS, replace `apache2` with `httpd` in each case. Now that you understand how Apache is installed and configured, we can move on to using modules.

Adding modules

As useful as Apache is out of the box, some functionality you'll likely require are not built in. Apache uses **modules** to extend its feature set. Examples of this may include installing the `php5` module to enable your site to use PHP, or perhaps the Python module if you develop in that language. Once a module is installed and activated, the features of that module will then become available to you.

The implementation of Apache between CentOS and Debian is different, and the ways in which modules are added between them is also different. In fact, Debian even includes its very own command for enabling and disabling modules, which is completely exclusive to Debian systems. These commands are `a2enmod` and `a2dismod`.

To work through the typical process of enabling a module in Debian, we can enable the PHP module on our server. I'll also detail this process in CentOS, but as I mentioned, this process is completely different between the two.

First, locate a package that contains the module you want. If you don't know the exact name of the package to install, you can print a list of available Apache modules to your terminal with the following command:

```
aptitude search libapache2-mod
```

By default, `aptitude` is not installed on most Debian systems. If the previous command results in a `command not found` error, you'll just need to install the `aptitude` package via `apt-get install`. The output may be too long depending on the size of your terminal window, so you may want to pipe the output into `less`:

```
aptitude search libapache2-mod |less
```

The following screenshot shows the search results of aptitude on a Debian system searching for `libapache2-mod`:

```
::  ▣                                    Terminal                                    – x
p   libapache2-mod-apparmor          - changehat AppArmor library as an Apache mo
p   libapache2-mod-apparmor:i386     - changehat AppArmor library as an Apache mo
p   libapache2-mod-apreq2            - generic Apache request library - Apache mo
p   libapache2-mod-apreq2:i386       - generic Apache request library - Apache mo
p   libapache2-mod-auth-cas          - CAS authentication module for Apache2
p   libapache2-mod-auth-cas:i386     - CAS authentication module for Apache2
p   libapache2-mod-auth-gssapi       - GSSAPI Authentication module for Apache2
p   libapache2-mod-auth-gssapi:i386  - GSSAPI Authentication module for Apache2
p   libapache2-mod-auth-kerb         - apache2 module for Kerberos authentication
p   libapache2-mod-auth-kerb:i386    - apache2 module for Kerberos authentication
p   libapache2-mod-auth-mellon       - SAML 2.0 authentication module for Apache
p   libapache2-mod-auth-mellon:i386  - SAML 2.0 authentication module for Apache
p   libapache2-mod-auth-ntlm-winbin  - apache2 module for NTLM authentication aga
p   libapache2-mod-auth-ntlm-winbin  - apache2 module for NTLM authentication aga
p   libapache2-mod-auth-openid       - OpenID authentication module for Apache2
p   libapache2-mod-auth-openid:i386  - OpenID authentication module for Apache2
p   libapache2-mod-auth-openidc      - OpenID Connect authentication module for A
p   libapache2-mod-auth-openidc:i38  - OpenID Connect authentication module for A
p   libapache2-mod-auth-pgsql        - Module for Apache2 which provides PostgreS
p   libapache2-mod-auth-pgsql:i386   - Module for Apache2 which provides PostgreS
p   libapache2-mod-auth-plain        - Module for Apache2 which provides plaintex
p   libapache2-mod-auth-plain:i386   - Module for Apache2 which provides plaintex
p   libapache2-mod-auth-pubtkt       - key-based single-sign-on authentication mo
:▮
```

There are quite a few modules available for Apache in Debian systems

By searching that way, you can press Enter or the up and down arrow keys to scroll through the output, and then press *Q* when you're finished. By perusing the output, you'll see that the PHP package is named `libapache2-mod-php5`. So, let's install it with the following command:

```
# apt-get install libapache2-mod-php5
```

Once the package is installed, check the output. It's very possible that Debian already installed the module for you, the logic being that if you specifically ask for a package to be installed, you'll probably want to have it usable right away. If you see output similar to the following, then the PHP module in this example is already installed:

```
apache2_invoke: Enable module php5
```

You can verify this by attempting to enable it anyway, by executing `a2enmod php5` in the shell. If it's enabled, you'll see output similar to the following:

```
Module php5 already enabled
```

In essence, the `a2enmod` and `a2dismod` commands work pretty much the same. As you can probably gather, one enables modules and the other disables them. In order to use an Apache module, it must be enabled. However, if you no longer need a module you can disable it (or better yet, remove it). Going over all the modules and the features they provide is outside the scope of this book. But in practice, you'll only enable modules that are required by your site, which differs from environment to environment. Before we move on to the same procedure when performed on CentOS systems, I'll leave you with this. To see a list of all modules that are installed on a Debian system, issue the following command:

```
# apache2ctl -M
```

Now, let's move on to CentOS. Most modules can be listed similar to how we did before in the Debian section, by using the package manager to list available module packages. In the CentOS, we can do so via the following command:

```
yum search mod_
```

Unfortunately, the PHP module isn't listed in this output. This is because we enable PHP in CentOS by simply installing the `php` package. This is where things start to get confusing; quite a few CentOS Apache module packages have a naming convention beginning with `mod_`, but not all of them do. A bit of research is sometimes necessary when determining which packages need to be installed to grant the system access to a module. If there are any other modules you may need for a site you're developing, such as `mod_ldap` for LDAP authentication, feel free to install those as well.

Unlike Debian, the `yum` package manager should have already enabled the modules you installed for you. Now that we've installed PHP in our CentOS system, we should have PHP available to us once we restart the `httpd` daemon. To verify this, we should be able to create an `info.php` file and store it in `/var/www/html/info.php`. The contents of the file are as follows:

```
<?php phpinfo();
?>
```

If you navigate to the URL `http://<your_server_IP>/info.php`, you should see a page containing information regarding your server's PHP implementation.

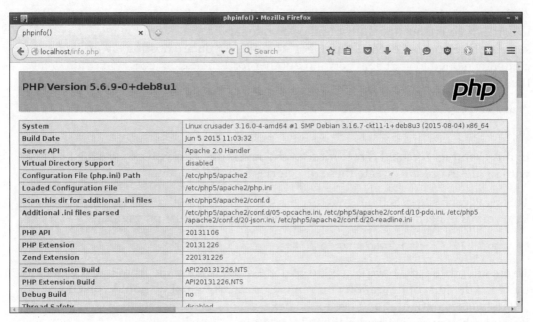

Viewing PHP server information on an Apache server

Although it's perfectly fine to use an info.php file in order to test PHP, do not leave it on the server—it is a security risk. You don't want to make it too easy for attackers to determine specific information regarding what your server is running. This procedure is merely to test that PHP is running properly.

Now that we've gone through installing Apache modules, it should be easy for you to customize your web server as you need in order to support any websites or applications you plan to run.

Setting up virtual hosts

It's very common for a single organization to host multiple sites. Each of these sites can live on their own server or virtual machine, but that's not very practical. Running just one site per server is very expensive and not very efficient. The concept of **virtual hosts** is that multiple sites can live on one web server, which saves infrastructure. Of course, it's always possible that you may have a website that generates so much traffic that sharing it with other high-traffic sites may not be a good idea, but when this is not the case, virtual hosts are recommended.

As mentioned before, `/var/www` is the default location where Apache looks for files to serve. If you're hosting multiple sites on one server, you would want to create a separate directory for each of them. For example, if you are hosting a website for a company named `tryadtech.com` and another for `linuxpros.com`, you could create the following directory structure:

`/var/www/tryadtech.com/html`

`/var/www/linuxpros.com/html`

In this example, I created directories several levels deep, so you can use the `-p` flag with `mkdir` in order to create these directories and their parents.

This way, each site gets their own directory so you can keep their content separate. Everyone will need to read these files, so we'll need to adjust permissions:

`# chmod 755 -R /var/www/<nameofsite>`

To create a virtual host, we'll need to create a configuration file from it. On Debian, there is a default configuration you can use as a starting point should you choose (I'll detail the configuration I use in the next section, so using this file is not required). If you wish, you can start with the following file:

`/etc/apache2/sites-available/000-default.conf`

This file serves as a good reference point for creating configuration for a virtual host. If you choose to use it, copy it to the directory you've created for your virtual host:

`# cp /etc/apache2/sites-available/000-default.conf /etc/apache2/sites-available/tryadtech.com.conf`

On CentOS, the `/etc/apache2/sites-available` directory doesn't even exist, so go ahead and create that. In order to tell Apache to load sites from this directory, we'll need to add the following line to the bottom of the `/etc/httpd/conf/httpd.conf` file:

`IncludeOptional sites-available/*.conf`

Now, here's an example virtual host configuration file. I've saved it as `/etc/apache2/sites-available/tryadtech.com.conf` on my Debian test system, but on CentOS just replace `apache2` with `httpd`. I took this example file from the `000-default.conf` file I mentioned previously, removing the commented lines for the sake of brevity. The first bold line was not originally present, and the second was modified:

```
<VirtualHost *:80>
        ServerAdmin webmaster@localhost
        ServerName tryadtech.com
```

```
DocumentRoot /var/www/tryadtech.com/html
ErrorLog ${APACHE_LOG_DIR}/error.log
CustomLog ${APACHE_LOG_DIR}/access.log combined
</VirtualHost>
```

As you can see here, we're calling out an `html` directory underneath the `tryadtech.com` directory. To develop your site, you would place your site's files into the `html` directory, and after restarting Apache, you should be able to access that directory from a web browser.

So, how does the Apache server know which directory to send visitors to? Notice the `ServerName` line that I added to the configuration file. In this line, I'm calling out a specific domain name that the files within this virtual host belong to. This requires that you already have DNS set up and pointing to this IP. For example, your DNS entry at your domain name registrar would be pointing each of these two virtual hosts to the same IP address. When a request comes in via the `tryadtech.com` domain, Apache should serve the user files from the `/var/www/tryadtech.com/html` directory. If you configure another virtual host and domain name, the same would apply to that domain as well.

Summary

In this chapter, we set up an Apache server that we can use to share information on a local intranet, or even the Internet if our machine is externally routable. We walked through installing Apache, customizing it, setting up modules, as well as setting up virtual hosts.

In the next chapter, we'll tackle advanced networking techniques such as subnetting, adding redundancy to DHCP and DNS, and routing. See you there!

8

Understanding Advanced Networking Concepts

As we've made our way through our journey into Linux network administration so far, we've covered everything from planning, setting up file servers, network services, and more. Now as we approach the end of this book, the last few chapters will round off this knowledge with information on advanced networking, security, and even troubleshooting. In this chapter, we'll take a look at several concepts that are a bit more advanced, such as subnetting, routing, and more!

In this chapter, we will cover:

- Dividing your network into subnets
- Understanding the CIDR notation
- Implementing **Quality of Service (QoS)**
- Understanding **Network Address Translation (NAT)**
- Routing TCP/IP traffic
- Creating redundant DHCP and DNS servers
- Configuring a network gateway

Dividing your network into subnets

Unless you're running a very small home or office network, subnetting is generally a good idea. Subnetting allows you to split your network into smaller pieces, each with their own IP addresses and resources. An example may include placing wireless traffic, servers, workstations, and company-issued mobile devices on their own subnets. In addition, if there is any specific service on your network that receives the most traffic, you can also place that service on its own subnet as well. There are endless possibilities, and every administrator will have his or her own ideas of the best way of splitting up the network.

In *Chapter 6, Configuring Network Services*, we set up a DHCP server. In it, I included an example of using a specific subnet for dynamically leased IP addresses. In that scheme, the network we used was `10.10.96.0/22`. This means that we have several networks available to us, which include `10.10.96.0`, `10.10.97.0`, `10.10.98.0`, and `10.10.99.0`. With this network, we can basically divide several services each into their own network. In our configuration, `10.10.99.0` was used for DHCP. But of course, there's nothing stopping you from using IP addresses `10.10.96.1` through `10.10.99.254` should you decide to do so. It really is up to you how you configure your network. In that chapter, we set some of the ground work that will be used in this chapter. But we didn't go over how we arrived at these numbers, or how to manually split up the network ourselves.

The magic in subnetting is all about the subnet mask, though this number is only glanced over by most. For quite a few networks, the subnet mask is left at its default (`255.255.255.0`) and no one really questions it. If you purchase a router from a store and put it into production without configuring it (bad idea), you're left with a 24-bit network and a `255.255.255.0` subnet mask. But what does this actually mean?

There are two different styles of subnets, **classful** and **classless**. In production networks, it's rare that anyone mentions actual classes anymore, as classless is how subnetting is done nowadays (more on that later). But before we get into classless networking, it's important to understand what came before. With our discussion on subnetting, we used the example subnet mask of `255.255.255.0` several times, which belongs to what is considered a Class C network. In total, there are five classes, Class A through Class E. Classes D and E aren't used for much, so we'll stick with Classes A through C for the sake of our discussion of classful IP addressing.

The subnet masks for classes A to C are as follows:

Class	Subnet mask
A	`255.0.0.0`
B	`255.255.0.0`
C	`255.255.255.0`

Each of these subnet masks corresponds to which portion of the IP address is designated for the network, and which part is designated for each individual node. For example, say we have a network configured with a network address 192.168.50.0 as a Class C network. This means that our network has a subnet mask of 255.255.255.0. As with all IPv4 IP addresses, our network address has four octets: 192, 168, 50, and 0. To illustrate how a subnet mask affects an IP address, I'll line up each octet in a table:

192	168	50	0
255	255	255	0

The purpose of a subnet mask is to *mask out* which octets of an IPv4 address correspond to the entire network and which correspond to individual nodes. The highest possible number in each octet is 255. If an octet within a subnet mask is set to 255, which takes up that entire octet and thus cancels it out. In this case, the IP address of every node will begin with 192.168.50, since the first three octets were canceled out. Notice that the last octet is a zero in both the network address and subnet mask. In IPv4 networking, a 0 means anything. Therefore, the last octet of the subnet mask being 0 tells us that it doesn't care about that octet, and the network address being 0 means that it doesn't either. Thus, any number in the last place is fair game.

In our case, IP addresses starting from 192.168.50.0 through 192.168.50.255 belong to this network (subnet). Well, almost. We could never begin our DHCP IP range with distributing the 192.168.50.0 IP address if our subnet mask was 255.255.255.0. This is because the first IP address of a subnet cannot be assigned to a node. The first IP address is designated as the **network identifier** and is reserved. It's certainly possible to have an IP address ending in 0, as long as it's not the first IP address in the block. But in a Class C network, an IP address of 192.168.50.0 is not valid since it is indeed the first address within that subnet.

Another IP address that cannot be assigned to any node is the last IP of a subnet. In our Class C example, that would be 192.168.255.255. This IP address is known as the **broadcast address** and is also reserved. If a broadcast message needs to be sent to the entire network, the broadcast address is used for that purpose. With that in mind, the maximum our DHCP range can be in a Class C network such as the one used in our example is 192.168.50.1 to 192.168.50.254.

You may be wondering about the purpose of a broadcast address. As mentioned, it allows for packets to be sent to an entire network. In practice, network services, such as DHCP, utilize broadcast. When you first plug in a computer to an Ethernet cable (a computer that is not programmed with a static IP), it will send a broadcast message requesting an IP address. Until it connects, it has no idea what the IP address is of your DHCP server. It could be `192.168.1.1`, or even `192.168.1.100`. It has no idea whatsoever. By sending broadcast messages, whichever server is responsible for DHCP should be able to hear the request and respond to it.

So, why was the IP address `192.168.50.0` chosen for the previous example? That number was just chosen at random in order to illustrate how the subnet mask impacts the IP addresses that are available. We could have used `172.16.254.0` as our network address and with the Class C subnet mask of `255.255.255.0`, which would still give us the same number of usable IP addresses (254). In this second example, we're still declaring a Class C network, but just with a different IP scheme. Since you're managing an internal network, you can choose whatever numbering system you want. As long as your IP addresses aren't publicly routable, it's all fair game as long as you don't use numbers above 255 in any octet, or the first or last IP address within a network. There are a few other IP addresses we can't use, but we'll get to those later.

To better understand how this works, we'll need to revisit subnet masks. As mentioned, a subnet mask helps determine which portion of an IP address scheme belongs to individual nodes and which portion belongs to the network itself. Think about it like this. A value of 255 is the maximum number that can be in any octet of a subnet mask or IP address. Each 255 within a subnet mask represents a number that cannot change. So, if you have an IP address `10.19.100.24` and a subnet mask `255.255.255.0`, you can tell right away that the first three octets of this network will never change. This means that every host that is a member of this subnet will have an IP address beginning with `10.19.100`. If the subnet mask was `255.255.0.0`, there would be more IP addresses available, since the last two octets are up for grabs. This would actually give us 65,534 IP addresses. The former would only allow us 254 IP addresses, since the last octet is the only one that could change and its maximum number is 255 (subtracting one for the broadcast address).

But you may have noticed that I used an example of a Class A IP address (`10.19.100.24`), but I used a Class C subnet mask (`255.255.255.0`). Is this valid? Sure! Regardless of the generally agreed upon class structure, the sole purpose of a subnet mask is to help you understand which portion is host and which portion of node. Thus, subnet masks of `255.255.0.0` and `255.255.255.0` are both valid for this network.

However, some IP addresses aren't considered valid for individual classes. While an internal IP network of 253.221.96.0 with a subnet mask of 255.255.255.0 fits all these rules, it's not considered valid for a Class C network. If you're only managing your IP addresses within your network, it may or may not work. So for each class in the classful style, there is a recommended scheme to stay within. I'll illustrate that in the following table:

Class	Beginning IP	Ending IP
A	0.0.0.0	127.255.255.255
B	128.0.0.0	191.255.255.255
C	192.0.0.0	223.255.255.255

 As with all things networking, there's an exception to keep in mind here as well and you cannot assign 127.0.0.0 or 127.0.0.1 to anything, since that refers to your local loop-back adapter.

In fact, it's very common with internal networks to start an IP address range with 10, within the Class A scheme. That's what we've done earlier in the book when we set up our DHCP server. In that example, we used the 10.10.96.0 network. But if you recall, we did not use a Class C subnet mask of 255.255.255.0; we used 255.255.252.0. This distinction will lead us right into our next topic, CIDR.

Understanding the CIDR notation

As I mentioned earlier, the concept of classful subnetting isn't used that often anymore. The main use of classful subnetting is in the default configuration of network appliances (such as routers) and also the default settings of most DHCP servers. In the case of home routers, the DHCP server is typically built in, and the default scheme is most often a Class C network (typically 192.168.1.0, with a couple of variations in between). But with most devices, home or enterprise, you'll probably get a Class C IP scheme if you don't change it to something else. There's nothing necessarily wrong with these default settings in a small network, but almost no one configuring a network nowadays uses the classful style. The reason for this is that classful networks are too limiting; in complex network roll-outs, it can be a pain to try to force your network plan to fit within one of these predetermined schemes.

The answer to the lack of flexibility in classful schemes comes in the form of
Classless Inter-Domain Routing (CIDR). With CIDR, we basically throw the
limitations of Class A, B, and C subnet masks out the window. Instead, we use a
binary system to determine how to divide our networks. So, rather than stick with
just three different subnet masks, we can *borrow* bits and change the subnet mask to
divide networks in more flexible ways.

To understand this concept, it's important to first understand the idea of bits. Each
octet within a subnet mask contains eight bits. Each bit is either a 1 or a 0 (binary).
Also, each of the eight bits has a value of worth. To illustrate this, take the number
255. This is the highest value any octet can be. Written in binary, 255 is 11111111.
Therefore, a Class C subnet mask of 255.255.255.0 written in binary would be
11111111.11111111.11111111.00000000.

To make this even easier to understand, see the following table where I outline one
of the four outlets (255) and show it in binary. In this table, the top row gives you the
point value of each bit. You can see that the rightmost bit is worth only 1, while the
leftmost is worth 128. Any bit that is a 1 on the bottom gets totaled up. In this case,
every bit is a 1 (since 255 is the maximum), so we add up every number on the top
row and come out with 255.

128	64	32	16	8	4	2	1
1	1	1	1	1	1	1	1

For another example, see the following table:

128	64	32	16	8	4	2	1
1	1	1	1	0	0	0	0

To convert this number into a decimal, start at the right and work your way to the
left. The first bit is a 0. Does it qualify for the point value of 1? Nope. Skip it. Next, it
doesn't qualify for 2, 4, or 8 either. So skip those. But it does qualify for the last four,
16, 32, 64, and 128. Add those together. The answer? 224. You just converted the
binary number of 1111000 into decimal.

Could we have used 1101000 for a value within a subnet mask? No way. The reason is because the bits that are a 1 in a subnet mask must be sequential. The following are all valid binary numbers in a subnet mask:

```
00000000
10000000
11000000
11100000
11110000
11111000
11111100
11111110
11111111
```

In fact, that's it. Since any 1's must be sequential (starting from the left to the right), those are the only numbers that are valid for any octet within a subnet mask. Therefore, the only valid decimal values for any octet of a subnet mask are 0, 128, 192, 224, 240, 248, 252, 254, and 255.

> If converting an IP address into binary, you'd follow the same point values in the tables previously, though the rule of sequential 1's wouldn't apply. Any number from 0 to 255 is valid in any octet in an IP address, as are any combination of 1's and 0's in each octet.

To *subnet* a network, we simply alter the number of sequential 1's. For example, the binary representation of 255.255.255.0 is 11111111.11111111.11111111.00000000. We could add an additional 1 to this mask, giving us 11111111.11111111.11111111.10000000, which gives us a subnet mask of 255.255.255.128. Using this subnet mask, we are able to divide our network into two parts. Let's break this down.

As I've mentioned several times, the purpose of a subnet mask is to *mask out* which portion of the IP address is for the network and which portion is for the individual nodes. As we already know, a subnet mask of 255.255.255.0 means that the first three octets cannot be used, but we can use it as the last one is a 0. If we apply this subnet mask to the 10.10.10.0 network, we can tell that every host will have an IP address of 10.10.10.x. The last octet is 0 and it tells us that IP addresses 10.10.10.1 to 10.10.10.254 are up for grabs. Again, we can't use the first IP of a subnet (10.10.10.0 in this case) or the last (10.10.10.255), as those correspond to the network identifier and broadcast address, respectively.

But what do we do with a subnet mask that does *not* end in 0? With a subnet mask of 255.255.255.128, the last octet is used but not exhausted, since it's not the maximum value of 255. We have some left over. This is because when an octet is *not* 255 in a subnet mask, it doesn't completely mask out that octet. Instead, it creates a dividing line. If we apply that subnet mask to our 10.10.10.0 network, the IP address of 10.10.10.128 cannot be used. What we've done is split that last octet in half. Remember, values 0 to 255 are valid in an octet; thus, 256 available numbers halved is 128. With that in mind, we created a scheme where we have two networks. One network contains IP addresses 10.10.10.1 to 10.10.10.126. The other allows us IP addresses 10.10.10.129 to 10.10.10.254. The reason for this is because 10.10.10.128 is the dividing line of our subnet and cannot be used. I also mentioned that the first and last IP addresses within a block can't be used either, because 10.10.10.0 and 10.10.10.128 are the identifiers for each network. The last IP addresses in each block are 10.10.10.127 and 10.10.10.255, respectively, and are off-limits because those are now the broadcast addresses for these two networks. If we write out these networks in the CIDR format, we get the following:

```
10.10.10.0/25
10.10.10.128/25
```

Remember, we count the number of sequential ones in the subnet mask to reach the *slash* number at the end. We could have written it as the following, but I'm sure you'll agree that CIDR is easier to type:

```
10.10.10.0/255.255.255.128
10.10.10.128/255.255.255.128
```

In binary, that subnet mask is 11111111.11111111.11111111.1 0000000. Since there are 25 1's, the CIDR notation for this subnet mask is 25. Hopefully, the concept is making sense now.

As for our classless style, there's nothing stopping you from using a subnet mask such as 255.255.255.0. Not everyone needs a large number of hosts. But instead of calling that a Class C subnet mask, in the CIDR style we would instead refer to it as a /24 network. In the table, I list the subnet masks used in discussion of classful networks, as well as their CIDR equivalent.

Class	Subnet mask	CIDR notation
A	255.0.0.0	/8
B	255.255.0.0	/16
C	255.255.255.0	/24

Now that we understand how subnetting works, how do we put this in action in our network? Fortunately, that part is easy. The magic for rolling out a subnet is all in your DHCP server. If you recall, in *Chapter 6, Configuring Network Services*, we used the following configuration in our DHCP server's /etc/dhcp/dhcpd.conf file:

```
default-lease-time 86400;
max-lease-time 86400;
option subnet-mask 255.255.252.0;
option broadcast-address 10.10.99.255;
option domain-name "local.lan";
authoritative;
subnet 10.10.96.0 netmask 255.255.252.0 {
  range 10.10.99.100 10.10.99.254;
  option routers 10.10.96.1;
  option domain-name-servers 10.10.96.1;
}
```

In the first bold line, I'm providing a subnet mask of 255.255.252.0 to each node that receives an IP address from this server. In the block of code toward the end, I've decided to issue IP addresses from 10.10.99.100 through 10.10.99.254. Therefore, each node will receive a 10.10.99.x IP address and a 255.255.252.0 subnet mask.

The only thing left when rolling out a subnet scheme is to ensure that every server or appliance that has a static IP address is also changed. Unless you've used a static lease (also known as a *reservation*), you'll have to find those hosts and change them manually. For this reason, I always prefer static leases over static IPs. With static leases, all you would have to do is edit your DHCP configuration and change the IPs distributed to your hosts. Refer to *Chapter 6, Configuring Network Services*, for how we set up our reservations.

Implementing Quality of Service

Not all network traffic is created equal nor are all services equally important. There are times when a network requires certain services to be treated with more urgency than others. Perhaps in a server environment, your web servers receive a high level of traffic from visitors and must prioritize MySQL, or perhaps your office uses **VoIP** (short for **Voice over IP**) and needs priority placed on the phone system. There are many reasons why your network may require a service to be treated with more urgency than others. **Quality of Service (QoS)** helps us achieve this.

While there are multiple ways of tweaking network adapters for QoS, the most typical is something known as **queuing discipline** (or more simply, **qdisc**). A queuing discipline is something an administrator can apply to a network adapter to use one of a multiple of schedulers, each with varying effects on how traffic is handled. To see which scheduler your network adapter is currently using, run the following command:

```
ip link list
```

Look for your default network card, which will likely either be eth0 (in Debian) or eno1 (in CentOS) or similar.

Viewing the output of IP link list in Debian

Most likely, you'll see qdisc pfifo_fast in the output, which tells us that the queuing discipline currently in use is pfifo_fast. This is basically a first-come first-serve scheduler (first in, first out). But rather than contain a single band, pfifo_fast it contains three — each separating traffic into three priorities. The first band (band 0) contains the highest priority traffic. Each band is handled only after the previous one has been serviced. Unless your distribution has changed the default scheduler, pfifo_fast, is most likely what is currently in use on your system out of the box.

The pfifo_fast scheduler is known as a classless scheduler. In other words, what you see is what you get — there is no configuration to be done when it comes to how classless schedulers filter traffic. Other classless disciplines include **Stochastic Fair Queuing (SFQ)**, **Extended Stochastic Fair Queuing (ESFQ)**, and **Token Bucket Filter (TBF)**.

The SFQ qdisc uses the concept of FIFO as we've mentioned before, but separates network traffic into more than one FIFO, handled in a round-robin fashion. This qdisc tries to be as fair as possible, using flows to schedule packet transmission. This gives each flow a turn to transmit, preventing any one of them from becoming saturated. ESFQ is very similar, but it gives the administrator more options in which to configure. Unlike SFQ, TBF does not actually manipulate packets nor does it do any scheduling. The main purpose of TBF is to set a rate at which transmission will occur, allowing you to set parameters, such as the rate, burst, peakrate, and more. For more in-depth information, on these qdiscs, see the main pages for `sfq` and `tbf`. Setting the preferred qdisc on a network adapter is done via the `tc` command. See the following example for setting `sfq` on Ethernet adapter `eno1`:

```
# tc qdisc add dev eno1 root sfq perturb 60
```

Here, we're calling the `tc` command with `qdisc` and clarifying that we would like to add (we can also `del`) a qdisc. We're going to execute this against interface `eno1`, and we're requesting this change to egress (`root`) while targeting the `sfq` qdisc for our interface. Finally, we're setting our qdisc specific parameters (in this case, `pertub`). The perturb parameter allows us to set the seconds in which the hashing algorithm for this qdisc will be reset. There are other sfq-specific values we can alter, such as the number of flows used, quantum, redflowlimit, and more. See `man sfq` for complete descriptions of the parameters that can be used with sfq or tbf.

Where the concept of classless qdiscs falls short is the fact that they don't allow you to classify traffic as granularly as one might like. While it is certainly useful to change how packets are scheduled, that concept doesn't allow you to pick and choose which type of traffic receives priority at any given time. Classful qdiscs solves this issue, and gives the administrator much more flexibility. With these, you're able to set parents and children, each with different rules. In fact, that is the primary difference between classful and classless qdiscs. It's not the case that classless qdiscs aren't configurable at all; they just don't have the options to support the flexibility of advanced use cases. Next, we'll explore the classful qdiscs and how they allow us this added flexibility.

By utilizing the power of classful qdiscs, you gain almost total control over how packets are handled on your network. I said *almost* because it's important to remember that the idea of queuing discipline affects only outbound traffic (egress) while little can be done to manage incoming traffic. However, on a production network, guaranteeing particular services a certain amount of bandwidth can be very beneficial. As we've discussed in the previous section, classless qdiscs allow us to manage the general way in which packets are handled, but classful qdiscs allow us more control by setting classes as well as filters.

A possible scenario you may run into is VoIP traffic becoming unstable, causing calls to sound fuzzy or drop altogether. In this case, you may want to guarantee more bandwidth to your VoIP server, even if that means sacrificing traffic from another source. In addition, SSH is also important on a Linux network. If your server is too inundated with packets to even respond to a request to connect to it via SSH, that could be a very bad problem since you wouldn't be able to log in and correct any issues that may come up. These are very real scenarios many face without prioritizing traffic. If there is a service your network or company depends on, it's a good measure to prioritize it.

The most popular qdisc to achieve this is **Hierarchical Token Bucket (HTB)**, which is a classful qdisc. HTB allows you to control the egress bandwidth used on a device, and it is based on the TBF style we discussed earlier. HBT features a number of classes that can be used to control traffic, such as setting the `parent`, `priority`, `rate`, `ceil`, and the number of burst bytes. See `man htb` to view a complete list.

Just as we did with configuring a classless qdisc, the setting of a classful qdisc like HTB is also done via the `tc` command. On most systems, this command is stored in `/sbin` and is likely not to be in a regular user's path. Type `which tc` to locate where this binary is on your distribution. In most cases, your system should recognize this command if run while logged in root. What follows is an example of the process of setting up HTB as the qdisc for a network device named `eth0`.

```
# tc qdisc add dev eth0 root handle 1: htb default 10
# tc class add dev eth0 parent 1: classid 1:1 htb rate 2mbit
# tc class add dev eth0 parent 1:1 classid 1:10 htb rate 1mbit ceil
1.5mbit
# tc class add dev eth0 parent 1:1 classid 1:20 htb rate 100kbps ceil
100kbps
```

In the first command, we're changing the qdisc from the default `pfifo_fast` to `htb`. In this command, `root` pertains to the fact we're setting this against egress traffic. The handle of `1:` is a name for this particular instance of `htb`. Setting a default of `10` means that any traffic that is not specifically classed elsewhere will be given a class ID of `1:10`. With the second command, we're creating class ID `1:1` and adjusting it to use a rate of `2mbit`. In the third, we're doing the same, except we're creating an ID of `1:10` with a ceiling, which will limit this class to `1.5mbit`. Because we set the default as `10`, this is the class that will be used if we don't specifically target traffic to use something else. Finally, I also threw in a third class, `1:20`, which has a much lower limit of `100kbps`. With both the `rate` and `ceil` values set to the same value, we can reasonably expect traffic under this class to consume `100kbps` but also be limited to `100kbps`. You can continue to add additional classes to the `1:` parent using this method, as many as you need to split up your bandwidth accordingly.

Now that we have our classes identified, we should put them to use. With our previous example, you'll likely notice your bandwidth is now less than it was (assuming your bandwidth is above the `1.5mbit` default that we set). But our other two classes are unused, so we can boost our limit our bandwidth for other services as we see fit. So, let's add a filter for SSH. Since SSH doesn't require a great deal of bandwidth, we can assign our `1:20` class to it. To do so, we'll again use the `tc` command:

```
# tc filter add dev eth0 parent 1: protocol ip prio 7 u32 match ip sport
22 0xffff classid 1:20
```

> It's possible to change the port that your server listens on for SSH connections, as we'll discuss in *Chapter 9, Securing Your Network*. If you changed your SSH port, adjust the `tc` command accordingly.

That leaves us with two classes, `1:1` and `1:10`. We can assign filters to those as well, depending on which port we would like to classify for the traffic:

```
# tc filter add dev eth0 parent 1: u32 match ip sport 80 0xffff classid
1:1
```

```
# tc filter add dev eth0 parent 1: u32 match ip sport 5060 0xffff classid
1:10
```

Here, I used ports `80` and `5060` for HTTP and VoIP traffic, respectively. Your ports may differ, so feel free to adjust the command accordingly to fit the needs of your network. But in this hypothetical example, traffic on port `80` will be classified as `1:1` and granted a maximum rate of `2mbit` (great for a web server), and traffic on port `5060` will be granted `1.5mbit`.

In summary, classless qdiscs allow you to control the general consensus of how packets are managed on your system. Depending on your environment, you may find that changing to a classless qdisc increases performance. But the real benefit comes in the form of classful qdiscs, which allows you more granular control over how packets are handled, as well as the rates your server's resources are provided. Tuning network performance is a time-consuming task and requires trial and error to determine which values, classes, and filters will improve performance on your network.

Routing TCP/IP traffic

The entire purpose of networking is to get traffic from point A to point B. When a computer requests information from another, packets are routed to the destination and then back. Sometimes, computers need a little guidance on how to get packets to the destination. This is known as **routing**. To assist with this, nodes utilize the concept of a **routing table** to help decide where packets should be sent given specific destinations. It would be very easy if every network in existence used the same IP scheme, but in truth, every network is completely different. To talk to a different network, your computer must know how to get to that network. Think of a routing table as a map of external destinations and the gateways to get to those destinations.

To better understand this, let's also talk about the concept of the **default gateway**. Typically, the default gateway is a router that understands how to talk to other networks. When you send a request for information over a network, packets traverse to the local default gateway and then onto other networks from there. In the case of a small office or home network, the default gateway is likely the router that sits in between your network and the rest of the world. In addition, it's also in between your local device and all other devices within your network. Without a default gateway, it's unlikely you'd be able to communicate over your network at all.

To view your default gateway, issue the `ip route` command and look for the line that reads `default via`.

```
root@crusader:/home/jay# ip route
default via 192.168.1.1 dev wlan0   proto static   metric 1024
169.254.0.0/16 dev docker0   scope link   metric 1000
172.17.0.0/16 dev docker0   proto kernel   scope link   src 172.17.42.1
192.168.1.0/24 dev wlan0   proto kernel   scope link   src 192.168.1.106
root@crusader:/home/jay#
```

Output of the ip route command

Without a default gateway (or with a default gateway that hasn't been properly configured), you're likely to find that you aren't able to communicate with other nodes on your network. In most cases, the default gateway is added to your routing table once you receive an address via DHCP. If you're using a static IP configuration, you can manually set the default gateway in Debian via `/etc/network/interfaces`, or the init script for your network card in CentOS (such as `/etc/sysconfig/network-scripts/ifcfg-eno1`). Here's a sample of these configuration files with the relevant line highlighted:

The `/etc/network/interfaces` file (Debian):

```
iface lo inet loopback

allow-hotplug eth0
iface eth0 inet dhcp

# The primary network interface
allow-hotplug eth1
iface eth1 inet static
   address 10.10.96.1
   netmask 255.255.252.0
   gateway 10.10.96.1
   broadcast 10.10.96.255
   dns-search local.lan
   dns-nameservers 10.10.96.1
```

The `/etc/sysconfig/network-scripts/ifcfg-eno1` file (CentOS):

```
TYPE=Ethernet
BOOTPROTO=static
DEFROUTE=yes
PEERDNS=yes
PEERROUTES=yes
IPV4_FAILURE_FATAL=no
NAME=eno1
UUID=8e6587dd-74ec-488f-8597-a04c4a4c5091
DEVICE=eno1
ONBOOT=yes
IPADDR="10.10.96.4"
NETMASK="255.255.252.0"
GATEWAY="10.10.96.1"
```

If you'd like to set your default gateway even more manually than that, you can also do so in your terminal via a shell command, as follows:

```
# route add default gw 10.10.10.1 eth0
```

 If the route command isn't recognized by your system, you'll need to install the `net-tools` package.

Simple enough. We use the route command to add a new route; in this case, we're adding our default gateway (`default gw`). In this case, we're setting that gateway to `10.10.10.1` and binding it to interface `eth0`. It probably goes without saying, but once you reboot this machine or restart networking, this setting will likely be lost unless you make it permanent by updating the `init` script for your interface card, as we discussed earlier.

To view your routing table, simply execute the `route -n` command without any arguments. If the command isn't found, you may need to call out the path (such as `/sbin/route`) or run it as root. When you execute this command, you'll see the routing table. This will also show you your default gateway.

```
* ▣                              Terminal                              _ ::
Destination     Gateway         Genmask         Flags Metric Ref    Use Iface
0.0.0.0         192.168.1.1     0.0.0.0         UG    1024   0        0 wlan0
169.254.0.0     0.0.0.0         255.255.0.0     U     1000   0        0 docker0
172.17.0.0      0.0.0.0         255.255.0.0     U     0      0        0 docker0
192.168.1.0     0.0.0.0         255.255.255.0   U     0      0        0 wlan0
root@crusader:/home/jay# █
```

Output of the route -n command

First up for discussion in regards to this table is the IP address of `0.0.0.0`. In terms of networking, this refers to everything. As you can see in the table shown in the previous example, the gateway for destination `0.0.0.0` on this network is `192.168.1.1`. Therefore, any communication is sent to this IP (after all, it is the default gateway). There are also other networks shown in this table as well. In my case, they refer to instances of Docker running on this test machine as well as KVM virtualization, and each have their own independent virtual networking. Since they are all running on this same machine, their gateway is local: `0.0.0.0`.

A Linux machine can easily act as a router itself, without the need for expensive networking equipment from companies such as Cisco. This flexibility makes Linux a very prominent choice for networking, and Linux-based hardware routers are becoming quite common. This is due, at least in part, to how easy it is to configure a Linux system to be a router. In a nutshell, all it takes to turn a Linux node into a router is multiple network interface cards. Each interface card can have its own default gateway, so you can actually configure routing the same way as how we've added a default gateway for `eth0` earlier in this section. You would just do the same for `eth1`, `eth2`, or for whatever other interfaces you may have on the system.

However, there is one caveat. With most Linux distributions, routing between network interfaces is typically disabled by default. This has caused your author much grief and frustration until this became known early on in my career, so I'll save you the trouble and show you how to enable routing between interfaces on your Linux system.

First, see if this has already been done for you. While I've found that many distributions don't have forwarding enabled by default, some do. Checking this is easy:

```
cat /proc/sys/net/ipv4/ip_forward
```

What is the output of that command? Is it 1? If so, you're all set. If not, we'll need to change this. To do so, simply replace the value with 1 (as root):

```
echo 1 > /proc/sys/net/ipv4/ip_forward
```

That's it, you're done. You just enabled routing between interfaces (forwarding). That wasn't so hard. But, I suppose you'd prefer this to be a permanent change. Once you reboot your system, it's likely that this setting will just revert back to its default. To make this change permanent, edit /etc/sysctl.conf with your favorite text editor (as root) and add the following line to the end of the file:

```
net.ipv4.ip_forward = 1
```

Now, whenever you reboot your system, you will keep this setting. Of all the networking tweaks I've had you do thus far, this was definitely the easiest.

Finally, let's spend a little bit of time on **Network Address Translation** (**NAT**). The concept of NAT is to alter packets that are destined for one host and alter them so that their destination becomes something else. This alteration is actually done by altering the packets themselves, and it can be quite useful for managing network routing. The most common use for NAT is to conserve IP addresses, which is especially important given the shortage of IPv4 addresses these days. If you have a router in your home, you're likely familiar with this concept already. Your **Internet Service Provider** (**ISP**) gives you an IP, and that IP is what the rest of the world sees you as. But within your local network, you probably have a dozen or so devices connected and using the same Internet connection. Each of your internal devices have an IP address given to them by your local DHCP server, but that address is just local and is not routable to the outside world. In this case your router keeps track of the packets coming to and from each of your devices, and it alters the packets so that they don't get mixed up and end up at the right place.

For example, say you have a laptop and a desktop (on the same network), and you visit https://www.packtpub.com/ on your laptop. Your router sends the request out to the Internet, and delivers the result. Basically, your router makes that request on behalf of your laptop. When the return packets arrive from https://www.packtpub.com/, the destination address of the packets is changed from your public IP address, back to the IP address of the machine that requested the information. This way, you can be reasonably sure your laptop will get the reply, since it was the one that asked for it in the first place.

The concept of NAT is clever, and this isn't even the only use-case. You could even manually alter the destination address yourself as well, which could assist you with sending packets to other networks that your internal computers would otherwise have no idea how to route to. To alter NAT manually, we use the `ip rule` command. Utilizing this command is just a matter of altering the destination based on where the traffic is originating from. Consider the following example:

```
# ip rule add nat 10.10.10.1 from 192.168.1.134
```

This couldn't be simpler. Here, we're telling our system to look for any packets that are from `192.168.1.134`, and rewrite them to flow to `10.10.10.1` instead. Repeat this for any other *NATing* you need to perform.

Creating redundant DHCP and DNS servers

In *Chapter 6, Configuring Network Services*, we set up DHCP and DNS servers. This is great, but unfortunately there's one major problem. Either one is a single point of failure. If the DHCP server were to go down, new devices wouldn't be able to receive an IP address, and clients that are currently connected will drop off the network as their current IP lease expires. If the DNS server were to go down, clients wouldn't be able to reach destinations by the hostname. Depending on the scope of your network, this downtime might be hard to deal with, so having redundancy for these services may be a good idea.

With a DHCP server configured for redundancy with another server, it will synchronize its list of IP addresses that were issued, and each will detect if the other stops responding. In this case, the secondary would take over the task of issuing new IP addresses. With DNS, it's just a matter of adding another DNS server on your network, but I'll talk more about that in just a bit.

Let's start with adding redundancy to our DHCP server. The initial one that was created earlier can be considered the primary server for the sake of simplicity. The next thing you would do is create another server to serve as the secondary. This can be another physical server or even a VM, the choice is yours. Install `isc-dhcp-server` as we discussed in *Chapter 6, Configuring Network Services*. Once you have the second server stood up, we can begin.

It's absolutely *imperative* to ensure the clocks are synchronized on both of your DHCP servers before they are placed into production. Before continuing, it may be a good idea to double check that NTP is configured and working on both. In *Chapter 6, Configuring Network Services,* information pertaining to setting up NTP was included.

Starting on our primary node, we should add some additional code to our /etc/ dhcp/dhcpd.conf file. I've bolded the lines of configuration that are new and for the purpose of adding redundancy:

```
default-lease-time 86400;
max-lease-time 86400;
option subnet-mask 255.255.252.0;
option broadcast-address 10.10.99.255;
option domain-name "local.lan";
authoritative;
failover peer "dhcp-failover" {
  primary;
  address 10.10.96.2;
  port 647;
  peer address 10.10.96.1;
  peer port 647;
  max-response-delay 60;
  max-unacked-updates 10;
  load balance max seconds 3;
  mclt 3600;
  split 128;
}
subnet 10.10.96.0 netmask 255.255.252.0 {
  option routers 10.10.96.1;
  option domain-name-servers 10.10.96.1;
  pool {
    failover peer "dhcp-failover";
    range 10.10.99.100 10.10.99.254;
  }
}
```

Note that the following line was removed:

```
range 10.10.99.100 10.10.99.254;
```

It was replaced by the pool { } block in the same section.

For the most part, the same configuration we've done on our primary server can be copied over to the secondary. Feel free to use the /etc/dhcp/dhcpd.conf file we have here as a base for starting the configuration on the second server. Again, I'll highlight what's different between the two. The code is as follows:

```
default-lease-time 86400;
max-lease-time 86400;
option subnet-mask 255.255.252.0;
option broadcast-address 10.10.99.255;
option domain-name "local.lan";
authoritative;
failover peer "dhcp-failover" {
  secondary;
  address 10.10.96.1;
  port 647;
  peer address 10.10.96.2;
  peer port 647;
  max-response-delay 60;
  max-unacked-updates 10;
  load balance max seconds 3;
}
subnet 10.10.96.0 netmask 255.255.252.0 {
  option routers 10.10.96.1;
  option domain-name-servers 10.10.96.1;
  pool {
    failover peer "dhcp-failover";
    range 10.10.99.100 10.10.99.254;
  }
}
```

The following lines were removed from the configuration of the secondary server:

mclt 3600;

split 128;

You should notice that the address of the primary and secondary are reversed in each. In the first configuration file, the primary is `10.10.96.1` and the secondary was set to `10.10.96.2`. In the second, this was changed to `10.10.96.2` and `10.10.96.1`, respectively. Also, pay careful attention to the IP addresses, subnet mask, and any other value that would likely be different from one network to the next. If you start the DHCP service on both your servers (on Debian, it's `isc-dhcp-server`, and on CentOS it's `dhcpd`) you should see them communicate via the logs. The specific logs to check would be `/var/log/syslog` in Debian-based systems and `/var/log/messages` in CentOS systems. You can easily test if this is working, by disabling the DHCP service on one of the servers and you should see the other issuing IP addresses in its place.

Now that we have redundancy configured for DHCP, let's do the same for DNS. In fact, this is a great deal easier. All you have to do is designate another server to act as your secondary DNS server (you can create a new machine, or just add it to your secondary DHCP server) and then copy over your configuration files and zone files to the new server. Again, *Chapter 6, Configuring Network Services*, has all the relevant details for these files. If you want to save a bit of time, you could even just clone your original DNS server into a new machine, which is easy to do if you're using virtualization or understand how to use the `dd` command. After whatever method you prefer for creating the secondary server and copying your zone files over, test that DNS is working on the new server. Once it is, we turn back to our DHCP configuration to deploy this secondary server to all of our nodes.

In our `/etc/dhcp/dhcpd.conf` file, look for the following line:

```
option domain-name-servers 10.10.96.1;
```

Change it to the following:

```
option domain-name-servers 10.10.96.1, 10.10.96.2;
```

You're done. Now, every time your clients' lease expires or they request a new IP address, they'll automatically be provided the secondary DNS address.

The only thing left to do at this point is to configure any nodes you may have set up with static IP addresses to use the secondary DNS server. As I've mentioned somewhere in the neighborhood of a thousand times by now, I highly prefer static leases (reserving IP addresses for various nodes on the DHCP server) to manual static IP assignments for this reason and more. You only need to configure them in the DHCP server. But if you do have any nodes you've configured networking by hand (to each their own), just update their `init` scripts. Again, you'll find this configuration in `/etc/network/interfaces` (Debian) or `/etc/sysconfig/network-scripts/<if-name>.cfg` (CentOS).

Summary

At this point in our journey, your network should be in much better shape. In this chapter, we accomplished quite a bit. We've discussed advanced topics such as routing, NAT, subnetting, Quality of Service, and we even set up redundancy for our DHCP and DNS servers. It would sure be a shame if something were to happen to our awesome network. That's why in the next chapter, I'll cover how to strengthen the security of our network. See you there!

9

Securing Your Network

Security vulnerabilities and the miscreants who take advantage of them are everywhere. With the millions of lines of code contained within software running on a typical network, it's statistically impossible to ever be 100 percent secure from all possible threats. However, a good network administrator pays attention to current trends in network security and takes all the possible precautions to help ensure the network is as secure as it possibly can be. In this chapter, we will take a look at some of the things that can be done to increase the security of your network.

In this chapter, we will cover:

- Limiting the attack surface
- Securing SSH
- Configuring the iptables firewall
- Protecting system services with fail2ban
- Understanding SELinux
- Configuring Apache to utilize SSL
- Deploying security updates

Limiting the attack surface

The most important rule of network security is limiting your attack surface. In a nutshell, this means that the less software you have installed and/or the less services you have running, the less it can be used against you. If that wasn't bad enough, in some cases an unpatched flaw in server software could allow a miscreant to use your server to attack someone else. By limiting the number of packages in use on your system, you're lowering the possibility of something bad happening.

This sounds simple enough, and it is, but it's important to keep in mind that this isn't just a matter of installing only what you need. Many Linux distributions ship with software that you may never need to use. This isn't just true for servers either. Even your end-user workstations could have unnecessary services running that would be a treasure trove for an attacker to use. One common example of this is having a **Mail Transfer Agent (MTA)** running on your system. It's surprising that many Linux distributions ship with an MTA running by default. Unless you specifically need an MTA (for example, you have scripts installed that need to send e-mail messages to administrators), you should remove these packages from your systems.

When rolling out Linux on any network, the first thing you should do is find out what is installed and what is running, and then decide what to turn off and/or uninstall. This is what is referred to as limiting your attack surface. It is true that Linux is one of most secure systems there are, but nothing will help you if you aren't keeping an eye on what is running and listening for connections on your network. For the remainder of this section, I'll go over a few ways in which you can limit your attack surface.

First, let's print out a list of all the packages installed on our system. This will allow us to see what is installed, and then we can remove anything that stands out that we're sure we don't need. This list will likely be huge, as it will include everything; I do mean everything—even the libraries and various packages that allow our system to function. You definitely won't understand what each of them packages are for, but as you learn more about Linux, you'll make more sense of these and know what needs to be removed. For example, I know to remove `exim` or `postfix` packages from all of my installations, as I don't personally need them anywhere. Since you won't understand the purpose of all of the packages installed on your system, I recommend you to take a quick look and remove the ones you know for sure you don't need. To print a list of installed packages, run one of the following commands:

For Debian-based sytems, execute the following command:

```
# dpkg --get-selections > installed_packages.txt
```

For CentOS systems, execute the following command:

```
# rpm -qa > installed_packages.txt
```

In either case, you'll end up with a text file called `installed_packages.txt` in your current working directory. This text file will contain a list of all the packages installed on your system. Feel free to check it and see if anything stands out as something that you can remove. In addition, this file serves as a handy backup as well. If you ever need to decommission a server and set up a new one with a similar purpose, you can compare the packages from one server to another to ensure the proper packages are installed.

Another neat trick to find out what is running on your system is with the `netstat` command. While we'll discuss this command further in *Chapter 10, Troubleshooting Network Issues*, let's try this out now:

`netstat -tulpn`

You should see a list of services running on the local computer that are actually listening for network connections. These should be given major attention, as anything listening for outside connections is a possible point of entry into your system. If you see something here that's listening for connections and you don't need it to be, remove the package. You can always disable a service, but removing the underlying package is better as they can't be accidentally started. Packages can always be reinstalled if you find that you actually did need them.

```
11:32:03 [crusader:~]$ netstat -tulpn
(Not all processes could be identified, non-owned process info
 will not be shown, you would have to be root to see it all.)
Active Internet connections (only servers)
Proto Recv-Q Send-Q Local Address          Foreign Address        State       PID/Program name
tcp        0      0 0.0.0.0:111            0.0.0.0:*              LISTEN      -
tcp        0      0 127.0.0.1:8080         0.0.0.0:*              LISTEN      11568/syncthing
tcp        0      0 192.168.1.106:53       0.0.0.0:*              LISTEN      -
tcp        0      0 172.17.42.1:53         0.0.0.0:*              LISTEN      -
tcp        0      0 127.0.0.1:53           0.0.0.0:*              LISTEN      -
tcp        0      0 0.0.0.0:22             0.0.0.0:*              LISTEN      -
tcp        0      0 127.0.0.1:631          0.0.0.0:*              LISTEN      -
tcp        0      0 127.0.0.1:953          0.0.0.0:*              LISTEN      -
tcp        0      0 0.0.0.0:47785          0.0.0.0:*              LISTEN      -
tcp6       0      0 :::111                 :::*                   LISTEN      -
tcp6       0      0 :::22000               :::*                   LISTEN      11568/syncthing
tcp6       0      0 :::53                  :::*                   LISTEN      -
tcp6       0      0 :::22                  :::*                   LISTEN      -
tcp6       0      0 ::1:631                :::*                   LISTEN      -
tcp6       0      0 ::1:953                :::*                   LISTEN      -
tcp6       0      0 :::34950               :::*                   LISTEN      -
udp        0      0 0.0.0.0:37269          0.0.0.0:*                          11568/syncthing
udp        0      0 0.0.0.0:21025          0.0.0.0:*                          11568/syncthing
udp        0      0 0.0.0.0:5353           0.0.0.0:*                          5536/chrome
```

The netstat command, listing running and listening services

In my case, I can see that I have Syncthing and Chrome listening for outside connections. This is expected. But in a production environment, such as a server, some things to watch out for would be the Apache web server (which would be a concern if the server is not actually a web server), postfix, or any file transfer utilities that shouldn't be installed.

Another useful tool is **ShieldsUP**, it is a service available on the Internet by GRC. This is not a Linux-specific tool by any means, but if you're using Linux on your router and want to ensure that you have it configured to be as stealthy as possible, this tool can be useful for testing. You can access this tool at the following URL:

`https://www.grc.com/shieldsup`

Please keep in mind that ShieldsUP is an online tool that is not under the control or management of the author or publisher. As a result, it's subject to change at any time. That being said, this site hasn't changed in quite some time and it's a very useful tool.

To use it, click on **Proceed** and then click on **All Service Ports**. This service works by checking to see which ports answer to outside requests. If a port is open, it will show red, and you should be able to click on it to find out more information on what the port is typically used for. This will provide you clues on what to disable. In the event that the service doesn't contain information regarding a specific port, simply search on Google to look for clues.

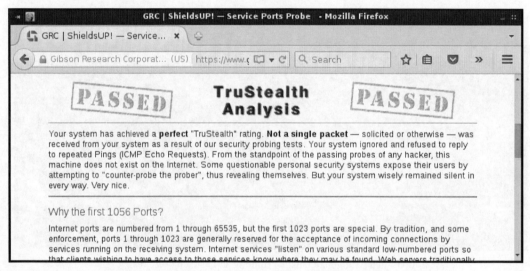

Using ShieldsUP! to see which ports answer from outside requests

Finally, the `systemctl` command can also be used to see what services are currently installed on your machine:

```
systemctl list-units -t service
```

Using the list the previous command will print to your terminal, you'll be able to see which unit files are currently installed, and their state.

That pretty much sums up how to interrogate your system to find out what is running. As you learn the typical names of services you may need to do a bit of Google search in order to learn the purpose of each service, but it gets easier with time. If you're at all unsure about what can be disabled or not, do your research first before you actually work on tweaking your running services. In the worst case, if you disable a necessary service, your server may not start the next time. As always, ensure you have good backups before altering system services.

Securing OpenSSH

OpenSSH is a wonderful tool; it's the Linux administrator's best friend. It saves you the trouble of having to walk into the server room and attach a monitor and keyboard in order to perform work on your network. Using any computer connected to the same network, you can pretty much do anything you want to as if you were standing right in front of the machine. The problem is that an unsecured SSH implementation gives miscreants the exact same luxury. Of all the things running on your network, SSH is definitely the one you want to give some major attention to.

The first and most common security tweak for SSH is to use only Version 2 of the protocol. To determine which version your Linux installation is using, `grep` the `/etc/ssh/sshd_config` file:

```
cat /etc/ssh/sshd_config |grep Protocol
```

If the answer is 1, you should edit this file and change the line that reads **Protocol 1** to **Protocol 2**, and restart SSH. The reason this is important is because Protocol 1 has considerably weaker security than Protocol 2. Thankfully, SSH Version 7 and later, now default to Protocol 2, so this isn't as common as it used to be. But at the time of this writing, Version 7 was just released and hasn't made its way into many distributions yet. Hopefully, by the time you read this, your distribution has upgraded to Version 7. But if not, it's important that you ensure all of your servers utilize only Protocol 2 for SSH. You can achieve this by changing the relevant line in your `sshd_conf` file and then restarting the SSH service.

Another worthwhile change to SSH is changing the port it listens on. By default, SSH is listening on **Port 22**. You can confirm this with the following command:

```
cat /etc/ssh/sshd_config |grep Port
```

Unless you changed it, the answer will be 22. Since 22 is the default port for SSH, that's the port everyone (including the bad guys) expects it to be on. In the /etc/ ssh/sshd_config file, there will be an option for the port near the top. If you change it to something else, it will be less obvious to outsiders. However, I don't want to lure you into a false sense of security here. Changing the port for SSH isn't a magical barrier against intrusion via SSH. In a targeted attack, a miscreant will scan every port on your server, so if they are determined, they'll figure out what port you changed it to. The reason why I recommend this change is because it's a very easy change to make. It requires only a few seconds to change your SSH port, and anything you can do to make your network less obvious to outsiders is a welcome change. The only time changing the SSH port can become a potential problem is if users of your network expect it to be on port 22. As long as you communicate this change to everyone, it should be a non-issue.

In order to connect to a server with a non-standard SSH port, use the -p flag:

```
ssh -p 63456 myhost.mynetwork
```

You can also designate the port while using scp as well:

```
scp -P 63456
```

> Note the -P parameter is uppercase in scp but not in the ssh command. This was intentional. The reason for this is because the lowercase -p option in scp was already taken, and it's used for preserving modification times when transferring files.

If you can't seem to get into the habit of requesting a different port for SSH, create an alias for it. However, this can be a problem if some of your hosts are still using port 22, so you would only use this alias if everything you connect to is on the same port. In the following example, we can set an alias to ssh to force it to always use port 63456:

```
alias ssh="ssh -p 63456"
```

Another very important change to your SSH configuration is to not allow root login. Under no circumstances should root login be allowed on any Linux server for any reason. If your configuration requires you to log in to a server as root via SSH, correct your configuration. To check to see if root login is enabled via SSH, run the following:

```
cat /etc/ssh/sshd_config |grep PermitRootLogin
```

If root login is enabled, disable it by correcting the following configuration line in
`/etc/ssh/sshd_config`. However, make sure you are able to access the server via
SSH with a normal user account first; otherwise, you'll be locked out. The following
configuration line in `sshd_config` will disallow root login:

`PermitRootLogin no`

> As always, restart `ssh` after you make any changes to its configuration.
> Don't worry about restarting SSH while you are using it, current
> connections will not be disrupted.
>
> For Debian systems, execute the following command:
>
> `# systemctl restart ssh`
>
> For CentOS systems, execute the following command:
>
> `# systemctl restart sshd`

Another practice worth implementing is locking SSH down to only allow
connections via specific users and/or groups. By default, any user with an
account on the system is available via SSH. To change this, add the following
line to the very bottom of the configuration file:

`AllowUsers jdoe`

If you have more than one user, you can add multiple users on the same line:

`AllowUsers jdoe bsmith`

You can also allow specific groups. First, create a group that you'll use for
SSH access:

`groupadd ssh_admins`

Next, add one or more users to the group:

`usermod -aG ssh_admins jdoe`

Finally, add the following line to the bottom of your SSH configuration file. After
you restart SSH, access will be restricted to those that are a member of this group.
Each time you need to grant SSH access to someone, all you'll need to do is add
their user ID to this group and you won't have to restart the `sshd_config`
configuration file each time.

`AllowGroups ssh_admins`

Finally, the most secure option for SSH is to not allow password-based authentication at all. Instead, users can use a public/private key pair for access. With this method, passwords are not transmitted over the network and those without a private key that matches an accepted public key are not allowed access. This is the practice that I recommend to everyone. On the down-side, it also comes with the most administrative overhead. To implement this change, each user will need to generate a key pair for SSH with the following command:

```
ssh-keygen
```

You'll be asked several questions, most of which you can leave as the default. For the passphrase, come up with something unique and ensure it's not the same as your password. You can leave it blank if you don't want to be asked for a passphrase while making connections, but I recommend creating one.

Next, the easiest way to configure a server to allow you to connect via a key is to import that key into the server, *before* you disable password authentication. To do that, use a variation of the following:

```
ssh-copy-id -i ~/.ssh/id_rsa.pub myserver.mynetwork.com
```

At this point, you'll be asked to log in to the server via your normal password. Then, the next time you connect to it, you will default to using the key pair you came up with and you'll be asked for your passphrase if you created one.

After all of your users have generated their key and imported it into the server, you can implement this change. Look for the line in the SSH configuration file that looks similar to the following:

```
PasswordAuthentication yes
```

Simply change that option to no, restart SSH, and you should be all set. The reason that this works is because when you copy over your SSH key using the `ssh-copy-id` command, what it's actually doing is copying the contents of your public key (`~/.ssh/id_rsa.pub`) on your local machine to the end of the `~/.ssh/authorized_keys` file on the remote machine. With password authentication disabled, SSH will check that the key listed there matches your private key (`~/.ssh/id_rsa`) and then allow you access.

With these tweaks, your SSH implementation should be reasonably secure. It certainly won't help you if you use weak passwords or passphrases, but these are the general steps you should take on all servers.

Configuring the iptables firewall

By default, Linux includes a firewall, **iptables**. This firewall should automatically be available on most (if not all) flavors of Linux. In this little activity, we'll set up a firewall on our Linux system. This should work fine regardless of which of the major distributions you use, but I'll call out anything that may be distribution specific. Before we get started though, I'll recommend that you play with this on a test machine, such as a VM or something you have physical access to. If you're using SSH, you may get disconnected when we enable the firewall, though I'll provide these steps in an order that hopefully, shouldn't drop your connection. Having a dedicated test machine to play around with is a good idea anyway.

With that out of the way, let's get started. Unfortunately, by default, iptables is wide open. It's so open, in fact, that it blocks nothing. To see this for yourself, issue iptables -L as root. Your output will probably look like this:

```
Chain INPUT (policy ACCEPT)
Chain FORWARD (policy ACCEPT)
Chain OUTPUT (policy ACCEPT)
```

What you're seeing here are three **chains** of iptables, each corresponding to input, output, and forwarding. If you haven't configured this yet (and your distribution doesn't offer any default configuration), you'll likely see the default policy for each being ACCEPT, which means exactly what it sounds like: it allows everything.

One of the first rules I like to implement is to allow for SSH:

```
# iptables -A INPUT -i eth0 -p tcp --dport 22 -j ACCEPT
```

With this command, we're appending a new rule (-A) to our INPUT chain on the interface eth0 using TCP and accepting traffic from dport (destination port) 22. If you changed your SSH port earlier, be sure to adjust this command accordingly. Also, if your interface is not eth0, change that too. Of course, our firewall allows anything anyway, since we've never changed the default policy. If you recall, it accepts everything by default. Let's change that with the following commands:

```
# iptables -P INPUT DROP
# iptables -P FORWARD DROP
# iptables -P OUTPUT DROP
```

Now, if we view the output of iptables -L, we should see the default policy is DROP on everything and SSH is allowed.

However, there's one problem—we can't do anything else. We're no longer able to install packages. Actually, we're unable to do anything on the Internet at all. For example, try pinging Google. You won't be able to. If you've followed along, we set our default policy to DROP and it really does mean DROP. No traffic is currently allowed to or from the server unless it's SSH. In order to restore networking, we'll need to allow a few more things. First, let's allow DNS, which utilizes port 53:

```
# iptables -I INPUT -s 10.10.96.0/22 -p udp --dport 53 -j ACCEPT
# iptables -I OUTPUT -s 10.10.96.0/22 -p udp --dport 53 -j ACCEPT
```

Here, we're allowing port 53, but only for our internal 10.10.96.0/22 network. Note that DNS uses UDP, so we included -p udp into our command. It goes without saying, but adjust the 10.10.96.0/22 portion for whatever your network scheme is.

At this point, we're still a bit more locked down on our system than we would like. For example, we have DNS now, but we wouldn't be able to browse the Internet without allowing ports 80 and 443. Let's take care of that next.

```
# iptables -A INPUT -i eth0 -p tcp --dport 80 -m state --state
NEW,ESTABLISHED -j ACCEPT
# iptables -A OUTPUT -o eth0 -p tcp --dport 80 -m state --state
ESTABLISHED -j ACCEPT
# iptables -A INPUT -i eth1 -p tcp --dport 443 -m state --state
NEW,ESTABLISHED -j ACCEPT
# iptables -A OUTPUT -o eth1 -p tcp --dport 443 -m state --state
ESTABLISHED -j ACCEPT
```

From this point forward, you should be able to browse the Internet on this machine and access it via SSH, though other ports and services shouldn't be accessible. If the machine in question is a router, you might want to configure port forwarding as well. Here's an example of port forwarding:

```
# iptables -t nat -A PREROUTING -i eth0 -p tcp --dport 65254 -j DNAT
--to-destination 10.10.96.10
```

In this example, we're forwarding traffic received on port 65254 to 10.10.96.10. This example is useful if you have something like SSH available on a port other than 22 and would like to be able to access a computer (in this case, 10.10.96.10) using that port. The server will now forward traffic it receives on that port to that computer. This uses the concept of PREROUTING, which handles incoming packets and is able to reassign them via NAT. In this case, we're using the firewall to create a NAT rule to send this traffic to the appropriate place.

If the server you're setting up this firewall on is destined to become a router, you'll want to enable routing between interfaces as well. We took care of that from a Linux level in the last chapter, but since we configured the firewall to DROP everything by default, we can no longer do that. To continue to route between interfaces, we'll need to enable routing within our firewall as well. To do that, we can use the following commands:

```
# iptables -t nat -A POSTROUTING -o eth0 -j MASQUERADE
# iptables -A FORWARD -i eth1 -j ACCEPT
```

In the previous command, we're allowing routing between interfaces eth0 and eth1. Adjust the previous commands to fit your distribution's network interface naming scheme so that it will fit your environment. We're also using POSTROUTING, which in terms of iptables is another word for outgoing traffic.

Another change that may be useful is allowing ping. With our configuration so far, ICMP ping packets are blocked. If you ping your server, you won't get a response. We can re-enable ping responses via the following commands. Be sure to change the IP address to match that of your server:

```
# iptables -A INPUT -p icmp --icmp-type 8 -s 0/0 -d 10.10.96.1 -m state
--state NEW,ESTABLISHED,RELATED -j ACCEPT
# iptables -A OUTPUT -p icmp --icmp-type 0 -s 10.10.96.1 -d 0/0 -m state
--state ESTABLISHED,RELATED -j ACCEPT
```

If for some reason you've made a mistake or if you'd like to start this activity again, issue the following commands to flush (reset) the iptables firewall:

```
# iptables -flush
```

Note that this won't undo your default policy, which you can explicitly set to ACCEPT if you'd like to undo everything we've done so far. We can set each table to it's default (ACCEPT) with the following commands:

```
# iptables -P INPUT ACCEPT
# iptables -P FORWARD ACCEPT
# iptables -P OUTPUT ACCEPT
```

We choose DROP for our default policy because in this mode, the firewall does not respond to the sending host with a status when rejecting traffic. In a sense, it's almost as if packets are sent to an endless black hole when a policy is set to DROP. This is a good thing, because miscreants can use the response they get back from the server to better target their attacks. It's best for them to get no response at all.

So, feel free to play around with `iptables` until you've gotten to a point where you are able to perform all the tasks that you normally were able to perform. Once you have a working and well-tested firewall, it's time to save the configuration. Otherwise, all this hard work would be lost when you reboot. Use the following command to save your firewall configuration:

```
# iptables-save > /etc/iptables.rules
```

To import these rules, we can use the following command:

```
# iptables-restore < /etc/iptables.rules
```

You'll probably want these changes restored automatically every time the system boots. Both Debian and CentOS have their own ways to accomplish this. Here are the methods in which to save the rules.

In Debian, first save the rules as we did before:

```
iptables-save > /etc/iptables.rules
```

Next, create the following file:

```
/etc/network/if-pre-up.d/iptables
```

Inside that file, place the following text:

```
#!/bin/sh
 /sbin/iptables-restore < /etc/iptables.rules
```

In CentOS, execute the following command:

```
# iptables-save > /etc/sysconfig/iptables
```

From this point onwards, your firewall rules should persist each time you reboot the server.

Protecting system services with fail2ban

A firewall is a great thing to have but it doesn't do much to protect services that are allowed. A firewall only goes as far as to allow or disallow access. But once access is allowed to a service, its security depends on its configuration and whether or not there are any security vulnerabilities. A service worth installing is **fail2ban**, which is a neat little tool that runs in the background and watches your logs for anything out of the ordinary, such as multiple failures to access a service. The most popular use of `fail2ban` is to protect SSH from those attempting to brute force it. In a lot of ways, `fail2ban` is the successor to **denyhosts**, which pretty much did the same thing. But `fail2ban` is able to protect more services than just SSH, another example being Apache.

When `fail2ban` sees that a source is attempting to access a service and is failing, it will set up a firewall rule on the fly to block that service from your server. To begin, install the `fail2ban` package on your server. In Debian systems, this is available in the default repositories. CentOS systems will find this package in the `epel` repository that we've set up in the past. Once installed, enable and start it with `systemctl` if it isn't already using the following command:

```
# systemctl start fail2ban
# systemctl enable fail2ban
```

Inside the `/etc/fail2ban` directory, you should see the main configuration file, `jail.conf`. It's a good idea to copy this configuration to a local copy, because if you edit `jail.conf`, it's always possible a package upgrade could overwrite it. The `fail2ban` service will read `jail.local` if it finds it and will not overwrite it if it were to be upgraded:

```
# cp /etc/fail2ban/jail.conf /etc/fail2ban/jail.local
```

Now that we have a local copy, we can now configure it to protect our services. Let's start with SSH. To do so, open `/etc/fail2ban/jail.local` in a text editor and look for the `[ssh]` section. On my system, this section looks like this:

```
[ssh]
enabled  = true
port     = 65256
filter   = sshd
action   = iptables[name=SSH, port=65256, protocol=tcp]
logpath  = /var/log/auth.log
maxretry = 6
```

As you can see, the configuration is fairly self-explanatory. The first line enables the SSH jail, it filters for traffic using `sshd`, and it looks in `/var/log/auth.log` for messages related to SSH. Although you've probably already noticed, we need to call out the SSH port in this file. If you stick with port 22, you can leave the relevant portions of the file as they are in your configuration. But if you changed your SSH port to something else, be sure to adjust accordingly. There are two places to place the port for SSH, the first on line three and the second on line five.

Now that we have our configuration in place, we can restart `fail2ban` in order to start securing SSH for us:

```
# systemctl restart fail2ban
```

Take a look at the configuration file for other services that we may want to enable. An example could be Apache for our web server or even NGINX if you have that set up. The default configuration file contains a great deal of examples you can use. To use one, simply change `enabled = false` to `enable = true` and then restart `fail2ban`.

Understanding SELinux

Security Enhanced Linux (**SELinux**) is a kernel module intended to increase security by enforcing the **Mandatory Access Control**. This concept gives you the control to ensure that users and applications are only able to access the things that they absolutely need to in order to complete the tasks they are designated to perform. While firewalls help protect the system against intrusion from the outside, SELinux helps prevent resources on the inside from doing things that they aren't supposed to be doing. This may sound vague, because it is how SELinux is used, and how you can benefit from it depends solely on how you implement it. Want to prevent a user from making a very private file world-readable? Sure, you can do that. Perhaps ensure Apache cannot access files outside of `/var/www`? You can do that too. Without SELinux, you would be relying solely on group and user permissions. SELinux helps you put more granular security restrictions in place by adding an additional layer of security to the mix.

SELinux is not exclusive to any one distribution, though you'll most commonly find it installed on Red Hat, Fedora, and CentOS systems. In a system such as Debian, you would need to install `selinux` if you wish to utilize it. Unfortunately, at the time of this writing, SELinux doesn't function properly in Debian due to the fact that a required package (`selinux-policy-default`) contained bugs that weren't fixed in time for Jessie's release, so this package was omitted in the official Debian 8.x "Jessie" repositories. However, the process for installing SELinux in Debian (should this package become available after publication) comes down to installing that package along with `selinux-basics`. After those packages are installed, you should be able to finish your SELinux installations by running the following commands and rebooting the system:

```
# selinux-activate
# systemctl enable selinux-basics.service
```

SELinux works with policies to determine whether or not an action is allowed. Policies are created with tools that exist in something known as the **SELinux userspace**, and the actual checking is done at the kernel layer. Each distribution that implements SELinux by default, will typically ship with a tested and supported set of policies, such that all the services you would reasonably expect to work will function as they should. Without a default set of policies, configuring SELinux by hand can be a real pain (if it even starts). As mentioned earlier, Debian's policies package is currently not a part of the main repository, so enabling SELinux in Debian may be chaotic at this time. In the case of CentOS though, everything you need to utilize SELinux will be working out of the box. In fact, unless you've disabled it, you're already using it!

There are three modes of operation for SELinux and those are **enforcing**, **permissive**, and **disabled**. By default, most installations I've seen lately are set to `enforcing`, but you can see which of these three yours is set to, by executing `sestatus`.

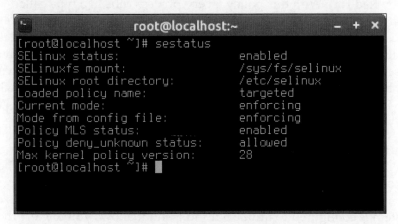

Output from sestatus on CentOS

With `enforcing`, SELinux is configured with its policy enabled and will act on anything that goes against that policy. If a violation occurs, SELinux will prevent the action and log it. In `permissive` mode, actions are not blocked but everything is still logged so you can audit your server yourself later. The `disabled` state is self-explanatory; in that mode, SELinux will not block or log anything while it is disabled. It's quite common that administrators will simply disable SELinux, assuming it to be too much of a burden if it gets in the way of a legitimate use case. But disabling SELinux isn't recommended unless you absolutely have to, as it's another layer of security that you could otherwise be benefiting from. At the very least, you may want to benefit from the `permissive` mode so that you would have more information available within your logs should something suspicious start to happen on your server.

To change the mode of operation for SELinux on the fly, use the `setenforce` command. For example, use `setenforce Enforcing` to change the mode to enforcing. Changes made via `setenforce` are not permanent. Once you reboot your machine, the mode will switch back to its default or whatever you have configured in its configuration file. The configuration file to change the mode permanently is the `/etc/sysconfig/selinux` file in Red Hat style distributions, or `/etc/selinux/config` in Debian. This file allows you to configure the two main settings to determine how SELinux is configured, the **mode** and the **type**. To change either permanently, update this file and restart the server. We already discussed the mode (it can be set to `enforcing`, `permissive`, or `disabled`), and the type is where we configure which policy we would like SELinux to use. This can be set to `targeted`, `minimum`, or multi-level security (`mls`).

In regards to updating the policy, `targeted` is the process that is in use by default on new installations (at least when it comes to Red Hat/CentOS), and it is fully supported by Red Hat. With this policy, every process runs in a type called `unconfined_t`, which is actually not restricted at all. Instead, processes will run under the Linux native **DAC** (short for **Discretionary Access Control**), which sandboxes them from other processes to help contain anything that may have been compromised. **MLS**, or **Multi-Level Security**, applies a sensitivity rating to objects, designated by `s0`, when it's enabled. (By executing `sestatus`, you can see whether or not MLS is enabled). We'll see some examples of context output shortly. With the minimum type, only processes we explicitly select will be safeguarded.

Every resource in a SELinux-enabled system contains a **label**, which is how SELinux identifies a resource and understands how to police it. You can see these labels (also known as contexts) yourself by using the `-Z` parameter with one or more commands, such as `ls`, `id`, or `ps`. This special parameter is available to these commands only when a system is configured to utilize SELinux, and it allows you to view the context as part of the normal output. For example, you can use the `-Z` parameter with the `ls` command on a SELinux system and you would see an output like this:

```
-rw-r--r--. root root unconfined_u:object_r:admin_home_t:s0 myfile
```

Normally, the output of the `ls` command would contain fields such as the modification date and size when viewing output of a command such as `ls`. But again, the `-Z` parameter is special. It implies that you would like to see the output of the command as it pertains to SELinux, rather than the output you would normally get. You can also try it with `id` (`id -Z`), and `ps` (`ps auxZ`) to have the output of those commands show you their SELinux context as well.

The label contains multiple fields. In the output from the `ls` command I pasted, we can see the fields `unconfined_u`, `object_r`, `admin_home_t`, and `s0`. To better understand this, look at the last few characters of each. The `_u` designates the user, `_r` designates the role, and `_t` represents the type. Therefore, we can see from the previous output that the file called `myfile` has a user context of `unconfined_u`; it's assigned the role of `object_r` and a type of `admin_home_t`. Let's look at another example. In the output of `ps auxZ` on my CentOS system, I see the following line for my SSH session:

```
unconfined_u:unconfined_r:unconfined_t:s0-s0:c0.c1023 jay 20575 0.0   0.0
135216 2080 ? S 10:40    0:00 sshd: jay@pts/0
```

Looking at the beginning of the line, we again have context for user, role, and type. In this case, each are named unconfined, but we can tell which is what by the last two characters.

The type is the most important part of the output, because this is how SELinux does its enforcing. Given the type, SELinux knows how to restrict (or not to restrict) the object. In the first example, we have `admin_home_t`, and we have `unconfined_t` in the second example. From this, we can gather that SELinux isn't enforcing anything with my SSH session (`unconfined_t`) but has a specific policy in place for my home directory, which is where the output of the file came from. Another context we have seen in the example output is the role, designated by a suffix `_r`. When applying a role, SELinux is able to group together various contexts and apply them to a user object with one call. This makes it easier to designate what users are able to do and how they're allowed to interact with other objects.

There are several commands that can be used to relabel the context information of an object. To begin, there's the `chcon` command. The `chcon` command is used with the `-t` parameter, which designates the type you would like to change the object to, followed by the name of the object:

```
# chcon -t admin_home_t myfile
```

Using `-R`, we tell the `chcon` command to make the changes recursively, which is great if you're changing the context of a directory. In addition, you can also use `-r` if you'd like to change the role instead of the type. If you make a mistake or you'd like to revert your changes, `restorecon` does exactly that. The `restorecon` command will revert an object to its default state, as defined in its policy. Another command for managing SELinux is `semanage`. With this command, we can make permanent changes to how objects are treated and labeled. It's important to note that changes via `chcon` might not always persist. While changes via `chcon` will likely survive a reboot, they persist if the filesystem gets relabeled. The `semanage` command allows us to make these changes more permanent. Using `semanage`, we can make changes to file contexts, user mappings, as well as user contexts.

First, an example of mapping user `jdoe` to the `sysadm_u` SELinux user:

```
# semanage login -a -s sysadm
```

Next, here's an example of using `fcontext` along with `semanage`, we can change what types file objects belong to:

```
# semanage fcontext -a -t  admin_home_t myfile
```

See the man pages for `semanage` for even more examples. SELinux is a large subject matter for which entire books have been written. A complete walkthrough of SELinux would take multiple chapters, but the information given here should serve as an adequate primer. When implemented properly, it can greatly enhance security on your servers.

Configuring Apache to utilize SSL

The *Chapter 7, Hosting HTTP Content via Apache* was all about Apache. There, we walked through how to get it running and configured in order to host a site on our network. But if we were to create a site that would potentially host personally identifiable information, we would want to make sure that we use proper security measures in order to protect that information. Using **SSL** certificates for our site allows it to be accessed over secure port 443, thus enhancing security. Utilizing SSL isn't the only measure we can make in order to increase security of our web server, but it's definitely a start.

There are two kinds of certificates we can use. We can create a self-signed certificate, or we can register a certificate with a **Certificate Authority (CA)**. The latter is preferred, though if you are only creating a site for internal use, it may be too much overhead. The difference is a self-signed certificate isn't trusted by any browser, since it wouldn't have come from a known CA. When you visit a site with such a certificate, it will complain that the certificate of the site isn't valid. This isn't necessarily true, because a self-signed certificate can certainly be valid; it's just that the browser has no way of knowing for sure. Getting a certificate registered with a CA would alleviate this, but at a cost. Registered certificates can be expensive, depending on the scope. The choice is yours.

 On Debian systems, make sure you enable SSL with the following command:
```
# a2enmod ssl
```

To begin, you would first choose a location on the filesystem of your webserver that will host the certificate files. There's no hard rule here, the only requirement is that Apache can access it (and preferably, no one else can!). Some good candidates include `/etc/apache2/ssl` in Debian and `/etc/httpd/ssl` in CentOS. I put mine in `/etc/certs`. Whichever path you choose, change into that directory and then we will continue.

If you've decided to create a self-signed certificate, you can do so with the following command:

```
openssl req -x509 -nodes -days 365 -newkey rsa:2048 -keyout server.key
-out server.crt
```

As your certificate gets generated, you will be asked for some information pertaining to your organization, contact information, and domain. Here's an example of the questions you'll be asked and some example answers:

- `Country name: US`
- `State or Province Name: Michigan`
- `Locality Name (City): White Lake`
- `Organization Name: My Company`
- `Organizational Unit Name: IT Dept`
- `Common Name (Fully Qualified Domain Name): myserver.mydomain.com`
- `Email Address: webmaster@mycompany.com`

This will create two files for you in your current working directory, `server.key` and `server.crt`. The filenames for those files is arbitrary, you can name them whatever you like. Now, we would need to make sure that our web server is able to find and use these files.

On Debian web servers, we can do this by editing `/etc/apache2/sites-available/default-ssl.conf`. In that file, there will be a section for us to add our directives that will enable our keys. Look for a section that has some comments regarding SSL. Within that section, add the following lines:

```
SSLCertificateFile /etc/certs/server.crt
SSLCertificateKeyFile /etc/certs/server.key
```

In CentOS, we would add the same lines to the `/etc/httpd/conf/httpd.conf` file, but with the `SSLEngine on` directive as well. This should go in it's own `VirtualHost` directive, similar to the example that follows. Just be sure to change the paths to match how your web server has been set up:

```
<VirtualHost *:443>

    SSLEngine On

    SSLCertificateFile /etc/certs/server.crt

    SSLCertificateKeyFile /etc/certs/server.key

    SSLCACertificateFile /etc/certs/ca.pem (Only include this line
    if the certificate is signed).

    DocumentRoot /var/www/

</VirtualHost>
```

Setting up a signed SSL certificate is similar, but the difference is in how you request it. The process entails creating a **Certificate Request (CSR)** that you will submit to your provider, which will in turn provide you with a signed certificate. The end result is the same—the files will end up in the same place. You'll just use the files given to you by your provider after submitting the CSR. Let's begin by creating a CSR, which we will use the `openssl` command to generate for us:

```
openssl req -new -newkey rsa:2048 -nodes -keyout server.key -out server.
csr
```

You'll be asked the same question as before, but notice that we're telling `openssl` to give us a `.csr`, so we will have a `server.csr` file in our working directory we will use to request a key from our CA. After you receive the files from your certificate provider, you would just update Apache as we have done earlier.

Deploying security updates

While it may seem like common sense to those of you more seasoned in security, updates for your distribution are released for a reason. In some cases, updates serve only to add new features or update software to the latest version. But in the case of Enterprise distributions such as CentOS and Debian, these are even more important.

This is one of the ways consumer-based distributions and Enterprise distributions differ. Distributions such as Ubuntu's non-LTS releases, Linux Mint, and Fedora receive more bleeding-edge packages than Enterprise distributions such as CentOS, Debian, and Red Hat. This is because the end user typically wants the latest versions of their web browser, e-mail client, word processor, or games. This doesn't matter much when it comes to the Enterprise. In the Enterprise, security updates are critical. While consumer-oriented distributions surely keep up to date with security patches on almost an equal level in most cases, these are intermixed with feature updates that may impair stability more than help it.

In the case of Debian, both styles are actually offered. The main distribution, which is known as **Debian stable**, receives little more than security patches. Even the default web browser (Iceweasel) isn't updated as often as Firefox would be on other platforms. The idea here is that change represents potential breakage. Quite a bit of work goes into ensuring that the packages you get in stable are tried and true, rather than the latest and greatest. This concept is similar to CentOS as well, though its packages generally tend to be older than those in Debian. To give you an idea of this, at the time of my writing this chapter, the latest Linux kernel is 4.1. Debian Jessie (the latest "Stable") includes kernel 3.16, while CentOS 7 is even older at 3.10. Not that there's nothing wrong with the kernel being old, I just mentioned it to give you an example. Both Red Hat and Debian have more bleeding-edge distributions available. **Fedora** is sponsored by Red Hat and includes more up to date packages. It's geared toward users who prefer to have the latest software. **Debian testing** also includes more up to date packages, though it's not nearly as stable as Fedora, facing package breakages from time to time. Debian testing is targeted toward those who would like to test the next release of Debian, as Debian testing eventually becomes the new Debian stable as it matures.

For security purposes, installing the latest security updates is critical. It's true that Linux is more secure and stable than many other platforms, but regardless of how secure the operating system is, at the end of the day, it's only as secure as how it's managed. An installation of a Linux distribution that's behind in updates is a sitting duck in the case of an exploitable vulnerability being discovered.

Given the existence of end-user and Enterprise distributions, managing their security updates can be a challenge. If your organization uses Linux on both servers as well as end-user machines, you may very well employ both types of distributions. This is because while CentOS is secure and stable, you're unlikely to be successful deploying it to end-user machines. Since the CentOS kernel is a bit older, it won't support all the new hardware that's available for end-user workstations today. In addition, there aren't as many customizations in place to make it reasonable for desktop or laptop use. While it can be done (and many people do), installing CentOS on an end-user device is typically an exercise in frustration. For end-user machines, you might opt for Ubuntu, Linux Mint, or Fedora instead. But with those, you would need to spend more time focusing on which updates are for security and which updates are for new features in applications. Depending on the nature of the update, you may choose to roll it out differently.

Ideally, in a perfect server room, all updates for servers would be installed immediately upon their release, there would never be any issues and everything would always go smooth. But in reality, there are challenges in keeping security updates current. Perhaps a regression may be present that stops an important application from running. Alternatively, perhaps an error in packaging actually breaks the RPM database (which is an extremely frustrating experience!), so while updates are important, some exercise in caution is needed as well.

The best policy, or at least one I've found that works well for me, is creating testing servers that can be used to test changes before you roll them out into production. In the case of virtual machine servers, you can even clone production servers and test updates or other changes on them to see how they will react if they were rolled out into production. Then, you can be reasonably confident that new updates won't break production servers. To be fair, these types of situations rarely happen. But given the flexibility of Linux and the fact that Linux servers are easy to clone, there's no reason not to do testing.

In CentOS systems, you can use the `yum update` command to update all the packages on your server. You can use `yum update` along with the name of a package to update just that package. In Debian systems, you can use `apt-get update` to refresh your sources, and then you can use `apt-get install` with a package name to update a package. To update everything, you would update your sources and then run `apt-get dist-upgrade`.

In real-world installations, you would probably not update all available packages on your server. Instead, one method is to update packages as needed. This requires a great deal of research on the part of the administrator, in order to pay attention to current security trends and then pick the security updates that impact services that are currently being used in production. For Debian and Red Hat based systems, there are two handy web sites pertaining to **Common Vulnerabilities and Exposures (CVE)** that you should have bookmarked.

For Red Hat use the following URL:

```
https://access.redhat.com/security/cve/
```

For Debian use the following URL:

```
https://security-tracker.debian.org/tracker
```

Both sites allow you to view individual CVE reports, which will inform you about vulnerable packages and whether or not they were patched. In some cases, a CVE may not even be exploitable in your particular distribution, in which case you wouldn't need to do anything. But by following these reports, you can make an informed decision regarding what potential vulnerabilities may affect your organization. This will allow you to create a plan to roll out the necessary patches onto your servers.

Summary

Security is a very complex subject. So complex that no one person can become an all-knowing expert, as even the top people in the industry are continually learning. Likewise, it's statistically impossible to create a bulletproof server that cannot be compromised. But as a network administrator, you have a role in doing the best you can to keep your nodes as secure as you're able to. Security is often reactionary, which requires you to be on your toes. In this chapter, we took a look at some of the ways you can help safeguard your network from risks. We covered concepts such as securing SSH, limiting your attack surface, securing Apache with SSL, fail2ban, and deploying security updates.

In the next chapter, we'll look into things you can do to troubleshoot issues when things go wrong.

10
Troubleshooting Network Issues

No network is perfect. Regardless of how well we plan and implement our infrastructure, problems can and will happen. The most important skill you will need in order to be successful as a network administrator is your ability to troubleshoot issues. When problems occur, your ability to think rationally and narrow down the issue by the process of elimination will carry you through. While it can certainly be stressful when things go haywire, network administrators enjoy the job security. In this chapter, we'll work through troubleshooting some common issues that may come up in Linux networks. In the final chapter of our journey, we will cover:

- Tracing routing issues
- Troubleshooting DHCP issues
- Troubleshooting DNS issues
- Displaying connection statistics with netstat
- Scanning your network with nmap and Zenmap
- Installing missing firmware on Debian systems
- Troubleshooting issues with Network Manager

Tracing routing issues

The entire purpose of a network is to get data from point A to point B. If for some reason we aren't able to get data where we need it, it can sometimes be a pain to pinpoint exactly where the issue manifests itself. But through the process of elimination, pinpointing where routing issues manifest themselves shouldn't be too difficult.

Whenever I experience issues with a node being unable to communicate to a specific server or network, I like to work my way from their workstation back to the switch stack until I find the issue. To start, I check the obvious things, such as what the IP address is (or if the machine even has one) and then I also check the routing table. If the problem is intermittent, you would likely want to test the cable. For some reason, I've come across quite a few instances where a problem resulted from a bad cable. I don't know why, but it seems that other administrators I know, don't have this luck. But it never hurts to run a cable tester on the network cable to check, just in case.

Assuming that you've already tried the easy stuff, next you would want to determine whether or not you can reach the default gateway. If you know the IP address of your local default gateway, simply ping it to see if you can reach it, and note the result. Does your attempt time out, or does it get through just fine? If you don't know the IP address of your gateway, run `route -n` in your terminal emulator to find out. If you can reach your default gateway by IP, try to reach it by hostname as well as the IP address of the target node you were trying to connect to in the first place. If you're able to reach resources by IP and not their hostname, this would most likely be a DNS issue. We'll talk about troubleshooting DNS later in this chapter. But for now, determining whether or not you can reach your DNS server and/or gateway would be good first steps. If you can't, you may have a resource that is down, and a line of angry co-workers waiting for you back at your desk.

If the problem is intermittent, we can start our troubleshooting by interrogating the local machine. The `ip address show` command will give us some details about the IP address of the local machine. We can actually shorten this command by abbreviating it to `ip addr show`, or if you really don't like typing, you can simplify it down further to just `ip a`. The following shows the output of `ip addr show` from an example system:

Investigating the IP address on a local machine

At this point in the book, there shouldn't be anything too surprising about the output of ip a. However, the output from my machine may look unique to what you may see in the wild, so it's worth going over. First, you can see that the Debian machine I used for testing has five network interfaces on it. The first is the local loopback adapter, lo; and the second is eth0. Since this machine is currently using Wi-Fi, it's no surprise that eth0 doesn't have an IP address. The next interface, wlan0, has an IP address of 192.168.1.106. The last two interfaces are unique; they exist as bridges for Docker and KVM virtualization to be able to perform their own networking. Even though Docker and KVM aren't within the scope of this book, I bring up the fact that they do their own networking because when one of these services is installed, you may see your Linux desktop environment report that you are connected to a network, even when technically you aren't. On my machine, if I disconnect wlan0, it would still show that I'm connected. This is because the GUI version of Network Manager that most graphical distributions ship with, does a terrible job of reporting an accurate status in regards to your connectivity, and this could confuse the situation.

Now that you've determined that the machine has an IP address, another step you can take is to use the traceroute command. Those of you that have used Windows, may be familiar with this concept already, as the Windows utility tracert works pretty much the same way. The traceroute utility is not always installed by default when you set up a Linux distribution, so you may need to install the traceroute package. From here, you should be able to use traceroute along with the hostname or IP of a resource, to see where the process drops out. You can also use traceroute against the URL of a website, if the issue is that your workstation isn't able to access the public Internet. In the following screenshot, a traceroute against google.com is shown:

```
14:00:17 [crusader:~]$ traceroute www.google.com
traceroute to www.google.com (192.122.185.38), 30 hops max, 60 byte packets
 1  m0n0wall.local (192.168.1.1)  2.357 ms  2.346 ms  2.351 ms
 2  172.21.0.1 (172.21.0.1)  2.346 ms  2.342 ms  3.502 ms
 3  wate.waterford.lib.mi.us (198.111.163.193)  3.789 ms  4.203 ms  4.670 ms
 4  198.111.175.120 (198.111.175.120)  8.650 ms  10.399 ms  10.391 ms
 5  198.108.22.150 (198.108.22.150)  10.357 ms  10.371 ms  10.374 ms
 6  * * *
 7  * * *
 8  * * *
 9  * * *
10  * * *
11  * * *
12  * * *
13  * * *
14  * * *
15  * * *
16  * * *
17  * * *
18  * * *
19  * * *
20  * * *
```

Running traceroute to troubleshoot accessing the public Internet

In the previous screenshot, I ran a `traceroute` to `www.google.com`. From the output, we can tell several things right away. First, we can see that the first `hop` our command tries to reach is a device called `m0n0wall.local` at an IP address of `192.168.1.1`. If I run `route -n`, I see that this is the default gateway of the network I'm currently using. The `m0n0wall` is a firewall distribution of FreeBSD, which is in use on this network. I discovered this when I ran the command. Next, we can see that we made it through the `m0n0wall` device to another private network of `172.21.0.1` and then `198.111.175.120`, but output stops when my request reaches `198.108.22.150`. After that, we just see asterisks, but we're not going beyond that. In a hypothetical example of my machine not being able to access the Internet, I may want to investigate the device at `198.108.22.150` and find out why it's not letting my traffic through. However, in my case this device is dropping ICMP packets, which is causing the `traceroute` command itself to fail.

One of the things you would definitely want to check when troubleshooting routing issues is your routing table. We covered routing in *Chapter 8, Understanding Advanced Networking Concepts,* and the routing table as well as adding routes was covered. But as a refresher, you can use `route -n` to print the routing table onto your shell. If the machine you're troubleshooting doesn't have a route to the network it needs to access, then the root-cause is easily apparent. You would then need to add a default gateway in order to allow the machine to reach that network.

Viewing the local routing table

Troubleshooting DHCP issues

If for some reason you have a machine that refuses to obtain an IP address, then this section is for you. DHCP issues aren't incredibly common, and thankfully aren't too hard to troubleshoot.

One of the most common issues I've seen with DHCP servers is the date and time of either the server or the client being wrong. In the Linux world, NTP is crucial and should always be working. In the case of DHCP, it only waits so long before the service times out a request for an IP address. If the clock is off by an hour and the incoming request is timestamped an hour ago, that confuses the server and the client will not receive an address. Always ensure that NTP is working on all your clients and servers. DHCP isn't the only service that would suffer with incorrect time on either end. Lot's of strange things can happen in this situation.

A reason for failure is the lack of available IP addresses. This may sound obvious, but you'd be surprised how often this happens. Even a /24 network of 254 available IP addresses can become saturated quickly these days, as everything from mobile devices to refrigerators (yes, refrigerators) want to claim an IP address these days. It's not uncommon for the average person to use three IP addresses without even noticing. A problem such as this can become increasingly annoying if you set your DHCP lease time to something greater than a day. In most cases, a lease time of 24 hours is adequate for most networks. Devices that need access will renew their lease when the time comes, while temporary devices won't attempt to renew the IP they were issued, which will cause it return to the pool.

I wish that I had a magic command you could run that would give you a printout of just how many IP addresses you have available. Unfortunately, I've never been able to find one, aside from possibly constructing a cumbersome Bash or Python script. The best thing for you to do while experiencing any issues with DHCP is to watch the log file and have the client try to connect again.

The output of a working DHCP server

In Debian, you can investigate by running `cat /var/log/syslog |grep dhcp` for messages relating to your DHCP server. On CentOS, you can use `journalctl -u dhcpd` to view these messages. What's better is to follow these logs in real time as the client tries to connect, so you can see the output as it happens. To do this, use `tail -f /var/log/syslog` in Debian or `journalctl -f -u dhcpd` in CentOS. Errors from your DHCP server should be fairly easy to follow, as the server is usually specific regarding what it is doing. You'll likely see it offer addresses to the client, or complain that there aren't enough IP addresses available. If you see the server offer an IP address to the client but the client never seems to finish the connection, then definitely check your NTP server on the client.

Troubleshooting DNS issues

DNS issues are typically rare, except in the case of an invalid configuration. In most cases, any troubleshooting you do would be done on your local DNS servers, as public DNS servers on the Internet are outside of your control. In the case of an external DNS server failing, such as that from your ISP, your only recourse might be to use a different DNS provider, such as utilizing Google's public DNS addresses of `8.8.8.8` and `8.8.4.4`. But in the case of your local DNS server failing, you have more control.

As always, you would start troubleshooting DNS issues by checking whether or not you can reach the DNS server. First, check `/etc/resolv.conf` to see which DNS server your machine is using. Is it the correct server? If not, correct this in your network scripts and restart networking. If it is the correct server, can you reach it? Try a simple ping, and as long as the server is configured to respond to ICMP echo requests, you should see a response. If you can reach the server, SSH into it and check its logs. Perhaps the daemon (`bind` in Debian, and `named` in CentOS) isn't running.

Moving beyond the simple things, there is a specific utility we can use to help troubleshoot bind-specific issues, and that utility is `nslookup`. Use the `nslookup` command along with the name of the resource you're trying to find, such as a hostname or the URL of a website.

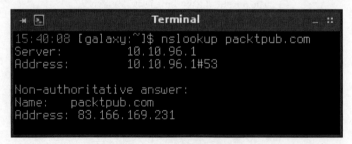

The output of a working DHCP server

The output of `nslookup` tells us a few useful things we can use to troubleshoot further. First, it will give us the IP address of the server that answered our request. In my case, `10.10.96.1` answered via port 53. Then, I can see the result of my query for `packtpub.com`, which gave me an external IP address of `83.166.169.231`. So far, so good. If your DNS server is reachable, the daemon is running and your local workstation is configured to point to it, a very common gotcha is the serial number in your domain record. If you've added a resource to your DNS server but forgot to increment the serial number, that can cause a lookup to fail even though you did add the configuration for that host. This may seem like common knowledge, but you'd be surprised how easy it is to forget.

In the event that `nslookup` doesn't return a record, check that you have actually added that record to the server. If it does respond with a record, then everything should be running smoothly as long as you have configured your local workstation to point to the correct server.

Displaying connection statistics with netstat

The `netstat` command is a useful utility to allow you to view some statistics regarding your current connection. We touched on it a bit in the last chapter. This command allows you to show useful networking information, such as showing you services that are listening for connections on your network card, and printing your routing table, among other things.

In the last chapter, I gave the example of `netstat -tulpn` to allow you to view currently connected and listening services. This command shows everything that's listening, as well as the port that it's listening on. Breaking this command down, we passed along some parameters. The first, `-t`, identifies that we would like to view information pertaining to TCP, `-u` represents UDP, `-l` requests listening sockets, `-p` attempts to show the name of the program, and `-n` also shows numeric values. Putting it all together, we get `netstat -tulpn`. In the industry, this is the most common usage of `netstat` that I've seen.

Other uses of `netstat` include showing your routing table (`netstat -r`), which gives you similar output as `route -n`. To view connection statistics, use `netstat -s`. Finally, you can also view a list of network interfaces on your system with `netstat -i`. For the most part though, this command is something you would use most often to print networking information to your terminal, that you would use for further analysis when trying to troubleshoot an issue or lock down a node.

Scanning your network with Nmap and Zenmap

The nmap utility is a network scanner that can give you a great deal of information regarding network resources. All you should have to do is install the nmap package. Once you have this utility in your arsenal, you can do some pretty neat things on your network. In most cases, nmap is used to interrogate systems and extract information. While nmap itself doesn't solve any actual problems, it helps you discover information you can use in order to build an understanding of what's happening on your network at any given time.

It also needs to be used with great care, as nmap is capable of disclosing information regarding a network that may be private, and unless you have express permission to use it, you should exercise discretion. Since nmap can be used for purposes of hacking, it's definitely a red flag to a network administrator (if that person isn't you) if they see this type of activity on the network. But in real-world scenarios, nmap can really be a life saver. In my experience, I found it quite useful in tracking down and interrogating machines that come up as hosting malware on the network, which strangely, always seems to be those that run Windows (go figure). If a vulnerability report only shows the IP address of an infected machine, it can be hard to track down whose machine it is. But with nmap, I can find out things such as which OS is running on that host, the hostname of the machine (which may even include the name of the user), and possibly the MAC address of that machine's network card.

There are many uses of nmap, but I'll start with some of my favorites. First, as I just mentioned, you can use nmap to try to determine which operating system a particular host is using. This will allow you to fine-tune further commands to specifically target the machine, as how you investigate nodes differs based on the OS they are running. To use nmap to attempt to find this information, use it with the -O parameter and the IP address of a host. Basically, execute the following command:

```
nmap -O 10.10.98.124
```

Another useful use case for nmap is scanning an entire subnet to determine which hosts are connected. If you're attempting to see which IP addresses are free, this is one way to do it (assuming no nodes have any firewalls that are blocking the scan):

```
nmap -sP 10.10.96.0/22
```

With the previous example, we can also use the --exclude option if we prefer a particular IP address not be scanned or included:

```
nmap -sP 10.10.96.0/22 --exclude 10.10.98.223
```

If a machine is behind a firewall, we can attempt to scan it anyway:

`nmap -PN 10.10.98.104`

As if we didn't already have enough utilities that can show us routing and interface information of our local machine, `nmap` can do that as well:

`nmap --iflist`

In addition to using `nmap` commands in a terminal, there is also **Zenmap**, which is more or less a GUI equivalent. Using it, we can do pretty much the same things as `nmap`, but in addition it allows you to save your scans, open previously saved scans, compare results between two saved scans, and even save command profiles for later use. If you find yourself using `nmap` on a usual basis, it may be useful for you to benefit from the added features of Zenmap.

Zenmap with a scan of a local network

One easy way to start testing Zenmap is to try it with any of the examples I've given in this chapter. You should be able to paste any of those commands in the third textbox at the top of the window, which reads **Command**. From here, you can click **Scan** to begin the scan. Once it's finished, you can save the results by clicking **Scan** and then **Save Scan**. As mentioned earlier, you can also compare scans to each other. This can be useful if you're curious which new devices were added to your network. You can run a scan of a subnet (using the `nmap -sP 10.10.98.0/24` example I gave earlier) on one day, and then run the scan again the next day. If you saved the results each time, you can compare them and then determine immediately if a new device was added to your network. This is a good practice to perform periodically anyway (especially if you're the person who is designated to approve new devices) to determine if there are any rogue or unauthorized devices present.

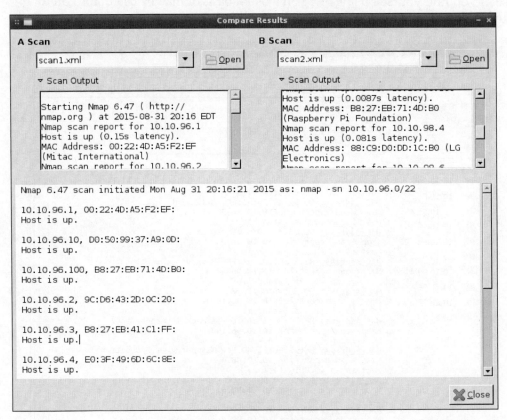

Comparing network scans in Zenmap

Deciding between using nmap and Zenmap is just a matter of preference. The features of Zenmap are quite nice, but the only thing it provides is ease of use. In nmap, for example, you can simply pipe the results into a text file yourself, and then you can run the diff command against the results of two output files without using a GUI application to perform this task.

```
nmap -sP 10.10.98.0/24 > scan1.txt
nmap -sP 10.10.98.0/24 > scan2.txt
diff scan1.txt scan2.txt
```

On a typical network administrator's desktop, you'd be using either a Linux or Windows installation with a graphical user interface; in this case, Zenmap may be a good fit to add to your tool set.

Installing missing firmware on Debian systems

Many distributions of Linux prefer to include only free software and drivers by default, and Debian falls into that category. The reason for this can be due to moral decisions or licensing restrictions, but the result may be that a specific network card or hardware device ceases to function out of the box. Commonly, this is very typical with wireless cards. One example of this is Intel wireless cards. While these typically work without any tinkering needed when it comes to end-user distributions (Ubuntu, Linux Mint, and so on), Enterprise distributions such as Debian often don't include these and force you to jump through additional hoops. The reason for this is because the software required for these cards to function isn't open-source, so the decision was made to not include it in the default repositories. Thankfully, this usually isn't too difficult to rectify providing you know the steps.

On Debian systems, there is a non-free parameter that can be added to your APT sources that tells the distribution that you would like such packages included when you search for and install software. But before you do this, make sure that you actually do need additional firmware. One dead giveaway is if Debian complains about missing firmware while booting. Without rebooting, you may see errors in the logs complaining about a lack of firmware for a hardware device. To view any output on your system that may be complaining about missing firmware, try the following command:

```
dmesg |grep firmware
```

To add the non-free component of your APT sources in Debian, first make a backup of your original sources.list file:

```
# cp /etc/apt/sources.list /etc/apt/sources.list.bak
```

Then, add the non-free parameter to the main repository. On my Debian Jessie system, the line looks like this:

```
deb http://ftp.us.debian.org/debian/ jessie main contrib non-free
```

Once that's done, refresh your sources with the following command:

```
# apt-get update
```

From this point forward, the non-free binary packages should be available to you. You can confirm this by searching for and listing available firmware packages on your system. The output should contain several nonfree packages. To perform this search, try the following command:

```
aptitude search firmware
```

For example, if firmware-linux-nonfree shows up in your list of available packages, then you've performed these steps correctly.

Unfortunately, detailing a full list of hardware compatibility for Debian and the required firmware for each would be beyond the scope of this book. However, the logs should give you a general idea of what firmware is missing, allowing you to search your package database for specific packages. Typically, copying a line of output from dmesg regarding failure to load firmware and doing a Google search will take you right to what package is needed to resolve the situation. In my case, the most commonly needed firmware package I run into is firmware-iwlwifi. Additionally, firmware-atheros and firmware-b43-installer are also common.

Troubleshooting issues with Network Manager

Network Manager is a tool that is used to manage network connections in Linux. It consists of a daemon that runs in the background, as well as an optional graphical utility that most desktop distributions include to show you your connection status at any given time. Network Manager is not required by any means, but it simplifies the management of your network interfaces and their configuration. In a lot of real-world networks, Network Manager is typically disabled and static IP addresses are used instead. As I've mentioned probably a hundred times so far, I always prefer static leases over static IPs. With a static IP, you do not have the central point of management, and would need to track down and change a server's IP address manually. It is for this reason that I recommend you to keep Network Manager running. It will watch for connections, activate your DHCP client, and then receive an IP address lease from your DHCP server. If you've set up a static lease (reservation) then you're already all set to go as soon as Network Manager initiates your connection.

In the case of networking issues that you've troubleshooted to be an issue local to Network Manager itself, there are several things you can do in order to pinpoint the problem.

First, on CentOS systems, ensure that your network interface is configured to come up on boot. For some reason I cannot understand, CentOS actually defaults to turning your network interface off during installation. Unless you turn it on while running the installer, it will also be disabled by default after you boot as well. If the interface is not enabled, then Network Manager wouldn't be able to manage it. Correcting this is simply a matter of editing the init script for the interface. You'll find init scripts for your network interface cards in CentOS at the following location: `/etc/sysconfig/network-scripts`. On my system, I find the `init` script for my interface card at `/etc/sysconfig/network-scripts/ifcfg-enp0s3`, though the name of your interface will of course differ.

Look at the last line, where you should see `ONBOOT="yes"`. If you don't see that, modify that line and then restart networking:

```
# systemctl restart network
```

Second, on Debian and CentOS systems, check to make sure that Network Manager is running. This is one of those rare occasions where the command to do something is the same in both distributions. With the following command, we can check the status of the NetworkManager daemon:

```
# systemctl status NetworkManager
```

While troubleshooting issues, `systemctl` can be very useful as it not only tells you whether or not the service is started, it also gives you a handful of lines from the logs that may be able to point you in the right direction if you're experiencing an issue.

To peruse Network Manager logs in their entirety, you can use `journalctl`:

```
journalctl -u NetworkManager
```

You can also use the `-f` flag to follow the log, so you'll see new entries as they happen. This is especially useful while troubleshooting why a machine isn't able to connect to a wireless network. Errors will appear as the user attempts to connect. The following example shows how to follow the output of NetworkManager output that gets written to the journal.

```
journalctl -f -u NetworkManager
```

As with most systemd units, we can restart Network Manager with one simple command:

```
# systemctl restart NetworkManager
```

The previous command may seem like a no-brainer, but for some reason, I've had to restart Network Manager more times than I would like. This is especially true while switching a machine from one network to another, or resuming from suspend (though those issues primarily only come up on end-user workstations).

For the most part, issues with Network Manager are rare and troubleshooting it is relatively straightforward. Using systemd's `journalctl`, we can watch Network Manager's output and determine the root cause. In most cases, the issue will come down to a misconfigured network card.

Summary

In this chapter, we covered some ways of troubleshooting issues that may come up on our Linux-based networks. While it's impossible to detail every possible thing that can go wrong, this chapter serves as a starting point for common issues that you might face. We started off by looking at routing issues as well as DHCP and DNS troubleshooting. In addition, we looked at useful troubleshooting tools such as `nmap`, as well as an overview of installing missing firmware that may be required to set up network cards in Debian. We closed off with information pertaining to troubleshooting Network Manager.

With this, this book comes to a close. Thank you for taking this journey through the world of Linux network administration with me. I hope that book has resonated with you and helped you get a better understanding. Working with Linux has been the single best career choice I have made, and I would like to thank all of my readers and colleagues for making it such a wonderful experience. To all of you, I wish for you, success, and it is my hope that your journey through Linux be as beneficial to you as it has been for me.

Index

A

ACK (acknowledge) packet 46
Apache
  about 159
  configuring 162-165
  configuring, for utilizing SSL 212-214
  installing 159-162
attack surface
  limiting 195-198
available memory
  checking 117-119

B

BIND (Berkeley Internet
    Name Domain) 145
broadcast address 175
broadcast domain 138

C

Caja 104
Canonical Name (CNAME) 150
CentOS 7
  acquiring 36-44
  installing 36-44
  URL 36
CentOS wiki
  URL 36
Certificate Authority (CA) 212
Certificate Request (CSR) 214
chains 203
CIDR notation
  defining 177-180
Cinnamon 31

classful 174
classless 174
Classless Inter-Domain Routing (CIDR)
    notation 93
Common Vulnerabilities and
    Exposures (CVE) 217
configuration file 58
connections
  managing, with Network Manager 64-68
connection statistics
  displaying, with netstat 225
CVE, Debian
  URL 217
CVE, Red Hat
  URL 217

D

Debian 8
  installing 10-35
  URL 10
Debian stable 215
Debian systems
  missing firmware, installing on 229, 230
Debian testing 215
deb package 2
default gateway 186
denyhosts 206
desktop environment 31
DHCP issues
  troubleshooting 222, 223
DHCP reservation 60
DHCP server
  about 54
  configuring 140-144
  installing 140-144

disabled 209
Discretionary Access Control (DAC) 210
disk cache 117
distributions
  defining 2
  reference 2
DNS issues
  troubleshooting 224, 225
DNS server
  about 3
  configuring 144-151
  installing 144-151
  URL 147
document root 163
Dolphin 104
Dolphin file manager 31
Domain Name System (DNS) 52, 144
dynamic DNS 52
Dynamic Host Configuration
      Protocol (DHCP) 52, 137

E

enforcing 209
error correction 46
Extended Stochastic Fair
      Queuing (ESFQ) 182
Extension Pack
  downloading 6-10
  installing 6-10
  URL 7
Extra Packages for Enterprise
      Linux (EPEL) 108

F

fail2ban
  about 206
  system services, protecting with 206, 207
Fedora 2, 215
file server
  considerations 87, 88
fstab
  used, for automatically mounting network
      shares 106, 107

G

GID (Group ID) 96
GNOME 31
GNOME System Monitor 119
GRUB (Grand Unified Bootloader) 33

H

Hierarchical Token Bucket (HTB) 184

I

idmapd 89
internal NTP server
  setting up 152-156
Internet Information Services (IIS) 159
Internet Service Provider (ISP) 145, 189
I/O wait 122
IP address layout
  planning 137-140
IP (Internet Protocol) 47
iproute2 suites 53-57
iptables 203
iptables firewall
  configuring 203-206
ISO image file, Debian 8
  acquiring 10-35

J

journald 129

K

KDE 31
KSysGuard 119
KVM 4

L

label 210
Linux downloads
  URL 4
Linux hostname resolution 51-53
Linux Mint 2

load average
  about 114
  defining 114-116
logging 128, 129
logrotate
  log size, maintaining with 129-131
log size
  maintaining, with logrotate 129-131
LXDEL 31

M

MAC address 54
Mail Transfer Agent (MTA) 196
Mandatory Access Control 208
MATE 31
mode 210
modules
  adding 166-169
  using 166
Mosh (mobile shell)
  about 84
  utilizing 84
mount command 105
Multi-Level Security (MLS) 210

N

nano 58
Nautilus 104
netinst 10
netstat
  connection statistics, displaying with 225
netstat command 225
net-tools 53-57
network
  dividing, into subnets 173-177
  scanning, with Nmap 226-229
  scanning, with Zenmap 226-229
Network Address
    Translation (NAT) 173, 189
network device
  naming 48-51
networked filesystems
  creating, with SSHFS 108
Network File System (NFS) 87

network hosts
  connecting, via openssh-client 72, 73
network identifier 175
network interfaces
  managing manually 57-63
Network Lock Manager (NLM) 89
network management 1, 2
Network Manager
  about 59, 230
  connections, managing with 64-68
  issues, troubleshooting with 230, 231
network shares
  mounting 104, 105
  mounting, via fstab 106, 107
  mounting, via systemd 106, 107
Network Time Protocol (NTP) 21, 137, 152
NFS 76, 97
NFS server
  setting up 89-97
NFS v3
  versus NFS v4 89
Nmap
  network, scanning with 226-229
NTP servers
  URL 155

O

OpenSSH
  about 199
  config file 74, 75
  configuring 71, 72
  installing 71, 72
  securing 199-202
  using 70
openssh-client
  network hosts, connecting via 72, 73

P

package manager 4
Pcmanfm 104
permissive 209
persist timer 47
physical machines
  versus virtual machines 3

Preboot Execution Environment (PXE) 6
processes
  inspecting 112-114
  managing 112-114
process identifier (PID) 112
protocol suite 46
public key authentication 80
public keys
  generating 80-82

Q

Quality of Service (QoS)
  about 173, 181
  implementing 181-185
queuing discipline (qdisc) 182

R

receive window 47
Red Hat Enterprise Linux (RHEL) 2, 5
redundant DHCP server
  creating 190-193
redundant DNS server
  creating 190-193
reservation 143
retransmission timer 46
root account 17
routing 186
routing issues
  tracing 219-222
routing table 186
rpm package 2

S

Samba 76, 87, 97, 98
Samba server
  setting up 98-103
scp (secure copy) command 75
scp utility
  defining 75, 76
  files, transferring to another node 76-78
  utilizing 75, 76
Secure Shell. *See* SSH
Security Enhanced Linux. *See* SELinux
security updates
  deploying 214-217

SELinux
  defining 208-211
SELinux userspace 209
Services for NFS 88
shell-based resource monitors
  using 119-125
ShieldsUP
  about 197
  URL 197
SIGTERM 113
sliding window 47
SMB protocol 88
SSH
  about 69
  traffic, tunneling via 78-80
SSH connections
  maintaining 82-84
sshd service 71
SSHFS
  about 87, 108
  networked filesystems, creating 108
SSH tunnel 78
SSL
  utilizing, via Apache configuration 212-214
SSL certificates 212
Start of Authority (SOA) 149
stateful 89
stateless 89
static lease 60
Stochastic Fair Queuing (SFQ) 182
stratum 154
subnet masks
  defining, for classes A to C 174
subnets
  network, dividing into 173-176
SUSE Enterprise Linux 2
SYN/ACK (synchronize
    acknowledgment) 46
SYN (synchronize) 46
systemd
  about 1
  used, for automatically mounting network
    shares 106-108
systemd init system
  defining 132-134
systemd journal
  defining 135

system services
protecting, with fail2ban 206, 207

T

TCP/IP protocol 1
TCP/IP protocol suite 46, 47
TCP/IP traffic
routing 186-189
three-way handshake 46
Time To Live (TTL) 149
Token Bucket Filter (TBF) 182
traceroute
defining 222
Transmission Control Protocol (TCP) 46
type 210

U

Ubuntu 2
Ubuntu Server 2
UDP (User Datagram Protocol) 47
UID (User ID) 96
Universally Unique Identifier (UUID) 106
used storage
scanning 126, 127

V

vim 58
VirtualBox
about 4
acquiring 4, 5

configuring 4
setting up 4
URL 4
virtual hosts
about 169
setting up 169-171
virtualization 3
virtual machines
about 2
versus physical machines 3
VM 3
VMware 4
VoIP (Voice over IP) 181

X

Xen 4
Xfce 31

Z

Zenmap
network, scanning with 226-229

Thank you for buying
Mastering Linux Network Administration

About Packt Publishing

Packt, pronounced 'packed', published its first book, *Mastering phpMyAdmin for Effective MySQL Management*, in April 2004, and subsequently continued to specialize in publishing highly focused books on specific technologies and solutions.

Our books and publications share the experiences of your fellow IT professionals in adapting and customizing today's systems, applications, and frameworks. Our solution-based books give you the knowledge and power to customize the software and technologies you're using to get the job done. Packt books are more specific and less general than the IT books you have seen in the past. Our unique business model allows us to bring you more focused information, giving you more of what you need to know, and less of what you don't.

Packt is a modern yet unique publishing company that focuses on producing quality, cutting-edge books for communities of developers, administrators, and newbies alike. For more information, please visit our website at www.packtpub.com.

About Packt Open Source

In 2010, Packt launched two new brands, Packt Open Source and Packt Enterprise, in order to continue its focus on specialization. This book is part of the Packt Open Source brand, home to books published on software built around open source licenses, and offering information to anybody from advanced developers to budding web designers. The Open Source brand also runs Packt's Open Source Royalty Scheme, by which Packt gives a royalty to each open source project about whose software a book is sold.

Writing for Packt

We welcome all inquiries from people who are interested in authoring. Book proposals should be sent to author@packtpub.com. If your book idea is still at an early stage and you would like to discuss it first before writing a formal book proposal, then please contact us; one of our commissioning editors will get in touch with you.

We're not just looking for published authors; if you have strong technical skills but no writing experience, our experienced editors can help you develop a writing career, or simply get some additional reward for your expertise.

Mastering Kali Linux for Advanced Penetration Testing

ISBN: 978-1-78216-312-1   Paperback: 356 pages

A practical guide to testing your network's security with Kali Linux, the preferred choice of penetration testers and trackers

1. Conduct realistic and effective security tests on your network.

2. Demonstrate how key data systems are stealthily exploited, and learn how to identify attacks against your own systems.

3. Use hands-on techniques to take advantage of Kali Linux, the open source framework of security tools.

Linux Mint Essentials

ISBN: 978-1-78216-815-7   Paperback: 324 pages

A practical guide to Linux Mint for the novice to the professional

1. Learn to use Linux Mint like a pro, starting with the installation and going all the way through maintaining your system.

2. Covers everything you need to know in order to be productive, including browsing the Internet, creating documents, and installing software.

3. Hands-on activities reinforce your knowledge.

Please check **www.PacktPub.com** for information on our titles

Kali Linux – Assuring Security by Penetration Testing

ISBN: 978-1-84-951-948-9   Paperback: 454 pages

Master the art of penetration testing with Kali Linux

1. Learn penetration testing techniques with an in-depth coverage of Kali Linux distribution.

2. Explore the insights and importance of testing your corporate network systems before the hackers strike.

3. Understand the practical spectrum of security tools by their exemplary usage, configuration, and benefits.

Kali Linux Cookbook

ISBN: 978-1-78328-959-2   Paperback: 260 pages

Over 70 recipes to help you master Kali Linux for effective penetration security testing

1. Recipes designed to educate you extensively on the penetration testing principles and Kali Linux tools.

2. Learning to use Kali Linux tools, such as Metasploit, Wire Shark, and many more through in-depth and structured instructions.

3. Teaching you in an easy-to-follow style, full of examples, illustrations, and tips that will suit experts and novices alike.

Please check **www.PacktPub.com** for information on our titles